상상 그 이상

모두의 새롭고 유익한 즐거움이
비상의 즐거움이기에

아무도 해보지 못한 콘텐츠를 만들어
학교에 새로운 활기를 불어넣고

전에 없던 플랫폼을 창조하여
배움이 더 즐거워지는 자기주도학습 환경을
실현해왔습니다

이제, 비상은
더 많은 이들의 행복한 경험과
성장에 기여하기 위해

글로벌 교육 문화 환경의
상상 그 이상을 실현해 나갑니다

상상을 실현하는 교육 문화 기업 비상

내 교과서, All that 에서 찾아보기 '의사소통 기능'

단원	비상교육 (김진완)	올댓	동아출판 (윤정미)	올댓	동아출판 (이병민)	올댓	천재교육 (이재영)	올댓	미래엔 (최연희)
Lesson 01	• 화가 난 감정 표현하기 • 오해 지적하기	20 80	• 경험 묻고 답하기 • 희망 표현하기	40	• 안부 묻고 답하기 • 기쁨, 유감 표현하기	60	• 감정 표현하기 • 동의·반대하기	60	• 의향 말하기 • 도움 제안하기
Lesson 02	• 기대하는 일 표현하기 • 알고 있는 정보 말하기	40 60	• 음식 주문하기 1 • 음식 주문하기 2		• 걱정 표현하기 • 방법 묻기	20	• 선호 묻고 답하기 • 설명 요청하기	20 100	• 이유 묻기 • 허락 요청하기
Lesson 03	• 알고 있는 내용 진술하기 • 허락 요청하기	100	• 설명 요청하기 • 반복 설명 요청하기	100 100	• 원하는 행동 묻기 • 당부하기		• 주제 소개하기 • 이유 묻고 답하기	60	• 안부 묻고 답하기 • 조언 구하기
Lesson 04	• 상대방의 의견 묻기 • 앞으로의 계획 묻기	80	• 교환 요청하기 • 환불 요청하기		• 의견 묻기 • 동의하기	80	• 궁금한 점 묻기 • 도움 제안하기	100	• 궁금한 것 묻고 답하기 • 설명 요청하기
Lesson 05	• 자세한 설명 요청하기 • 의견에 대한 이유 묻기	100 60	• 빈도 묻고 말하기 • 제안이나 권유하기	100	• 기대 표현하기 • 거절하기	40	• 추천 요청하기 • 기대 표현하기	40	• 걱정하기 • 의무 부인하기
Lesson 06	• 상대방을 안심시키기 • 상상한 내용 묻기	20 80	• 축하, 유감 표현하기 • 감정 표현하기	20	• 감사하기 • 금지하기	40	• 충고하기 • 허락 구하기	20 100	• 불만족 표현하기 • 다짐 말하기
Lesson 07	• 어떤 것에 만족하거나 불만이 있는지 묻기 • 후회하는 일 말하기	40 100	• 방법, 절차 묻고 답하기 • 감사 표현하기	40	• 궁금함 표현하기 • 보고하기		• 당부하기 • 부탁하기		• 이해 확인하기 • 바람·소원 표현하기
Lesson 08	• 어떤 일이 실제로 가능한지 묻기 • 이루어지기를 바라는 일 표현하기	60 80	• 선호 표현하기 • 의견 표현하기	20 80	• 후회 표현하기 • 기원하는 말 하기	100 40	• 후회 표현하기 • 수정하기	100	
Lesson 09									

올댓	능률교육 (김성곤)	올댓	천재교육 (정사열)	올댓	YBM (박준언)	올댓	YBM (송미정)	올댓	지학사 (민찬규)	올댓
100	• 바람에 대해 묻고 답하기 • 만족이나 불만족에 대해 묻기	80 40	• 기쁨이나 슬픔에 대해 묻기 • 기쁨 표현하기	60 60	• 가장 좋아하는 것 말하기 • 궁금증 표현하기		• 정보 묻고 답하기 • 알고 있는지 묻기	60	• 걱정·염려 묻기 • 기원하기	20 40
60 100	• 알고 있는지 묻기 • 놀람 표현하기	60	• 주제 소개하기 • 감사하기	40	• 충고 구하기 • 경고하기	20	• 동의나 이의 여부 표현하기 • 안심시키기	20	• 의견 제시하기 • 선호에 대해 묻기	80 20
20	• 궁금증 표현하기 • 경고하기, 주의 주기		• 기대 표현하기 • 기원하기	40 40	• 확실성 정도 표현하기 • 의견 표현하기	80	• 강조하기 • 안타까움, 후회 표현하기	100	• 알고 있는지 묻기 • 관심 표현하기	60
100	• 고민이나 불만족의 원인에 대해 묻기 • 확실성 정도 표현하기		• 슬픔, 불만족, 실망의 원인에 대해 묻기 • 충고 구하기	20	• 충고하기 • 불허하기	20 100	• 의무 표현하기 • 가능성 정도 표현하기	60	• 만족이나 불만족 묻기 • 이유 묻기	40 60
20	• 의견 표현하기 • 희망, 기대 표현하기	80 40	• 궁금증 표현하기 • 정의하기		• 알고 있는지 묻기 • 희망, 기대 표현하기	60 40	• 설명 요청하기 • 대안 묻기	100	• 가능성 정도 묻기 • 길 묻기	60
40	• 선호에 대해 묻고 답하기 • 상기시키기	20	• 선호에 대해 묻기 • 싫어하는 것 표현하기	20	• 주제 소개하기 • 제안·권유하기	100	• 허가 여부 묻기 • 제안, 권유, 요청에 답하기	100 100	• 의견 묻기 • 동의하거나 이의 제기 하기	80
80 80	• 설명 요청하기 • 가능성 정도 표현하기	100 60	• 의견 묻기 • 이의 제기하기	80	• 요청하기 • 감사하기	40	• 궁금증 표현하기 • 생각할 시간 요청하기		• 바람·소원 표현하기 • 상상하여 말하기	80 80
			• 화냄 표현하기 • 화냄에 응대하기	20 20	• 관심 표현하기 • 만족이나 불만족에 대해 묻기	40	• 반복 요청하기 • 추천하기	100	• 상술하기 • 이해 점검하기	80
					• 가능성 정도 묻기 • 바람, 소원 말하기	60 80				

콕 강의 30회 자유 수강권

교재 속 원하는 부분만 콕 찍어 골라 듣자!

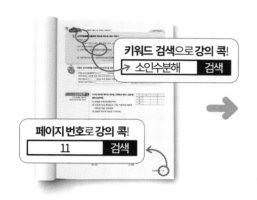

키워드 검색으로 강의 콕!
소인수분해 [검색]

페이지 번호로 강의 콕!
11 [검색]

수박씨닷컴에서
비상교재 강의 무료 수강!

┃ 비상교재 구매자 전용 혜택 ┃

혜택 ❶
콕 강의 30회 자유 수강권

※ 콕 강의 자유 수강권은
ID당 1회만 사용할 수 있습니다.

콕 강의 30회 무료 수강 쿠폰번호

※ 박스 안을 연필 또는 샤프펜슬로 칠하면 번호가 보입니다.

이용 방법

수박씨닷컴 접속
www.soobakc.com
→ 메인 중앙
'비상교재 혜택존' 클릭
→ 쿠폰 번호 입력
→ 강의 수강 및
당첨 경품 확인!

혜택 ❷
수강권만 등록해도
100% 선물 당첨

※ 당첨 경품은 매월 변경됩니다.

족보닷컴
기출문제
다운로드권
↓

수행평가
자료
다운로드권
↓

문의 1544-7380 | www.soobakc.com

The무한수강 α 알파
중학 생활의 든든한 내신 플래너

PLAN & WORK (1학기)

TIME & DATA	
3월 개학	자기주도학습 동기 유발, 전 과목 100% 우리 학교 맞춤 학습
4월 영어듣기평가	영어 듣기 실전 모의고사, 비법 특강 및 해설 특강 학습
5월 중간고사	중간 시험대비 & 서술형 특강, 족보닷컴 기출문제 제공
6월	SKY 멘토 고민 상담, 상위권 심화 학습, 수행평가 가이드 & 자료 포털 제공
7월 기말고사	시험 전략 제공, 기말 시험대비 & 서술형 특강
8월 여름방학	SLS 자기주도학습, 학습 성향 4종 검사 진행

PLAN & WORK (2학기)

TIME & DATA	
9월 개학, 영어듣기평가	포트폴리오 점검, 영어 듣기 실전 대비, 영/수 단계별 전문 학습
10월 중간고사	최고득점 내신관리, 중간 시험대비 내맘대로 테스트
11월 기말고사	골든 클래스 프리미엄, 기말 시험 특강, 족보닷컴 쿠폰 제공
12월 겨울방학	포트폴리오 코칭, 취약과목 보충, 학습 방향 및 진로 탐색
1월 (새해)	시기별 맞춤 학습 계획 스마트플랜, 방끝생끝 플래너 제공
2월	프리미엄 진로 컨설팅 진행, 신학기 내신 진도강좌, 학습법 코칭

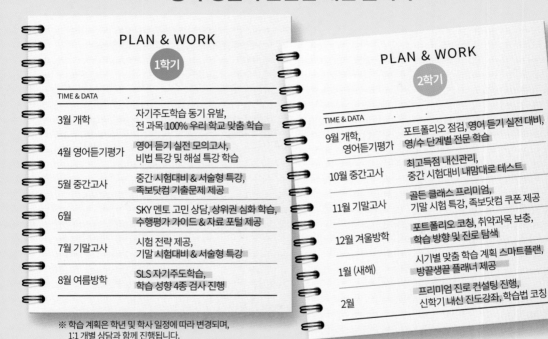

※ 학습 계획은 학년 및 학사 일정에 따라 변경되며, 1:1 개별 상담과 함께 진행됩니다.

POINT 1

학원의 학습 관리를 내 방 안에서
실시간 학습 관리 알파ON

POINT 2

만족도 100%* 검증된 스타 선생님의
우리 학교 교과서 맞춤 강좌
*2019년 수박씨닷컴 회원 대상 조사 결과

POINT 3

24시간 평균 10분 내 답변 도착!
명문대 튜터의 실시간 질답 ON

전 학년 전 강좌 무제한 수강	최신 학습 기기 무료 제공	프리미엄 진로 컨설팅	과목/유형별 수행평가 자료 포털	족보닷컴 기출문제 다운 쿠폰

성적장학생 294%* 증가, 성적 향상률 97.1%**
결과로 증명한 수박씨닷컴 The무한수강 α 의 내신 맞춤 플랜

*2019년 1학기까지의 장학생 참여 기준 **알파ON클래스를 1년 동안 경험한 회원 전수조사 결과(2019.09 기준)

문의 1544-7380 | www.soobakc.com

수박씨닷컴은 최고 실력의 강사진이 대한민국 1위 교과서*와 1위 교재**로 강의하며, 1:1 담임제 학습관리로 최상의 교육 서비스를 제공합니다.
*2015~2019 대한민국 교육기업 대상 <초중등 교과서> 부문 **2014~2016 국가브랜드 대상 <중고등 교재> 부문

VISANG

중학 영어의 모든 것

All
that
중학 영어 3-1

구성과 특징

PART I 실력 다지기

All that Grammar

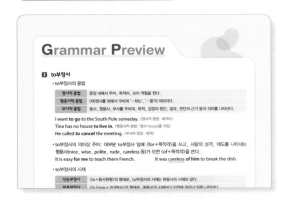

- 단원을 학습하기 전에 꼭 알아야 할 핵심 문법 개념을 소개하는 자기주도적 학습 장치

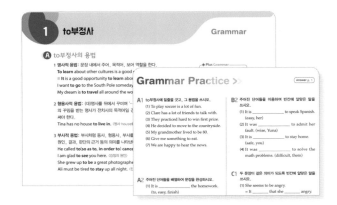

- 주요 교과서를 철저히 분석하여 구성한 체계적인 문법 목차
- [개념 소개] → [Grammar Practice] → [Grammar Test] 3단계로 구성된 체계적인 문법 학습 시스템
- 출제 빈도가 높은 기출 문항들을 엄선하여 수록한 연습 문제

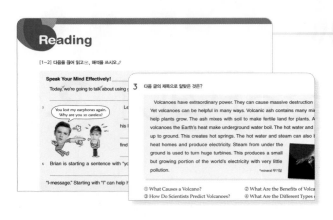

All that Reading

- 재미있고 다양한 소재의 지문 수록
- 교과서 지문을 이용한 끊어 읽기, 해석 연습
- 실제 시험과 유사한 독해 문항 유형을 다양하게 수록

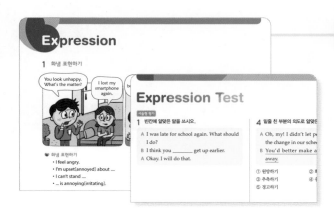

All that Expression

- 주요 교과서에 소개된 의사소통 기능을 엄선하여 소개
- 대화 상황을 재미있는 만화로 생생하게 제시
- 다양한 유형의 기출 문항들을 엄선하여 수록

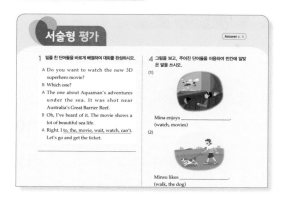

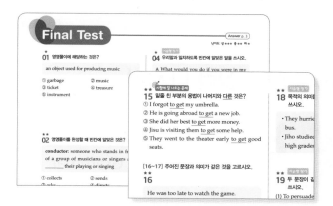

- 문법과 표현을 적용한 서술형 평가 제공
- 학교 서술형 평가 완벽 대비를 위한 다양한 문제 수록

- 실제 시험과 동일한 유형으로 구성된 종합 평가
- 여러 난이도의 문제를 빈출 유형 위주로 수록

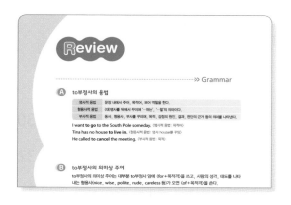

- 단원에서 학습한 문법과 의사소통 기능 복습
- 학습 내용을 도식화하여 신속한 이해 점검 가능

PART II 듣기 실전 모의고사

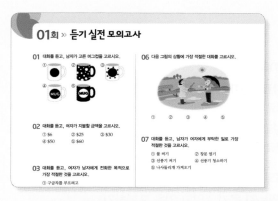

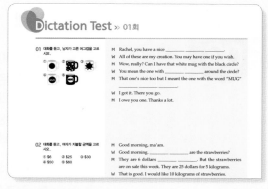

- 시·도 교육청 영어 듣기능력평가를 분석하여 반영한 듣기 실전 모의고사 5회 수록
- 실제 시험과 유사한 분량 및 녹음속도의 듣기 자료를 통해 실전 적응력 향상
- 듣기 능력을 향상시켜줄 Dictation Test 제공

차례

How To Study

* 월간, 주간, 일간 학습 계획을 세운 후 공부하는 습관을 가져 보세요. 무턱대고 공부하는 것보다 훨씬 체계적이고 계획적으로 공부할 수 있어요.
* 먼저, 구체적으로 공부할 분량을 파악한 후에 학습 목표를 세워 보세요. 목표를 세울 때는 막연하거나 장황하지 않게 구체적으로 세우는 것이 중요해요. 그렇게 해야 계획대로 공부할 수 있고 목표한 만큼은 반드시 끝낸다는 마음으로 공부할 수 있어서 효율적이에요.

60일 완성 학습 계획표

Lesson 01 to부정사

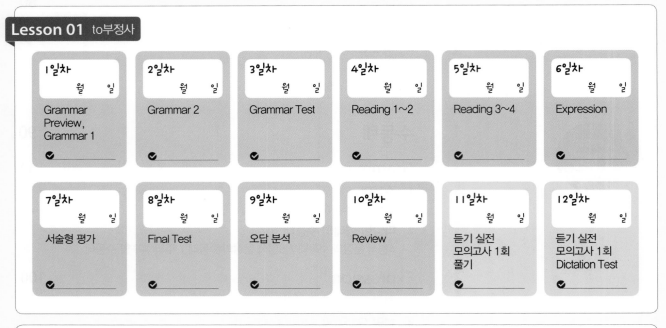

1일차 월 일	2일차 월 일	3일차 월 일	4일차 월 일	5일차 월 일	6일차 월 일
Grammar Preview, Grammar 1	Grammar 2	Grammar Test	Reading 1~2	Reading 3~4	Expression

7일차 월 일	8일차 월 일	9일차 월 일	10일차 월 일	11일차 월 일	12일차 월 일
서술형 평가	Final Test	오답 분석	Review	듣기 실전 모의고사 1회 풀기	듣기 실전 모의고사 1회 Dictation Test

Lesson 02 동명사

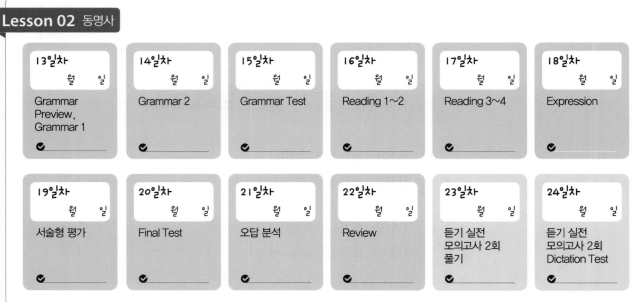

13일차 월 일	14일차 월 일	15일차 월 일	16일차 월 일	17일차 월 일	18일차 월 일
Grammar Preview, Grammar 1	Grammar 2	Grammar Test	Reading 1~2	Reading 3~4	Expression

19일차 월 일	20일차 월 일	21일차 월 일	22일차 월 일	23일차 월 일	24일차 월 일
서술형 평가	Final Test	오답 분석	Review	듣기 실전 모의고사 2회 풀기	듣기 실전 모의고사 2회 Dictation Test

Lesson 03 시제

25일차 월 일	26일차 월 일	27일차 월 일	28일차 월 일	29일차 월 일	30일차 월 일
Grammar Preview, Grammar 1 ✓	Grammar 2 ✓	Grammar Test ✓	Reading 1~2 ✓	Reading 3~4 ✓	Expression ✓

31일차 월 일	32일차 월 일	33일차 월 일	34일차 월 일	35일차 월 일	36일차 월 일
서술형 평가 ✓	Final Test ✓	오답 분석 ✓	Review ✓	듣기 실전 모의고사 3회 풀기 ✓	듣기 실전 모의고사 3회 Dictation Test ✓

Lesson 04 관계사

37일차 월 일	38일차 월 일	39일차 월 일	40일차 월 일	41일차 월 일	42일차 월 일
Grammar Preview, Grammar 1 ✓	Grammar 2 ✓	Grammar Test ✓	Reading 1~2 ✓	Reading 3~4 ✓	Expression ✓

43일차 월 일	44일차 월 일	45일차 월 일	46일차 월 일	47일차 월 일	48일차 월 일
서술형 평가 ✓	Final Test ✓	오답 분석 ✓	Review ✓	듣기 실전 모의고사 4회 풀기 ✓	듣기 실전 모의고사 4회 Dictation Test ✓

Lesson 05 수동태

49일차 월 일	50일차 월 일	51일차 월 일	52일차 월 일	53일차 월 일	54일차 월 일
Grammar Preview, Grammar 1 ✓	Grammar 2 ✓	Grammar Test ✓	Reading 1~2 ✓	Reading 3~4 ✓	Expression ✓

55일차 월 일	56일차 월 일	57일차 월 일	58일차 월 일	59일차 월 일	60일차 월 일
서술형 평가 ✓	Final Test ✓	오답 분석 ✓	Review ✓	듣기 실전 모의고사 5회 풀기 ✓	듣기 실전 모의고사 5회 Dictation Test ✓

🍎 미리보는 2학기 차례

실력 다지기

Lesson 01

to부정사

Grammar Preview

❶ to부정사

• to부정사의 용법

명사적 용법	문장 내에서 주어, 목적어, 보어 역할을 한다.
형용사적 용법	(대)명사를 뒤에서 꾸미며 '…하는', '…할'의 의미이다.
부사적 용법	동사, 형용사, 부사를 꾸미며, 목적, 감정의 원인, 결과, 판단의 근거 등의 의미를 나타낸다.

I want **to go** to the South Pole someday. 〈명사적 용법: 목적어〉
Tina has no house **to live in**. 〈형용사적 용법: 명사 house를 꾸밈〉
He called **to cancel** the meeting. 〈부사적 용법: 목적〉

• to부정사의 의미상 주어: 대부분 to부정사 앞에 〈for+목적격〉을 쓰고, 사람의 성격, 태도를 나타내는 형용사(nice, wise, polite, rude, careless 등)가 오면 〈of+목적격〉을 쓴다.
It is easy **for me** to teach them French.   It was <u>careless</u> **of him** to break the dish.

• to부정사의 시제

단순부정사	〈to+동사원형〉의 형태로, to부정사의 시제는 본동사의 시제와 같다.
완료부정사	〈to have+과거분사〉의 형태로, 본동사의 시제보다 이전에 일어난 일을 나타낸다.

❷ to부정사의 활용

• 의문사+to부정사

what + to부정사	무엇을 …할지	how + to부정사	어떻게 …할지
where + to부정사	어디서(로) …할지	when + to부정사	언제 …할지

• enough to / too … to

형용사(부사)+**enough**+to부정사	**too**+형용사(부사)+to부정사
= so+형용사(부사)+that+주어+can …	= so+형용사(부사)+that+주어+can't …
…할 만큼 충분히 …한(하게)	너무 …해서 …할 수 없는

• 독립부정사

to be sure 확실히   to be brief 간단히 말하면
needless to say 말할 필요도 없이   so to speak 말하자면
to tell the truth 사실을 말하자면   strange to say 이상한 말이지만
to make matters worse 설상가상으로   to be frank with you 솔직히 말해서

A to부정사의 용법

1 명사적 용법: 문장 내에서 주어, 목적어, 보어 역할을 한다.

To learn about other cultures is a good opportunity. 〈주어〉

= **It** is a good opportunity **to learn** about other cultures. 〈가주어 it〉

I want **to go** to the South Pole someday. 〈목적어〉

My dream is **to travel** all around the world. 〈보어〉

2 형용사적 용법: (대)명사를 뒤에서 꾸미며 '…하는', '…할'의 의미이다. to부정사의 꾸밈을 받는 명사가 전치사의 목적어일 경우 to부정사 뒤에 반드시 전치사를 써야 한다.

Tina has no house **to live in**. 〈명사 house를 꾸밈〉

3 부사적 용법: 부사처럼 동사, 형용사, 부사를 꾸미며, 문맥에 따라 목적, 감정의 원인, 결과, 판단의 근거 등의 의미를 나타낸다.

He called **to(so as to, in order to) cancel** the meeting. 〈목적〉

I am glad **to see** you here. 〈감정의 원인〉

She grew up **to be** a great photographer. 〈결과〉

Ali must be tired **to stay** up all night. 〈판단의 근거〉

> **Plus Grammar**
> · **to부정사를 목적격보어로 취하는 동사**
> ask, want, allow, advise, cause, tell, expect 등
> I **asked** my mom **to take** me to the movies. (나는 엄마께 나를 영화관에 데려가 달라고 부탁했다.)
> · **가목적어 it**
> 5형식 문장에서 to부정사가 목적어로 쓰일 경우, to부정사를 뒤로 보내고 그 자리에 가목적어 it을 쓴다.
> Jack found **it** interesting **to take** pictures. (Jack은 사진 찍는 것이 재미있다는 것을 알았다.)

B to부정사의 의미상 주어

to부정사의 의미상 주어는 대부분 to부정사 앞에 〈for+목적격〉을 쓰고, 사람의 성격, 태도를 나타내는 형용사가 오면 〈of+목적격〉을 쓴다. 단, 의미상 주어가 일반인이거나 문장의 주어와 일치하는 경우 생략할 수 있다.

It is easy **for me** to teach them French.

It was careless **of him** to break the dish.

It is impossible **(for us)** to live without water.

> **Plus Grammar**
> 사람의 성격, 태도를 나타내는 형용사
> nice, wise, brave, polite, rude, foolish, careful, careless 등

C to부정사의 시제

1 단순부정사: 〈to+동사원형〉의 형태로, to부정사의 시제는 본동사의 시제와 같다.

Maria seems **to be** ill.

= It seems that Maria **is** ill.

2 완료부정사: 〈to have+과거분사〉의 형태로, 본동사의 시제보다 이전에 일어난 일을 나타낸다.

He seems **to have been** a teacher.

= It seems that he **was** a teacher.

Grammar Practice >>

Answer p. 1

A1 to부정사에 밑줄을 긋고, 그 용법을 쓰시오.

(1) To play soccer is a lot of fun.

(2) Clare has a lot of friends to talk with.

(3) They practiced hard to win first prize.

(4) He decided to move to the countryside.

(5) My grandmother lived to be 80.

(6) Give me something to eat.

(7) We are happy to hear the news.

A2 주어진 단어들을 배열하여 문장을 완성하시오.

(1) It is _____ the homework.
(to, easy, finish)

(2) Elizabeth found _____ to persuade him. (stupid, it, to, try)

(3) John thinks _____ a good education. (important, to, get, it)

(4) Ms. Smith _____ to my friends. (be, me, advised, to, nice)

B1 괄호 안에서 알맞은 것을 고르시오.

(1) It is important (for, of) Jim to know the truth.

(2) It is nice (for, of) him to share his lunch with his partner.

(3) It was foolish (for, of) you to accept his proposal.

(4) It is natural (for, of) us to take off our shoes in the house.

(5) It is rude (for, of) her to do such a thing.

B2 주어진 단어들을 이용하여 빈칸에 알맞은 말을 쓰시오.

(1) It is _____ to speak Spanish. (easy, her)

(2) It was _____ to admit her fault. (wise, Yuna)

(3) It is _____ to stay home. (safe, you)

(4) It was _____ to solve the math problems. (difficult, them)

C1 두 문장이 같은 의미가 되도록 빈칸에 알맞은 말을 쓰시오.

(1) She seems to be angry.
= It _____ that she _____ angry.

(2) Mike seems to have majored in biology.
= It _____ that Mike _____ in biology.

(3) He seemed to be sick.
= It _____ that he _____ sick.

(4) Jonathan seemed to have been rich.
= It _____ that Jonathan _____ _____ rich.

C2 우리말과 일치하도록 주어진 단어를 이용하여 빈칸에 알맞은 말을 쓰시오.

(1) 그녀는 나쁜 꿈을 꿨던 것 같다.
→ She seems _____ a bad dream. (dream)

(2) 그 간호사가 사건을 목격했던 것 같다.
→ The nurse seems _____ the accident. (see)

(3) Hana는 그것에 대해 알고 있는 것 같다.
→ Hana seems _____ about it. (know)

교과서 **South Pole** 남극 **cancel** 취소하다 **impossible** 불가능한 **ill** 아픈 **first prize** 1등상 **countryside** 시골 지역 **persuade** 설득하다
어휘 **share** 공유하다 **accept** 받아들이다 **proposal** 제안, 제의 **take off** 벗다 **admit** 인정하다 **major in** …을 전공하다

D to부정사의 부정 / 대부정사

1 to부정사의 부정: to부정사 앞에 not(never)을 써서 부정의 의미를 나타낸다.
Mom told me **not to eat** too many candies.

2 대부정사: 앞에 나온 동사의 반복을 피하기 위해 to부정사의 동사를 생략하고 남겨진 to가 to부정사 전체를 대신한다.
You can have a bite if you want **to** (have).

E to부정사의 관용 표현

1 의문사+to부정사: 문장 내에서 주어, 목적어, 보어로 쓰이며 〈의문사+주어+should+동사원형〉으로 바꿔 쓸 수 있다.

what+to부정사	무엇을 …할지	how+to부정사	어떻게 …할지
where+to부정사	어디서(로) …할지	when+to부정사	언제 …할지

I don't know **what to get** mom for her birthday.
= I don't know **what I should get** mom for her birthday.

2 enough to / too … to

형용사(부사)+enough+to부정사	too+형용사(부사)+to부정사
= so+형용사(부사)+that+주어+can …	= so+형용사(부사)+that+주어+can't …
…할 만큼 충분히 …한(하게)	너무 …해서 …할 수 없는

Jimmy is smart **enough to read** difficult books.
= Jimmy is **so** smart **that** he **can read** difficult books.
The digital camera is **too** expensive for me **to buy**.
= The digital camera is **so** expensive **that** I **can't buy** it.

> ◆ **Plus** Grammar
> 〈so that+주어+can(may)〉은 '…하기 위해서'의 뜻으로 목적을 나타낸다.
> He studied hard **so that** he **could** get better grades. (그는 더 좋은 성적을 받기 위해서 열심히 공부했다.)

F 독립부정사

문장 전체를 꾸미는 to부정사 구문으로 일종의 관용적 표현이다.

to be sure 확실히	to be brief 간단히 말하면
needless to say 말할 필요도 없이	so to speak 말하자면
to tell the truth 사실을 말하자면	strange to say 이상한 말이지만
to make matters worse 설상가상으로	to be frank with you 솔직히 말해서

Needless to say, health is the most important thing.
To tell the truth, I don't like the color.

Answer p. 1

D1 괄호 안에서 알맞은 것을 고르시오.

(1) He told the kids (not to, to not) touch the toy.

(2) I bought an alarm clock (never to, to never) be late again.

(3) You can have this cake if you'd love (at, to).

(4) It was foolish of me (to follow not, not to follow) her advice.

D2 생략된 표현을 찾아 빈칸에 쓰시오.

(1) A Will you visit her tomorrow?
   B I'd like to (_____ _____
   _____), but I'm not sure.

(2) You can go if you want to (_____).

E1 우리말과 일치하도록 빈칸에 알맞은 말을 쓰시오.

(1) 네 파티에서 무엇을 입어야 하는지 말해 줘.
   → Tell me _____ _____ wear at your party.

(2) 그녀는 어떻게 이 상자를 여는지 궁금했다.
   → She wondered _____ _____ open this box.

(3) 낚시하러 갈 수 있을 만큼 날씨가 좋다.
   → It's fine _____ _____ go fishing.

(4) 그 벌레는 너무 빨라서 내가 잡을 수 없었다.
   → The worm was _____ quick for me _____ catch.

(5) 이 알약은 너무 써서 나는 그것을 삼킬 수 없다.
   → This pill is _____ bitter _____ I _____ swallow it.

E2 두 문장이 같은 의미가 되도록 빈칸에 알맞은 말을 쓰시오.

(1) The students asked me how to solve the question.
   = The students asked me _____ they _____ solve the question.

(2) The flag is too huge for me to raise.
   = The flag is _____ huge _____ I _____ raise it.

(3) My smartphone is small enough to fit in my hip pocket.
   = My smartphone is _____ small _____ it _____ fit in my hip pocket.

(4) Jack doesn't know how he should fix the computer.
   = Jack doesn't know _____ _____ _____ the computer.

F1 밑줄 친 부분에 주의하여 문장을 우리말로 옮기시오.

(1) <u>Strange to say</u>, he seems to like me.
   → _____

(2) <u>Needless to say</u>, I can't go to the festival.
   → _____

(3) <u>To make matters worse</u>, I got a bad cold.
   → _____

(4) <u>To be sure</u>, he was impolite.
   → _____

(5) <u>To be frank with you</u>, he isn't honest.
   → _____

교과서 **have a bite** 한 입 먹다 **wonder** 궁금해하다 **worm** 벌레 **pill** 알약 **bitter** 맛이 쓴 **swallow** 삼키다 **hip pocket** 뒷주머니
어휘 **fix** 고치다, 수리하다

Grammar Test

01 빈칸에 알맞지 <u>않은</u> 것은?

> It was _____ of her to do that.

① kind   ② honest
③ foolish   ④ difficult
⑤ wise

[02~03] 빈칸에 알맞은 것을 고르시오.

02

> He is interested in flying airplanes, so he wants _____ a pilot.

① be   ② to being
③ to be   ④ to is
⑤ to have been

03

> Ms. Kim told _____ during the class.

① the students not to talk
② the students to talking
③ the students to not talk
④ the students to talk not
⑤ not the students to talk

04 밑줄 친 부분 중 어법상 어색한 것은?

> ①Andy ②found ③a large flat ④rock ⑤to sit.

서술형 평가
05 밑줄 친 부분에 주의하여 문장을 우리말로 옮기시오.

> <u>To be frank with you</u>, she is not attractive at all.

→ _____

06 밑줄 친 부분의 용법이 나머지와 <u>다른</u> 것은?
① He needs <u>to take</u> some rest.
② His goal is <u>to win</u> a gold medal.
③ <u>To teach</u> me how to swim is her job.
④ Tony grew up <u>to be</u> a famous singer.
⑤ It was stupid of her <u>to lose</u> her patience.

07 괄호 안에서 알맞은 것을 고르시오.
(1) The device made it easier (find, to find) the direction.
(2) A man asked me (give, to give) him some money.
(3) Is it possible (generate, to generate) electricity from wind?

서술형 평가
08 생략된 표현을 찾아 빈칸에 쓰시오.

> A Your uncles are coming this evening. Can you be back by seven?
> B I will try to (_____ _____ _____ _____).

교과서 **pilot** 조종사, 비행사   **flat** 평평한   **attractive** 매력적인   **take a rest** 쉬다   **job** 일, 책임   **patience** 인내심   **device** 장치, 기구
어휘   **direction** 방향   **generate** 발생시키다

09 두 문장이 같은 의미가 되도록 빈칸에 알맞은 말을 쓰시오.

(1) The novel is so exciting that I can't stop reading it.

= The novel is _____ exciting for me _____ _____ reading.

(2) The chair was so strong that it could support his weight.

= The chair was strong _____ _____ _____ his weight.

10 빈칸에 알맞은 것은?

A Did you hear something last night?
B I'm not sure, but I seem _____ someone knock on the window.

① heard   ② to hear
③ having heard   ④ to have heard
⑤ to having heard

11 빈칸에 알맞은 말을 쓰시오.

• It is natural _____ them to worry about their children.
• How nice _____ you to let me stay here!

12 짝지어진 문장의 의미가 <u>다른</u> 것은?

① To speak when you're eating is rude.
   = It's rude to speak when you're eating.
② I came here to say goodbye.
   = I came here in order to say goodbye.
③ They will tell you what to do.
   = They will tell you what you might do.
④ I'll never learn how to tie a necktie.
   = I'll never learn how I should tie a necktie.
⑤ He got up early to watch the sunrise.
   = He got up early so as to watch the sunrise.

13 빈칸에 들어갈 말이 바르게 짝지어진 것은?

• Tell me _____ to bring on the camping trip.
• It's not easy to understand _____ to play chess.

① where – when   ② what – where
③ how – what   ④ what – how
⑤ when – how

14 주어진 문장과 같은 의미가 되도록 빈칸에 알맞은 말을 쓰시오.

I'm slow. I can't run 100 meters in eighteen seconds.

(1) I'm _____ slow _____ run 100 meters in eighteen seconds.
(2) I'm not fast _____ _____ run 100 meters in eighteen seconds.

교과서 **support** 지탱하다, 지지하다 **natural** 당연한, 자연스러운 **rude** 무례한 **tie** 묶다 **necktie** 넥타이 **sunrise** 해돋이, 일출
어휘 **second** (시간 단위인) 초

Reading

[1~2] 다음을 끊어 읽고 ☑, 해석을 쓰시오. ✎

The Junk Orchestra

"The world sends us garbage, we send back music." This was written on the back of a concert

3 ticket I was given. "The Junk Orchestra" played instruments made entirely out of garbage. I was so

moved by the music that I met Favio Chávez, the conductor, and asked him about the orchestra.

Why did you start The Junk Orchestra?

6 **Favio Chávez** When I went to a small town called Cateura in Paraguay in 2005, I saw children

living in a town that was mostly filled with garbage. I wanted to add something positive to their

lives, so I decided to share my love of music with them.

9 **Why did you use garbage to make instruments?**

Favio Chávez One person's garbage is another person's treasure. Nicolás

Gómez, a garbage picker, helped me a lot. He @play, made, to, it, for, possible,

12 children, music by making instruments out of garbage. I want people to know

that even something worthless can make inspiring music.

---

1 밑줄 친 @를 어순에 맞게 배열하시오.

_____

2 위 글의 Favio Chávez에 관한 내용과 일치하지 <u>않는</u> 것은?
① 정크 오케스트라의 지휘자이다.　　　　　　② 2005년에 파라과이에 갔다.
③ 파라과이 아이들과 오케스트라를 구성했다.　④ 악기를 만드는 데 쓰레기를 이용했다.
⑤ 다른 사람의 도움 없이 악기를 만들었다.

교과서 **instrument** 악기 **entirely** 전적으로, 완전히 **treasure** 보물 **worthless** 가치 없는 **inspire** 영감을 주다
어휘🎧

3 빈칸에 알맞은 것은?

환경

Today, many of the world's largest cities face two similar challenges: environmental pollution and crime. What are urban planners doing **to fix** these problems? Hyderabad, a city in India, _____, is planting trees. Adding green to a city has a number of advantages. Trees remove pollution from the air and make it cleaner. The streets in Hyderabad were gray and ugly a few years ago. However, today they are filled with trees and flowers. The green areas make the city cleaner and more colorful. They are also places for people **to relax**. A study in the U.S. showed something else interesting: the greener a neighborhood is, the less crime there is.

① therefore   ② however   ③ for example
④ in addition   ⑤ on the contrary

4 다음 글의 주제로 알맞은 것은?

직업

Every year, hundreds of people die and lose their homes because of forest fires. Smoke jumpers are helping **to stop** this. Smoke jumpers are a special type of firefighter. They jump from planes into areas that are difficult **to reach** by car or on foot, like the middle of a mountain forest. At a fire site, smoke jumpers first examine the land and decide **how to fight** the fire. Their main goal is **to stop** a fire from spreading. Using basic equipment such as shovels and axes, smoke jumpers clear land of burnable material like plants and other dry material. They carry water with them too, but only a limited amount.

① what smoke jumpers do   ② what makes a fire spread fast
③ how to become a smoke jumper   ④ the best ways to prevent forest fires
⑤ the first thing to do to put out fires

---

3   **challenge** 과제, 난제   **pollution** 오염   **urban** 도시의   **remove** 제거하다   **neighborhood** 주위, 지역
4   **reach** …에 도달하다   **examine** 조사하다, 검토하다   **spread** 퍼지다   **burnable** 태울 수 있는   **material** 물질

Expression

1 화냄 표현하기

💗 화냄 표현하기
- I feel angry.
- I'm upset(annoyed) about ....
- I can't stand ....
- ... is annoying(irritating).

💗 화냄에 응대하기
- Calm down.
- Take it easy.
- Don't get so angry.
- There's nothing to get angry about.

2 충고 구하기 / 충고하기

💗 충고 구하기
- What should I do?
- What do you think I should do?
- Do you think I should keep trying?
- Can I get your advice on this matter?
- What would you do if you were in my shoes?

💗 충고하기
- I think you should apologize to her.
- You should(had better) take a taxi.
- If I were you, I would study harder.
- Why don't you get some exercise?
- I suggest you keep trying.
- I advise you to be nice to others.

Expression Test

Answer p. 2

1 빈칸에 알맞은 말을 쓰시오.

A I was late for school again. What should I do?

B I think you _____ get up earlier.

A Okay. I will do that.

2 빈칸에 알맞은 것은?

A That man is throwing trash.

B _____

① Why is he so upset?

② You should think of others.

③ I can't stand people like him.

④ I think you should not throw trash.

⑤ There's nothing to get angry about.

3 밑줄 친 부분과 바꿔 쓸 수 있는 것은?

A My younger brother spilt milk on my new shirt. I can't stand it.

B Calm down. He's only three years old.

① Same here.

② How sad.

③ Take it easy.

④ I have no idea.

⑤ Don't worry.

4 밑줄 친 부분의 의도로 알맞은 것은?

A Oh, my! I didn't let people know about the change in our schedule.

B You'd better make all the calls right away.

① 원망하기 　　② 확신하기

③ 추측하기 　　④ 충고하기

⑤ 경고하기

5 우리말과 일치하도록 빈칸에 알맞은 말을 쓰시오.

A What's wrong, Jina?

B I'm _____ _____ my sister Sujin. (나는 내 여동생 수진이에게 화가 나.) She broke my favorite cup.

A Oh, I'm sorry to hear that.

6 자연스러운 대화가 되도록 A의 말에 이어질 (A)-(C)를 바르게 배열한 것은?

A I have a math test in the afternoon. I'm too nervous.

(A) But I always make mistakes when I feel too nervous. What should I do?

(B) Don't worry. Just do your best.

(C) You should do the easy questions first. Then you will feel better.

① (A) – (C) – (B)

② (B) – (A) – (C)

③ (B) – (C) – (A)

④ (C) – (A) – (B)

⑤ (C) – (B) – (A)

서술형 평가

1 주어진 단어들을 이용하여 밑줄 친 우리말을 영어로 옮기시오.

> **A** You look very tired, Judy. What's wrong?
> **B** I couldn't sleep well last night.
> **A** Why not?
> **B** My neighbor played music so loudly at night. (1) 나는 그것에 대해 화가 나. (upset, about)
> **A** Did you try to talk to your neighbor about it?
> **B** I'm not sure how to tell him. (2) 너는 좋은 생각이 있니? (any, ideas)
> **A** Well, why don't you bring some snacks and kindly tell him that you can't sleep at night because of the noise?
> **B** That's a good idea. I'll do that.

(1) _____

(2) _____

2 그림을 보고, 주어진 단어들을 이용하여 목적을 나타내는 문장을 완성하시오.

(1)

I visited Hawaii _____.
(enjoy, water sports)

(2)

I went to Busan _____.
(visit, grandmother)

3 빈칸에 알맞은 말을 <보기>에서 골라 알맞은 형태로 쓰시오.

> ─ 보기 ─
> ask   play   visit

(1) I want _____ you something.

(2) Lisa plans _____ her friend in the hospital.

(3) Mom told my brother _____ outside because it was raining.

4 두 문장이 같은 의미가 되도록 빈칸에 알맞은 말을 쓰시오.

(1) The pie was too big for me to eat alone.
= The pie was so _____.

(2) The quiz was easy enough to be solved in two minutes.
= The quiz was so _____ in two minutes.

(3) To say sorry first is a wise thing.
= _____ to say sorry first.

5 어법상 <u>어색한</u> 부분을 찾아 바르게 고쳐 쓰시오.

> Mina and Minho are my cousins. Mina is just four years old, but she is very smart. She is too smart to read books and she likes to read books. Her brother Minho is seven years old. He's very talkative. He is talkative enough to listen to others. He should listen carefully to others.

(1) _____ → _____

(2) _____ → _____

Final Test

Answer p. 3

난이도: 상 ★★★ 중 ★★ 하 ★

01 ★ 영영풀이에 해당하는 것은?

an object used for producing music

① garbage　　　　② music
③ ticket　　　　　④ treasure
⑤ instrument

02 ★★ 영영풀이를 완성할 때 빈칸에 알맞은 것은?

conductor: someone who stands in front of a group of musicians or singers and _____ their playing or singing

① collects　　　　② sends
③ asks　　　　　④ directs
⑤ appreciates

03 ★★ 짝지어진 대화가 <u>어색한</u> 것은?

① A I want to lose weight. What should I do?
　 B You'd better exercise regularly.
② A He is making fun of me again. I can't stand it.
　 B Calm down. He is just joking.
③ A I'm so tired and sleepy now.
　 B If I were you, I would go home and rest.
④ A That woman is cutting in line.
　 B I can't stand people like her.
⑤ A Do you think I should apologize to him?
　 B Thank you for your advice.

04 ★ 〔서술형 평가〕 우리말과 일치하도록 빈칸에 알맞은 말을 쓰시오.

A What would you do if you were in my shoes?
B If _____ _____ _____, I would never go there again.
(내가 너라면 거기에 다시는 가지 않을 거야.)

05 ★ 빈칸에 알맞은 것은?

A _____ my friend, Jessica.
B What's wrong?
A She talks about me behind my back.

① I really like　　　② I'm curious about
③ I agree with　　　④ I'm upset with
⑤ I can't wait to meet

06 ★★ 〔서술형 평가〕 그림을 보고, 주어진 단어들을 배열하여 문장을 완성하시오.

A What's wrong, Sally? You look sick.
B I don't feel well. I think I have a fever.
A Why _____?
(you, don't, the school nurse, go, to)
B Okay. I will do that.

교과서　**object** 물건, 물체　**produce** 만들어 내다, 생산하다　**regularly** 규칙적으로　**make fun of** …을 놀리다　**cut in line** 줄에 새치기하다
어휘　**fever** 열

Final Test

★★ 서술형 평가

07 자연스러운 대화가 되도록 (A)-(D)를 바르게 배열 하시오.

(A) Not at all. Please let me watch the basketball game.

(B) I can't stand this science program. It's so boring.

(C) Okay. No problem.

(D) Really? I thought you were enjoying it.

_____ → _____ → _____ → _____

★★ 시험에 잘 나오는 문제

08 의도하는 바가 나머지와 다른 것은?

① I advise you to get up early in the morning.

② I think you should get up early in the morning.

③ Why don't you get up early in the morning?

④ You had better get up early in the morning.

⑤ I'm sure you'll get up early in the morning.

★

09 빈칸에 알맞은 것은?

She is looking for a roommate _____.

① to live

② to live in

③ to live of

④ to live for

⑤ to live with

★★ 서술형 평가

10 우리말과 일치하도록 빈칸에 알맞은 말을 쓰시오.

사실을 말하자면, 나는 그와 잘 지내는 것이 어려워.

→ _____, it is difficult for me to get along with him.

★★ 서술형 평가

[11~12] 어법상 어색한 부분을 찾아 바르게 고쳐 쓰시오.

★★

11

He told his dog to not bark, but it kept barking.

_____ → _____

★★

12

I want you to thinking about it once more.

_____ → _____

★

13 빈칸에 알맞지 않은 것은?

It was _____ for Barbara to finish it by herself.

① hard

② easy

③ difficult

④ stupid

⑤ impossible

★

14 우리말 뜻이 알맞지 않은 것은?

① She is, so to speak, like an angel.
  (말하자면)

② To be brief, he quit his job.
  (간단히 말하면)

③ Strange to say, I saw them in my dreams.
  (이상한 말이지만)

④ To make matters worse, the light went off.
  (다행히도)

⑤ To be frank with you, I don't agree with you.
  (솔직히 말해서)

교과서 어휘 🎧 **roommate** 방을 함께 쓰는 사람, 룸메이트 **get along with** …와 잘 지내다 **bark** 짖다 **quit** 그만두다 **go off** (불·전기 등이) 나가다

 시험에 잘 나오는 문제

15 밑줄 친 부분의 용법이 나머지와 다른 것은?

① I forgot to get my umbrella.

② He is going abroad to get a new job.

③ She did her best to get more money.

④ Jisu is visiting them to get some help.

⑤ They went to the theater early to get good seats.

[16~17] 주어진 문장과 의미가 같은 것을 고르시오.

16

He was too late to watch the game.

① He didn't want to watch the game.

② He was very late, but he could watch the game.

③ He wasn't late, so he could watch the game.

④ He was so late that he couldn't watch the game.

⑤ He wasn't late, but he couldn't watch the game.

17

It seems that he knew the truth.

① He seems to know the truth.

② He seemed to know the truth.

③ He seems to have known the truth.

④ He doesn't seem to know the truth.

⑤ He seemed to have known the truth.

서술형 평가

18 목적의 의미를 나타내도록 빈칸에 각각 알맞은 말을 쓰시오.

• They hurried so _____ to catch the last bus.

• Jiho studied very hard in _____ to get high grades.

서술형 평가

19 두 문장이 같은 의미가 되도록 빈칸에 알맞은 말을 쓰시오.

(1) To persuade him is useless.

= _____ is useless _____ _____ him.

(2) I can't decide where to put this desk.

= I can't decide where _____ _____ _____ this desk.

(3) He can run fast enough to catch the thief.

= He can run so fast _____ he _____ catch the thief.

20 밑줄 친 부분의 용법이 〈보기〉와 같은 것은?

보기

She has nothing to do today.

① It is fun to play baseball.

② I'm happy to see you again.

③ My hobby is to take pictures.

④ There are many things to eat on the table.

⑤ I came home early to watch the soccer game.

교과서 어휘 **abroad** 해외로 **theater** 극장 **hurry** 서두르다 **useless** 소용없는 **thief** 도둑

★★ 서술형 평가

21 우리말과 일치하도록 주어진 단어들을 배열하여 문장을 완성하시오.

나는 그녀에게 전화하지 말라고 말했다.
(told, I, to, call, not, her)

→ _____

★★

22 빈칸에 들어갈 말이 나머지와 다른 것은?

① It was rude _____ you to go away.
② It was careless _____ Susie to lose her wallet again.
③ It was kind _____ you to send Kate some flowers.
④ It was impossible _____ him to get a good grade in the last test.
⑤ It was nice _____ David to help poor people.

[23~24] 어법상 어색한 것을 고르시오.
★★★
23

① This book is great for us to read.
② Betty has a lot of work to do.
③ Michael has many friends to play.
④ Sora seems to make mistakes.
⑤ There are lots of beautiful places to visit.

★★★
24

① To make planes is my favorite hobby.
② She is too young to finish it without help from others.
③ It is necessary to examine the case in detail.
④ Peter knows exactly what to do for his goal.
⑤ Anthony considered it easy master the subject.

★★

25 빈칸에 알맞은 것은?

An animal's eyes are sensitive enough to lose their sight easily. If they are attacked, it can cause blindness and put the creature's life in danger. For this reason, some animals have "_____ eyes". Fruit bats, for example, have white hairs beneath their ears to protect their eyes during fights. Attackers go for these instead of their real eyes. Others hide their eyes in bold patterns. The eyes of butterfly fish are hidden in a dark stripe across their faces.

① bright   ② real   ③ naked
④ false   ⑤ blind

★

26 필자가 주장하는 바로 알맞은 것은?

A balanced diet is a diet that includes the right amount of food from each of the food groups. Having a balanced diet will ensure that your body receives all the nutrients that it needs to stay healthy. Therefore, it is important for us to eat a variety of foods in order to get all of the nutrients that our bodies need. In short, we should try to balance our diet.

① 지방 섭취를 자제해야 한다.
② 식습관을 바꾸는 것은 어렵다.
③ 하루 권장량을 섭취해야 한다.
④ 건강을 위해 운동을 해야 한다.
⑤ 균형 잡힌 식습관을 가져야 한다.

교과서 **consider** 여기다, 생각하다 **sensitive** 민감한 **sight** 시력 **attack** 공격하다 **balance** 균형을 유지하다 **diet** 식사 **include** 포함하다
어휘 **receive** 받다 **nutrient** 영양소

[27~28] 다음을 읽고, 물음에 답하시오.

Herb Casey wanted (A) becoming/to become mayor of his city. So he put up signs, knocked on doors, and (B) send/sent letters to thousands of people in his city, that said "Please vote for me." It was finally election day. Herb put up even more signs. He called people on the phone and told them, "Today is election day. Please vote for me." At eight o'clock, Herb went to vote and arrived at the voting booth ten minutes after eight. However, he wasn't allowed (C) to vote/vote because voting ended at eight o'clock. The next day, the votes were counted. Did he win the election? No, he didn't. He lost the election by one vote. He made the biggest mistake in his life.

★★
27 Herb Casey의 심정 변화로 알맞은 것은?
① sad → upset
② worried → delighted
③ indifferent → relieved
④ hopeful → disappointed
⑤ embarrassed → pleased

★★
28 (A)–(C)에서 어법에 맞는 말이 바르게 짝지어진 것은?

	(A)	(B)	(C)
①	becoming	– send	– to vote
②	becoming	– sent	– vote
③	to become	– send	– to vote
④	to become	– sent	– to vote
⑤	to become	– sent	– vote

[29~30] 다음을 읽고, 물음에 답하시오.

Exercising is ⓐone of the most important ways to keep your body healthy. When you exercise, you strengthen your bones, muscles, and heart. You also burn off excess fat and improve your balance and mood. Today, many people don't get ⓑenough exercise. They usually watch TV, play video games, or use the Internet for several hours. Does that sound like you? If it does, it's time ⓒto get up and get moving! Playing soccer or dancing are all great ways ⓓto work out. To stay healthy, try to do about one hour of exercise a day. And try ⓔto not be inactive for more than two hours at a time.

★★
29 위 글의 내용을 요약할 때, 빈칸 (A)와 (B)에 들어갈 말이 바르게 짝지어진 것은?

It is important to ___(A)___ in order to keep your body ___(B)___.

① stay inside – safe
② stay inside – healthy
③ do exercise – healthy
④ do exercise – warm
⑤ eat less – in shape

★★
30 밑줄 친 ⓐ–ⓔ중 어법상 어색한 것은?
① ⓐ   ② ⓑ   ③ ⓒ   ④ ⓓ   ⑤ ⓔ

교과서 **mayor** 시장 **vote** 투표; 투표하다 **election** 선거 **voting booth** 기표소 **end** 끝나다 **count** 세다 **strengthen** 강화하다
어휘 **inactive** 활동하지 않는

·· >> Grammar

Ⓐ to부정사의 용법

명사적 용법	문장 내에서 주어, 목적어, 보어 역할을 한다.
형용사적 용법	(대)명사를 뒤에서 꾸미며 '…하는', '…할'의 의미이다.
부사적 용법	동사, 형용사, 부사를 꾸미며, 목적, 감정의 원인, 결과, 판단의 근거 등의 의미를 나타낸다.

I want **to go** to the South Pole someday. 〈명사적 용법: 목적어〉
Tina has no house **to live in**. 〈형용사적 용법: 명사 house를 꾸밈〉
He called **to cancel** the meeting. 〈부사적 용법: 목적〉

Ⓑ to부정사의 의미상 주어

to부정사의 의미상 주어는 대부분 to부정사 앞에 〈for+목적격〉을 쓰고, 사람의 성격, 태도를 나타내는 형용사(nice, wise, polite, rude, careless 등)가 오면 〈of+목적격〉을 쓴다.
It is easy **for me** to teach them French.   It was careless **of him** to break the dish.

Ⓒ to부정사의 시제

1 **단순부정사**: 〈to+동사원형〉의 형태로, to부정사의 시제는 본동사의 시제와 같다.
Maria seems **to be** ill.
= It seems that Maria **is** ill.

2 **완료부정사**: 〈to have+과거분사〉의 형태로, 본동사의 시제보다 이전에 일어난 일을 나타낸다.
He seems **to have been** a teacher.
= It seems that he **was** a teacher.

Ⓓ to부정사의 부정 / 대부정사

1 **to부정사의 부정**: to부정사 앞에 not(never)을 써서 부정의 의미를 나타낸다.
Mom told me **not to eat** too many candies.

2 **대부정사**: 앞에 나온 동사의 반복을 피하기 위해 to부정사의 동사를 생략하고 남겨진 to가 to부정사 전체를 대신한다.
You can have a bite if you want **to** (have).

E to부정사의 관용 표현

1 의문사+to부정사

what+to부정사	무엇을 …할지	how+to부정사	어떻게 …할지
where+to부정사	어디서(로) …할지	when+to부정사	언제 …할지

2 enough to / too ... to

형용사(부사)+enough+to부정사	too+형용사(부사)+to부정사
= so+형용사(부사)+that+주어+can ...	= so+형용사(부사)+that+주어+can't ...
…할 만큼 충분히 …한(하게)	너무 …해서 …할 수 없는

F 독립부정사

to be sure 확실히	to be brief 간단히 말하면
needless to say 말할 필요도 없이	so to speak 말하자면
to tell the truth 사실을 말하자면	strange to say 이상한 말이지만
to make matters worse 설상가상으로	to be frank with you 솔직히 말해서

>> Expression

1 화냄 표현하기

💗화냄 표현하기
- I feel angry.
- I'm upset(annoyed) about ....
- I can't stand ....
- ... is annoying(irritating).

💗화냄에 응대하기
- Calm down.
- Take it easy.
- Don't get so angry.
- There's nothing to get angry about.

2 충고 구하기 / 충고하기

💗충고 구하기
- What should I do?
- What do you think I should do?
- Do you think I should keep trying?
- Can I get your advice on this matter?
- What would you do if you were in my shoes?

💗충고하기
- I think you should apologize to her.
- You should(had better) take a taxi.
- If I were you, I would study harder.
- Why don't you get some exercise?
- I suggest you keep trying.
- I advise you to be nice to others.

Lesson 02

동명사

Grammar Preview

❶ 동명사

- 동명사: 〈동사원형＋ing〉의 형태로 명사 역할(주어, 목적어, 보어)을 한다.
  Taking a walk is good exercise. 〈주어〉
  Emma enjoys **baking** some cookies on Sundays. 〈동사의 목적어〉
  My bad habit was **biting** my fingernails. 〈주격보어〉

- 동명사의 의미상 주어: 보통 동명사 바로 앞에 소유격으로 나타내며, 목적격을 쓰기도 한다.
  I'm sure of **Bill's**(Bill) **being** honest with you.   Nick felt bad about **her cheating** on the test.

- 동명사의 관용 표현

be busy -ing …하느라 바쁘다	be used to -ing …하는 데 익숙하다
look forward to -ing …하는 것을 고대하다	on -ing …하자마자
feel like -ing …하고 싶다	be worth -ing …할 만한 가치가 있다
spend＋시간(돈)＋(in) -ing …하는 데 시간(돈)을 쓰다	
keep(prevent, stop) ... from -ing …가 …하지 못하게 하다	
have trouble(difficulty) (in) -ing …하는 데 어려움을 겪다	
cannot help -ing (= cannot but＋동사원형) …하지 않을 수 없다	
It is no use -ing (= It is of no use to＋동사원형) …해도 소용없다	

❷ 동명사, to부정사, 현재분사

- 동명사와 to부정사를 목적어로 쓰는 동사

동사 + 동명사	finish, enjoy, give up, avoid, mind, put off, consider, admit, deny 등
동사 + to부정사	want, hope, plan, decide, refuse, choose, agree, promise, expect 등
동사 + 동명사[to부정사]	love, like, begin, start, hate, continue 등 〈뜻이 동일함〉 remember, forget 〈동명사: 과거에 대한 내용 / to부정사: 미래에 대한 내용〉 try 〈동명사: 시험 삼아 …해 보다 / to부정사: …하려고 애쓰다〉

- 동명사와 현재분사

	역할	예문
동명사	명사(주어, 목적어, 보어)	My hobby is **collecting** old coins.
현재분사	형용사(보어, 수식어)	Jane is **collecting** materials for a report.

- 병렬 구조: 문법적으로 동일한 성질의 것들이 접속사로 연결된 것을 말한다. 접속사 앞에 동명사가 오면 뒤에도 동명사가 와야 하고, 앞에 to부정사가 오면 뒤에도 to부정사가 와야 한다.
  Playing soccer <u>or</u> **dancing** is my way of relieving stress.

1 동명사

A 동명사의 역할

동명사는 〈동사원형+ing〉의 형태로, 문장에서 명사처럼 주어, 목적어, 보어 역할을 한다. 또한 동사처럼 목적어, 수식어구 등과 함께 쓸 수 있다.

Taking a walk is good exercise. 〈주어〉
Emma enjoys **baking** some cookies on Sundays. 〈동사의 목적어〉
He greeted me by **shaking** his hand. 〈전치사의 목적어〉
My bad habit was **biting** my fingernails. 〈주격보어〉

cf. 동명사의 부정은 동명사 바로 앞에 not(never)을 쓴다.
I regret **not buying** the book.

> ● Plus Grammar
> 주어 자리에 오는 동명사는 단수 취급한다.
> **Speaking** English fluently <u>is</u> very difficult.

B 동명사의 의미상 주어

동명사의 의미상 주어는 보통 동명사 바로 앞에 소유격으로 나타내며, 목적격을 쓰기도 한다.

I'm sure of **Bill's**(Bill) **being** honest with you.
I'll not forget **his**(him) **helping** me with my experiment.
Nick felt bad about **her cheating** on the test.

cf. 의미상 주어가 문장의 주어와 같거나 일반적인 대상(we, they, people)일 경우 의미상 주어를 생략한다.
I'm sorry for (**my**) not cleaning the room.
(**Our**) Eating fast is bad for our health.

C 동명사의 관용 표현

be busy -ing …하느라 바쁘다	be used to -ing …하는 데 익숙하다
look forward to -ing …하는 것을 고대하다	on -ing …하자마자
feel like -ing …하고 싶다	be worth -ing …할 만한 가치가 있다
spend+시간(돈)+(in) -ing …하는 데 시간(돈)을 쓰다	
keep(prevent, stop) ... from -ing …가 …하지 못하게 하다	
have trouble(difficulty) (in) -ing …하는 데 어려움을 겪다	
cannot help -ing (= cannot but+동사원형) …하지 않을 수 없다	
It is no use -ing (= It is of no use to+동사원형) …해도 소용없다	

I don't **feel like studying** tonight.
It is no use crying over spilt milk.

> ● Plus Grammar
> **be used to -ing**: …하는 데 익숙하다
> **used to+동사원형**: …하곤 했다 〈과거의 규칙적인 습관 · 상태〉
> I **am used to eating** kimchi. (나는 김치 먹는 것에 익숙하다.)
> He **used to take** a short walk in the morning. (그는 아침에 짧은 산책을 하곤 했다.)

Grammar Practice >>

Answer p. 4

A1 밑줄 친 부분의 문장 성분을 〈보기〉에서 고르시오.

> 보기
> ⓐ 주어   ⓑ 목적어   ⓒ 보어

(1) He is interested in <u>making</u> model airplanes.
(2) What I like best is <u>listening</u> to the radio.
(3) <u>Meeting</u> new friends is very exciting.
(4) Jack's job is <u>fixing</u> broken machines.
(5) <u>Feeling</u> tired easily is his weak point.
(6) We usually enjoy <u>swimming</u> in the pool.

A2 괄호 안에서 알맞은 것을 고르시오.

(1) I remember (closing not, not closing) the door.
(2) Minji is proud of (to win, winning) first prize.
(3) (Making never errors, Never making errors) is impossible for her.
(4) (Drink, Drinking) enough water is good for your health.

B1 우리말과 일치하도록 주어진 단어를 이용하여 빈칸에 알맞은 말을 쓰시오.

(1) 그는 우리가 그 도시를 방문하는 것을 제안했다.
  → He suggested _____ _____ the city. (visit)
(2) 나는 그녀가 피아니스트로서 성공할 것을 확신한다.
  → I'm sure of _____ _____ as a pianist. (succeed)
(3) 제가 여기 앉아도 괜찮나요?
  → Do you mind _____ _____ here? (sit)

C1 밑줄 친 부분을 알맞은 형태로 쓰시오.

(1) I couldn't help <u>shout</u> at him.
(2) He looked forward to <u>get</u> letters from his friends.
(3) I am used to <u>wear</u> a necktie.
(4) Jenny spent her money in <u>decorate</u> the house.
(5) It is no use <u>argue</u> with him.
(6) I don't feel like <u>play</u> tennis today.
(7) This activity keeps you from <u>feel</u> blue.
(8) Bob is busy <u>take</u> care of animals.
(9) The British museum is worth <u>visit</u>.
(10) She is far from <u>keep</u> quiet.

C2 두 문장이 같은 의미가 되도록 빈칸에 알맞은 말을 쓰시오.

(1) It is of no use to try to persuade him.
  = It is no _____ _____ to persuade him.
(2) I could not help crying at the last scene.
  = I could not but _____ at the last scene.
(3) As soon as I know the result, I'll let you know.
  = _____ _____ the result, I'll let you know.
(4) I would like to drink cold water.
  = I feel _____ _____ cold water.

교과서 **greet** 인사하다 **shake** 흔들다 **bite** 물다 **fingernail** 손톱 **experiment** 실험 **cheat** 부정행위를 하다 **spill** 흘리다, 쏟다
어휘 **fix** 수리하다, 고치다 **weak point** 약점 **suggest** 제안하다 **shout** 소리 지르다 **decorate** 장식하다 **blue** 우울한

⒟ 동명사와 to부정사

1 동명사나 to부정사만 목적어로 취하는 동사

동사＋동명사	동사＋to부정사
finish, enjoy, give up, avoid, mind, put off, consider, admit, deny 등	want, hope, plan, decide, refuse, choose, agree, promise, expect 등

Did you **finish writing** your essay?

She **decided to write** a report about globalization.

> **＋Plus Grammar**
> **need＋to부정사**: 능동의 의미
> **need＋동명사**: 수동의 의미
> I **need to fix** my car.
> (나는 내 차를 수리할 필요가 있다.)
> My car **needs fixing.**
> = My car needs to be fixed.
> 　(내 차는 수리될 필요가 있다.)

2 동명사와 to부정사를 모두 목적어로 취하는 동사

- 의미 차이가 없는 동사: love, like, begin, start, hate, continue 등

  I **began to enjoy(enjoying)** teatime in the afternoon.

- 의미 차이가 있는 동사

동사	동명사를 취하는 경우	to부정사를 취하는 경우
try	시험 삼아 …해 보다	…하려고 애쓰다
remember(forget)	…했던 것을 기억하다(잊다)	…할 것을 기억하다(잊다)

He **tried breaking** the rock. 〈시도〉　　He **tried to break** the rock. 〈노력〉

I **remember meeting** you last week. 〈과거〉

I **remember to meet** you tomorrow. 〈미래〉

> **＋Plus Grammar**
> **stop＋동명사**: …하기를 멈추다
> **stop＋to부정사**: …하기 위해 멈추다
> My father **stopped smoking.**
> (나의 아버지는 담배를 끊었다.)
> My father **stopped to smoke.**
> (나의 아버지는 담배를 피우기 위해 멈췄다.)

⒠ 동명사와 현재분사

동명사는 명사 역할을 하여 주어, 목적어, 보어로 쓰이고, 현재분사는 형용사 역할을 하여 명사를 꾸미거나 주어, 목적어의 보어로 쓰인다.

My hobby is **collecting** old coins. 〈동명사: 모으기〉

Jane is **collecting** materials for a report. 〈현재분사: 모으고 있는〉

cf. 명사 앞에 쓰일 때, 동명사는 뒤의 명사의 목적이나 용도를 나타내는 또 다른 명사의 역할을 하며, 현재분사는 뒤의 명사를 꾸미는 형용사 역할을 한다.

　a **sleeping** bag (= a bag for sleeping) 〈동명사＋명사〉

　a **sleeping** baby (= a baby who is sleeping) 〈현재분사＋명사〉

> **＋Plus Grammar**
> 현재분사에 목적어나 수식어구가 붙는 경우, 뒤에서 명사를 꾸민다.
> I know the girl **sitting on the bench.**

⒡ 병렬 구조

병렬 구조란 문법적으로 동일한 성질의 것들이 접속사로 연결된 것을 말한다. 접속사 앞에 동명사가 오면 뒤에도 동명사가 와야 하고, 앞에 to부정사가 오면 뒤에도 to부정사가 와야 한다.

Playing soccer <u>or</u> **dancing** is my way of relieving stress.

I went to college **to study** more <u>and</u> **to get** a better job.

> **＋Plus Grammar**
> 문장에서 단어, 구, 절이 등위접속사, 상관접속사, 콤마(,) 등으로 연결되는 경우 연결되는 단어, 구, 절은 문법적 성질이 동일해야 한다.
> She is good at <u>not only</u> **playing** the guitar, <u>but also</u> **writing** poems.

Grammar Practice >>

Answer p. 4

D1 괄호 안에서 알맞은 것을 고르시오.

(1) She promised never (lying, to lie) again.

(2) I forgot (meeting, to meet) him two years ago.

(3) I decided (going, to go) to the library on Saturdays.

(4) He refused (accepting, to accept) their advice.

(5) I agreed (undertaking, to undertake) the project.

D2 어법상 어색한 부분을 찾아 고쳐 쓰시오.

(1) Would you mind to take a picture of me?

_____ → _____

(2) Don't forget coming back before dinner.

_____ → _____

(3) Jessica tried doing her best to solve the math problem.

_____ → _____

E1 밑줄 친 부분이 동명사인지 현재분사인지 쓰시오.

(1) Jake's working place is full of dirt.

(2) Pour the egg mixture into the frying pan.

(3) I'd like to buy him running shoes.

(4) The dancing bear seems to have hurt its ankle.

E2 밑줄 친 부분에 주의하여 문장을 우리말로 옮기시오.

(1) Look at the flying bird.

→ _____

(2) My mother bought a washing machine.

→ _____

(3) She is taking care of a crying child.

→ _____

F1 괄호 안에서 알맞은 것을 고르시오.

(1) He enjoys playing computer games and (to watch, watching) movies.

(2) I feel like going out and (get, getting) some fresh air.

(3) How about playing the guitar or (play, playing) the piano?

(4) She began to have trouble in seeing, hearing and (to walk, walking).

(5) I decided to save some money and (buy, buying) a new bike.

F2 두 문장을 한 문장으로 바꿔 쓸 때 빈칸에 알맞은 말을 쓰시오.

I like to play soccer. And I like to swim.

→ I like playing soccer and _____.

교과서 **essay** 과제물, 에세이 **globalization** 세계화 **collect** 모으다, 수집하다 **material** 자료 **relieve** 없애 주다, 완화하다
어휘 **undertake** (일·책임 등을) 맡다

Grammar Test

01 괄호 안에서 알맞은 것을 고르시오.

(1) I feel like (taking, to take) a walk after supper.

(2) She spent a lot of time in (cleaning, to clean) the room.

(3) That Chinese class is worth (taking, to take).

02 빈칸에 알맞지 <u>않은</u> 것은?

> They _____ drawing cartoons.

① enjoyed
② stopped
③ finished
④ wanted
⑤ loved

서술형 평가

03 우리말과 일치하도록 주어진 단어들을 바르게 배열하여 문장을 완성하시오.

> 제시간에 도착하지 않은 것에 대해 미안해.
> (arriving, for, not, on, time)

→ Excuse me _____.

04 밑줄 친 부분이 어법상 <u>어색한</u> 것은?

① The students stopped <u>talking</u>.
② David is fond of <u>taking</u> pictures.
③ <u>Playing</u> tennis is a good hobby.
④ Angela had to put off <u>to meet</u> him.
⑤ I hope <u>to visit</u> England someday.

서술형 평가

05 그림을 보고, 빈칸에 알맞은 말을 쓰시오.

> A What do you do in your free time?
> B I enjoy _____ books.

06 밑줄 친 부분의 쓰임이 나머지와 <u>다른</u> 것은?

① Are you considering <u>meeting</u> him?
② He is good at <u>speaking</u> Spanish.
③ Her plan is <u>throwing</u> a surprise party.
④ <u>Washing</u> hands is what you should do first.
⑤ The <u>burning</u> candles on the cake are very beautiful.

07 짝지어진 문장의 우리말 해석이 <u>잘못된</u> 것은?

① The baby does not stop crying.
  → 그 아기는 우는 것을 멈추지 않는다.
② I'm used to using chopsticks.
  → 나는 젓가락을 쓰는 데 익숙하다.
③ I'm looking forward to seeing her.
  → 나는 그녀를 보려고 앞쪽을 응시한다.
④ It's no use crying over your failure.
  → 너의 실패에 대해 울어도 소용없다.
⑤ Tom had difficulty counting numbers.
  → Tom은 숫자를 세는 데 어려움을 겪었다.

교과서 **supper** 저녁 식사 **cartoon** 만화 **be fond of** …을 좋아하다 **put off** …을 미루다, 연기하다 **consider** 고려하다
어휘 **throw a party** 파티를 열다 **burn** (불이) 타오르다 **candle** 양초 **count** 세다

08 빈칸에 들어갈 말이 바르게 짝지어진 것은?

> Paul gave up _____ the computer and decided _____ a new one.

① fix – buy
② to fix – buying
③ to fix – to buy
④ fixing – to buy
⑤ fixing – buying

서술형 평가

09 두 문장이 같은 의미가 되도록 빈칸에 알맞은 말을 쓰시오.

> I'm sure that she will win the game.
> = I'm sure of _____ _____ the game.

서술형 평가

10 우리말과 일치하도록 주어진 표현을 이용하여 문장을 완성하시오.

(1) 나는 수학 공부하는 것을 마쳤다.
　→ I _____.
　　 (finish, study math)

(2) 그들은 캠핑 가는 것을 원했다.
　→ They _____.
　　 (want, go camping)

11 어법상 어색한 것은?

① I finished doing my math homework.
② Billy likes to go to museum alone.
③ They began to run a restaurant together.
④ Susan is good at speaking and write English.
⑤ I'm looking forward to seeing my uncle.

12 짝지어진 문장의 의미가 서로 <u>다른</u> 것은?

① I feel like playing soccer.
　= I would like to play soccer.
② He began to repair the computer.
　= He began repairing the computer.
③ John remembers visiting the park.
　= John remembers to visit the park.
④ On arriving, he called me.
　= As soon as he arrived, he called me.
⑤ I couldn't help obeying my father.
　= I couldn't but obey my father.

13 어법상 옳은 것은?

① He continued plant the herb.
② Would you mind share the recipe?
③ I'll keep trying to improve my English.
④ Stretching before work out is important.
⑤ I remember to see her in front of the office yesterday.

14 밑줄 친 부분의 쓰임이 〈보기〉와 같은 것은?

> ┌─보기────────────────────┐
> │ I'll stop <u>complaining</u> about my meals. │
> └──────────────────────────┘

① It was a very <u>surprising</u> event.
② Jack was scared of the <u>barking</u> dog.
③ I know the woman <u>playing</u> the guitar there.
④ Studying animals <u>living</u> underwater is interesting.
⑤ <u>Discovering</u> new energy sources is important.

교과서　**give up** …을 포기하다　**run** 운영하다　**repair** 수리하다, 고치다　**obey** 따르다, 순종하다　**plant** 심다　**herb** 허브, 약초
어휘　**share** 공유하다　**recipe** 조리법　**complain** 불평하다　**discover** 발견하다

Lesson 02 동명사　**37**

Reading

[1~2] 다음을 끊어 읽고 ☑, 해석을 쓰시오. ✎

Why We Buy What We Buy

Have you wondered why you've bought things that you don't even want

3 or need? Let's consider what affects us when it comes to buying things.

Why do I buy pants and a bag after I have bought a coat?

Lisa buys a coat that she really loves. Immediately, she realizes that her pants do not ⓐmatch

6 her new coat. So, she buys new pants that go perfectly with her new coat. But she sees that

none of her bags match her new clothes. So, she buys a new bag. Most of her money is spent

on (A)buy the new items to complete her new ⓑlook.

9 What made Lisa search for new items ⓒimmediately after buying a new coat? The "Diderot

effect" may ⓓexplain it. Denis Diderot, a French writer, received a new gown as a gift. Soon after

receiving the gift, he noticed that all of his furniture did not go well with his new gown. So,

12 he ended up (B)replace most of it. The Diderot effect, therefore, is the concept that purchasing a

new item often leads to more ⓔplanned purchases.

---

1 밑줄 친 (A)와 (B)를 알맞은 형태로 쓰시오.

(A) _____   (B) _____

2 밑줄 친 ⓐ-ⓔ 중 문맥상 의미가 어색한 것은?

① ⓐ   ② ⓑ   ③ ⓒ   ④ ⓓ   ⑤ ⓔ

교과서 **wonder** 궁금해하다 **affect** 영향을 미치다 **complete** 완성하다 **search for** …을 찾다 **receive** 받다 **replace** 교체하다, 바꾸다
어휘 ♫ **concept** 개념 **purchase** 구매; 구매하다

3 빈칸에 알맞은 것은?

인물

Jacob and Wilhelm Grimm — two young men from Germany — loved **writing** traditional folktales of adventure and magic. Their tales reflected traditional life and beliefs in Germany. For example, for medieval Germans, the forest was a dangerous place. In Grimms' fairy tales, witches, talking animals, and other magical beings live in the forest. Although Grimms' fairy tales are now considered children's stories, the brothers first wrote them mainly for adults. Many of the early tales were dark and a little scary. Later, the brothers _____ many of the tales and also added drawings. This made them more appropriate for children.

① heard   ② confused   ③ softened
④ copied   ⑤ published

4 (A)–(C)의 순서로 알맞은 것은?

동물

Imagine **driving** through Yellowstone. You see a bear by the side of the road. Your parent stops the car to get a closer look. Before you can blink, the bear sticks its nose through your car window. The bear is looking for your picnic lunch.

(A) To **keep** people and bears **from getting** too close to each other, people are not allowed to feed them and they must stay at least 91 meters away from bears.

(B) But things have changed as many bears and people were injured as a result of this closeness.

(C) It's hard to believe, but this kind of interaction between humans and bears used to be common.

① (A) – (C) – (B)   ② (B) – (A) – (C)   ③ (B) – (C) – (A)
④ (C) – (A) – (B)   ⑤ (C) – (B) – (A)

---

3 folktale 설화 reflect 반영하다 medieval 중세의 appropriate 적절한
4 blink 눈을 깜박이다 stick 집어넣다 injure 부상을 입히다 interaction 상호 작용

Expression

1 희망, 기대 표현하기

💬 희망, 기대 표현하기

- I hope ....
- I can't wait to(for) ....
- I'm looking forward to ....

- I expect that ....
- It'll be nice to ....
- I'm really eager to ....

2 기원하기

💬 기원하기

- I wish(hope) ....
- I'll keep my fingers crossed!
- Good luck (with your ...)!

Expression Test

Answer p. 6

1 밑줄 친 부분의 의도로 알맞은 것은?

> A Which class are you going to take?
> B I'm going to take the cooking class. I'm looking forward to it.

① 충고하기
② 놀람 표현하기
③ 화냄 표현하기
④ 유감 표현하기
⑤ 기대 표현하기

2 의도하는 바가 나머지와 다른 것은?
① Good luck to you!
② I'm glad to hear that.
③ I wish you all the best.
④ I hope everything goes well.
⑤ I'll keep my fingers crossed for you.

3 빈칸에 알맞은 것은?

> A Today is very hot. How about going to the beach?
> B Sounds great! We haven't been there for a long time.
> A You're right. _____

① I went there last week.
② I'm not ready to go there.
③ I can't wait to see the beach.
④ I prefer to go to the amusement park.
⑤ I'm worried that the beach is crowded.

4 빈칸에 알맞지 <u>않은</u> 것은?

> A _____
> B I'll keep my fingers crossed for you.

① I have a marathon race tomorrow.
② I have a speech contest this weekend.
③ I have an interview on TV this Friday.
④ I have just finished all my homework.
⑤ I have a big basketball game this Saturday.

5 밑줄 친 부분과 바꿔 쓸 수 있는 것은?

> A How long has it been since you last saw your aunt?
> B Two years. I can't wait to see her.

① It'll be nice to wait for her.
② I'm anxious to wait for her.
③ I'm going to wait to see her.
④ I'm looking forward to seeing her.
⑤ I expect that she will wait for me.

6 자연스러운 대화가 되도록 (A)–(D)를 바르게 배열한 것은?

> (A) Just do your best. I'll keep my fingers crossed for you.
> (B) You look worried.
> (C) Yes. I have a bicycle race tomorrow.
> (D) Thanks.

① (A) – (C) – (B) – (D)
② (B) – (A) – (C) – (D)
③ (B) – (C) – (A) – (D)
④ (C) – (A) – (B) – (D)
⑤ (C) – (B) – (A) – (D)

서술형 평가

1 밑줄 친 단어들을 바르게 배열하여 대화를 완성하시오.

A Do you want to watch the new 3D superhero movie?

B Which one?

A The one about Aquaman's adventures under the sea. It was shot near Australia's Great Barrier Reef.

B Oh, I've heard of it. The movie shows a lot of beautiful sea life.

A Right. I <u>to, the, movie, wait, watch, can't.</u> Let's go and get the ticket.

_____

2 주어진 단어를 알맞은 형태로 쓰시오.

(1) _____ a true friend is hard. (find)

(2) Thank you for _____ me. (not forget)

(3) I'm interested in _____ about new culture. (learn)

3 밑줄 친 두 문장을 한 문장으로 바꿔 쓸 때 빈칸에 알맞은 말을 쓰시오.

A What would you like to do in your free time?

B I'd like to go fishing. It is my favorite thing to do.

→ _____ is my favorite thing to do.

4 그림을 보고, 주어진 단어들을 이용하여 빈칸에 알맞은 말을 쓰시오.

(1)

Mina enjoys _____.
(watch, movies)

(2)

Minsu likes _____.
(walk, the dog)

5 Molly의 새해 계획 메모를 보고, 글을 완성하시오.

My New Year's Resolutions
- exercise twice a week
- don't eat fast food
- write on my work-out diary
- drink 2 liters of water a day

Do you have any New Year's resolutions? Well, here are mine. First, I plan (1)_____ twice a week. Second, I will stop (2)_____. Next, I'll keep on (3)_____ my work-out diary. Also, I will try (4)_____ 2 liters of water a day. I'm sure I will become healthy by the end of this year.

Final Test

Answer p. 6

난이도: 상 ★★★ 중 ★★ 하 ★

★★
01 영영풀이가 <u>잘못된</u> 것은?

① receive: to be given something
② unplanned: not planned or expected
③ purchase: to buy something
④ immediately: without delay
⑤ replace: to become different

★★ 서술형 평가
02 빈칸에 알맞은 단어를 〈보기〉에서 골라 쓰시오.

┌─보기─────────────────────┐
│   realize   buy   match   │
└───────────────────────────┘

(1) Where did you _____ that dress?
(2) The coat does not _____ the hat.
(3) Amy didn't _____ that he was unhappy.

★★
03 짝지어진 대화가 <u>어색한</u> 것은?

① A I hope to visit all the museums in the world.
  B Wow! Good luck.
② A What are you looking forward to doing this winter?
  B I'm looking forward to going skiing.
③ A I have an important interview tomorrow.
  B I wish you all the best!
④ A Have you ever been to Dokdo?
  B I can't wait to visit Dokdo.
⑤ A Today, I'm going to tell John I like him.
  B Really? I'll keep my fingers crossed for you.

★ 서술형 평가
04 주어진 단어를 이용하여 빈칸에 알맞은 말을 쓰시오.

A He will come home tomorrow.
B I'm _____ _____ _____ seeing him at home. (look)
A Me too. I can't wait to see him.

★
05 빈칸에 알맞지 <u>않은</u> 것은?

A What are your hopes for this year?
B _____

① I hope to be healthier.
② I want to make a lot of friends.
③ I hope to grow taller.
④ I hope I can learn to play the violin.
⑤ I'm interested in drawing pictures.

★★ 서술형 평가
06 우리말과 일치하도록 빈칸에 알맞은 말을 쓰시오.

A Jack is going to take part in a speech contest tomorrow.
B Really? Let's keep our _____ _____ for him. (그의 행운을 빌어 주자.)

★ 서술형 평가
07 주어진 단어들을 배열하여 문장을 완성하시오.

A What do you want to do this year?
B I _____ for children.
  (write, to, a book, hope)

교과서   **delay** 지연, 지체   **different** 다른   **unhappy** 불행한   **take part in** …에 참가하다
어휘

Final Test

08 빈칸에 알맞지 <u>않은</u> 것은?

A You look worried.
B Yes. I have an important test tomorrow.
A Just do your best. _____
B Thanks.

① I wish you good luck.
② I wish you all the best.
③ I'll never forget your help.
④ I hope everything goes well.
⑤ I'll keep my fingers crossed for you.

★
09 우리말과 일치하도록 할 때 빈칸에 알맞은 것은?

기차로 여행하는 것은 매우 재미있다.
→ _____ is very interesting.

① Travel by train
② Traveled by train
③ To traveling by train
④ To traveled by train
⑤ Traveling by train

★ ★
10 빈칸에 들어갈 말이 바르게 짝지어진 것은?

• You should consider _____ a used car.
• Trees can keep rivers from _____.

① to buy – to overflow
② to buy – overflowing
③ buying – to overflow
④ buying – to overflowing
⑤ buying – overflowing

★ ★ 시험에 잘 나오는 문제
11 밑줄 친 부분의 쓰임이 나머지와 <u>다른</u> 것은?

① It was an <u>exciting</u> discovery.
② The boy <u>taking</u> pictures is Jiho.
③ No one spits on a <u>smiling</u> face.
④ The man <u>standing</u> at the door is my father.
⑤ We are looking forward to her <u>coming</u> back.

★ 서술형 평가
12 밑줄 친 부분을 알맞은 형태로 고쳐 쓰시오.

Eric tried to stop <u>play</u> online games, but he couldn't stop it.

→ _____

서술형 평가
[13~14] 어법상 어색한 부분을 찾아 고쳐 쓰시오.
★ ★
13

He doesn't have much interest in grow flowers in a garden.

_____ → _____

★ ★
14

She regrets having not worked harder while young.

_____ → _____

15 빈칸에 알맞지 <u>않은</u> 것은?

Sejin _____ taking piano lessons.

① stopped ② continued
③ wanted ④ gave up
⑤ liked

16 빈칸에 알맞은 것은?

Jim insisted on _____ coming to the meeting.

① they ② to them
③ for them ④ their
⑤ theirs

17 괄호 안에서 알맞은 것을 고르시오.

(1) I don't care about (his to come, his coming) here.
(2) She promised (giving, to give) me her old dress.
(3) I think he avoided (answering, to answer) my question.

18 밑줄 친 부분이 어법상 <u>어색한</u> 것은?

① I don't feel like <u>to have</u> lunch.
② His father decided to <u>stop</u> smoking.
③ We look forward to <u>going</u> on a field trip.
④ Would you mind <u>repeating</u> your question?
⑤ She has difficulty in <u>solving</u> the problem.

19 밑줄 친 부분의 쓰임이 〈보기〉와 같은 것은?

〈보기〉
The girl <u>dancing</u> on the stage is Juliet.

① Brad has forgotten <u>meeting</u> me.
② I know the man <u>wearing</u> a red shirt.
③ He has trouble in <u>focusing</u> on the lecture.
④ <u>Playing</u> badminton is good for your health.
⑤ <u>Predicting</u> the earthquake completely was impossible.

시험에 잘 나오는 문제
20 짝지어진 문장의 의미가 서로 <u>다른</u> 것은?

① I forgot that I met her before.
  = I forgot meeting her before.
② It is no use waiting for him any more.
  = It is of no use to wait for him any more.
③ I found that my car needed fixing.
  = I found that my car needed to be fixed.
④ She cannot help having her son's birthday party.
  = She cannot but have her son's birthday party.
⑤ He doesn't feel like going shopping today.
  = He can't imagine going shopping today.

서술형 평가
21 우리말과 일치하도록 주어진 단어들을 이용하여 빈칸에 알맞은 말을 쓰시오.

Molly는 어제 시험 삼아 쿠키를 만들어 보았다.
→ Molly _____ yesterday.
  (try, make, cookies)

교과서
어휘 **insist on** …을 주장하다 **repeat** 반복하다 **stage** 무대 **focus on** …에 집중하다 **lecture** 강의 **predict** 예측하다
earthquake 지진

★★

22 두 문장의 의미가 같도록 할 때 빈칸에 알맞은 것은?

> I can't remember that I turned the alarm off.
> = I can't remember _____ the alarm off.

① turn
② to turn
③ turning
④ turned
⑤ to be turned

★★★

23 어법상 옳은 것은?

① I am used to eat raw fish.
② They just started set the table.
③ Joe wants having a sincere partner.
④ Andy couldn't help to go there first.
⑤ I like going shopping and chatting with my friends.

★★★

24 어법상 어색한 것은?

① I won't avoid working with him.
② She has been busy repairing her car.
③ We'll finish looking around here soon.
④ He spends his money collect paintings.
⑤ I hope to read his short stories in English.

★★

25 다음 글의 주제로 알맞은 것은?

> Do animals have a "sixth sense" for earthquakes? Some scientists think that animals may sense weak tremors before a quake. Other scientists think that they may sense electrical signals set off by the shifting of underground rocks. People reported that some animals behaved strangely before the May 2008 earthquake in China. Elephants swung their trunks wildly. Peacocks screeched. Some pandas started marching around.   *tremor 미진(微震), 진동

① 지진의 발생 원인
② 지진이 잦은 지역
③ 지진 대피 훈련
④ 지진 피해
⑤ 동물들의 지진 감지 능력

★★

26 빈칸 (A)와 (B)에 들어갈 말이 바르게 짝지어진 것은?

> You might think sitting calmly before a big test gets your brain ready for the strain. Wrong! In Beilock's experiments, sitting quietly led to worries about the test and doubts about the outcome. This stress made critical thinking more ___(A)___. Her solution is to spend at least ten minutes before each test ___(B)___ about your thoughts or feelings. Participants who wrote before a stressful test ended up scoring an average of five percent better than their grades on a much easier test.

① common – talking
② common – writing
③ difficult – talking
④ difficult – writing
⑤ important – writing

교과서
어휘🎧

raw 날것의 signal 신호 screech 꽥 하는 소리를 내다 march 행진하다 strain 부담, 압박 critical 비판적인 average 평균

[27~28] 다음을 읽고, 물음에 답하시오.

According to a recent study, creative thinking ⓐimproves while a person is walking and shortly thereafter. The study found that (A)walking indoors and outdoors similarly boosted creative inspiration. The act of walking itself, and not the environment, was the ⓑmain factor. Creativity levels were significantly ⓒlower for those walking compared to those sitting. In the U.K., schools are signing up to be part of a new movement called the Daily Mile. The goal is to have all of the students at each school run or ⓓwalk for at least 15 minutes before the start of class every day. This will help students to ⓔachieve academic and social success.

★★
27 밑줄 친 ⓐ-ⓔ 중 문맥상 의미가 어색한 것은?

① ⓐ　　② ⓑ　　③ ⓒ　　④ ⓓ　　⑤ ⓔ

★★
28 밑줄 친 (A)와 쓰임이 다른 것은?

① He started walking down the hill.
② Walking around here at night is dangerous.
③ A man walking down the street looks strange.
④ Walking gives you energy for the rest of the day.
⑤ I'm looking forward to walking along the beach.

[29~30] 다음을 읽고, 물음에 답하시오.

The Forbidden City served as the home of emperors, and ⓐas the scene for religious and official ceremonies. For centuries, only the emperor's family and officials ⓑcould enter the Forbidden City. Since its opening in 1925, thousands of visitors ⓒhave passed through its gates. They visit it not only ⓓbecause of its historical importance but also because of its huge size and magnificent architecture. The site also houses ⓔastonish imperial treasures that comprises nearly 50,000 paintings, 320,000 pieces of porcelain, and so on.

*porcelain 자기(磁器)

★★★
29 밑줄 친 ⓐ-ⓔ 중 어법상 어색한 것은?

① ⓐ　　② ⓑ　　③ ⓒ　　④ ⓓ　　⑤ ⓔ

★★
30 Forbidden City에 관한 위 글의 내용과 일치하지 않는 것은?

① 황제들의 집으로서 역할을 했다.
② 황제의 가족과 관리들만 들어갈 수 있었다.
③ 1925년에 재건축이 완료되었다.
④ 개방된 이후, 많은 사람들이 방문하고 있다.
⑤ 황제의 보물들을 보유하고 있다.

교과서 **thereafter** 그 후에　**significantly** 상당히　**academic** 학문의　**emperor** 황제　**magnificent** 웅장한, 훌륭한　**architecture** 건축(술)
어휘 **astonish** 깜짝 놀라게 하다　**imperial** 황제의　**comprise** …으로 구성되다

.... >> Grammar

A 동명사의 역할

동명사는 〈동사원형＋ing〉의 형태로, 문장에서 명사처럼 주어, 목적어, 보어 역할을 한다. 또한
동사처럼 목적어, 수식어구 등과 함께 쓸 수 있다.

Taking a walk is good exercise. 〈주어〉
Emma enjoys **baking** some cookies on Sundays. 〈동사의 목적어〉
My bad habit was **biting** my fingernails. 〈주격보어〉

cf. 동명사의 부정은 동명사 바로 앞에 not(never)을 쓴다.
I regret **not buying** the book.

B 동명사의 의미상 주어

동명사의 의미상 주어는 보통 동명사 바로 앞에 소유격으로 나타내며, 목적격을 쓰기도 한다.
I'm sure of **Bill's(Bill) being** honest with you.
Nick felt bad about **her cheating** on the test.

cf. 의미상 주어가 문장의 주어와 같거나 일반적인 대상(we, they, people)일 경우 의미상 주어
를 생략한다.
I'm sorry for (**my**) not cleaning the room.
(**Our**) Eating fast is bad for our health.

C 동명사의 관용 표현

be busy -ing …하느라 바쁘다	be used to -ing …하는 데 익숙하다
look forward to -ing …하는 것을 고대하다	on -ing …하자마자
feel like -ing …하고 싶다	be worth -ing …할 만한 가치가 있다
spend＋시간(돈)＋(in) -ing …하는 데 시간(돈)을 쓰다	
keep(prevent, stop) ... from -ing …가 …하지 못하게 하다	
have trouble(difficulty) (in) -ing …하는 데 어려움을 겪다	
cannot help -ing (= cannot but＋동사원형) …하지 않을 수 없다	
It is no use -ing (= It is of no use to＋동사원형) …해도 소용없다	

D 동명사와 to부정사

1 동명사나 to부정사만 목적어로 취하는 동사

동사+동명사	동사+to부정사
finish, enjoy, give up, avoid, mind, put off, consider, admit, deny 등	want, hope, plan, decide, refuse, choose, agree, promise, expect 등

Did you **finish writing** your essay?

She **decided to write** a report about globalization.

2 동명사와 to부정사를 모두 목적어로 취하는 동사

- 의미 차이가 없는 동사: love, like, begin, start, hate, continue 등
- 의미 차이가 있는 동사

동사	동명사를 취하는 경우	to부정사를 취하는 경우
try	시험 삼아 …해 보다	…하려고 애쓰다
remember(forget)	…했던 것을 기억하다(잊다)	…할 것을 기억하다(잊다)

E 동명사와 현재분사

	역할	예문
동명사	명사(주어, 목적어, 보어)	My hobby is **collecting** old coins.
현재분사	형용사(보어, 수식어)	Jane is **collecting** materials for a report.

F 병렬 구조

병렬 구조란 문법적으로 동일한 성질의 것들이 접속사로 연결된 것을 말한다. 접속사 앞에 동명사가 오면 뒤에도 동명사가 와야 하고, 앞에 to부정사가 오면 뒤에도 to부정사가 와야 한다.

Playing soccer or **dancing** is my way of relieving stress.

I went to college **to study** more and **to get** a better job.

·························· >> Expression

1 희망, 기대 표현하기

- I hope ....
- I can't wait to(for) ....
- I'm looking forward to ....
- I expect that ....
- It'll be nice to ....
- I'm really eager to ....

2 기원하기

- I wish(hope) ....
- I'll keep my fingers crossed!
- Good luck (with your ...)!

Lesson 03

시제

Grammar Preview

1 현재완료, 현재완료진행

- 현재완료: 과거에 일어난 일이 현재까지 영향을 미치고 있을 때 쓰는 시제로 〈have(has)＋과거분사〉의 형태로 쓴다.

  I <u>lost</u> my wallet. 〈과거 – 현재 지갑을 찾았는지 알 수 없음〉

  I **have lost** my wallet. 〈현재완료 – 현재에도 지갑을 잃어버린 상태임〉

- 현재완료의 용법

용법	의미	함께 쓰이는 표현
완료	막 …했다	just, already, yet 등
경험	…해 본 적이 있다	ever, never, before, once 등
계속	(지금까지) …해 왔다	for, since, how long 등
결과	…해 버렸다 (그 결과 지금 …하다)	–

The famous singer **has** just **arrived** here.　　We **have been** to the book exhibition <u>once</u>.

The lawyer **has worked** here <u>for</u> 7 years.　　I **have lost** my smartphone.

- 현재완료진행형: 과거에 시작해서 현재에도 계속하고(되고) 있는 일을 표현할 때 〈have(has)＋been＋-ing〉의 형태로 쓴다.

  It **has been raining** for 3 days.

2 과거완료, 과거완료진행

- 과거완료: 과거의 어느 시점을 기준으로, 그 이전부터 기준 시점까지 일어난 일을 나타낼 때 쓰는 시제로 〈had＋과거분사〉의 형태로 쓴다. 현재완료와 마찬가지로 완료, 경험, 계속, 결과의 네 가지 용법이 있다.

용법	의미	예문
완료	(그 전에) …했었다	The show **had** just **ended** by the time I got there.
경험	(그때까지) …해 본 적이 있었다	I couldn't read the book because I **had** never **learned** Spanish.
계속	(그때까지 계속) …하고 있었다	He **had worked** for the company for two years.
결과	…했었다 (그 결과 그때 …인 상태였다)	He **had gone** abroad before I arrived at the airport.

- 대과거: 과거에 일어났던 일의 순서를 나타낼 때 더 이전에 일어났던 일을 대과거라고 하며, 과거완료로 표현한다.

  He <u>said</u> that the dog **had attacked** him before.

- 과거완료진행형: 어떤 동작이 대과거에서 시작되어 과거의 어느 시점까지 계속되었음을 강조할 때 〈had＋been＋-ing〉의 형태로 쓴다.

  Lily **had been doing** her homework when her father came back.

1 현재완료, 현재완료진행

Ⓐ 현재완료

1 현재완료: 과거에 일어난 일이 현재까지 영향을 미치고 있을 때 쓰는 시제로 〈have(has)＋과거분사〉의 형태로 쓴다.

부정문	have(has)＋not＋과거분사
의문문	Have(Has)＋주어＋과거분사 …?

I lost my wallet. 〈과거 – 현재 지갑을 찾았는지 알 수 없음〉
I **have lost** my wallet. 〈현재완료 – 현재에도 지갑을 잃어버린 상태임〉
James **hasn't arrived** yet.
Have you ever **heard** of the concert? — Yes, I have. / No, I haven't.

2 현재완료의 용법

용법	의미	함께 쓰이는 표현
완료	막 …했다	just, already, yet 등
경험	…해 본 적이 있다	ever, never, before, once 등
계속	(지금까지) …해 왔다	for, since, how long 등
결과	…해 버렸다 (그 결과 지금 …하다)	–

The famous singer **has** just **arrived** here. 〈완료〉
We **have been** to the book exhibition once. 〈경험〉
The lawyer **has worked** here for 7 years. 〈계속〉
I **have lost** my smartphone. 〈결과〉

3 현재완료와 함께 쓸 수 없는 부사(구): 명백한 과거를 나타내는 부사(구)(ago, yesterday, last year 등)와 의문사 when은 현재완료와 함께 쓸 수 없다.
He has caught the criminal two weeks ago. (×)
→ He **caught** the criminal two weeks **ago**. (○)

cf. 막연한 시간을 나타내는 부사 before는 현재완료와 함께 쓸 수 있다.

> **✦ Plus** Grammar
> have gone to는 '…에 가고 없다'라는 뜻으로 결과를 나타낸다.
> Yuri **has gone to** France.
> (Yuri는 프랑스에 가 버렸다. (그래서 현재 여기에 없다.))

Ⓑ 현재완료진행

1 현재완료진행형: 과거에 시작해서 현재에도 계속하고(되고) 있는 일을 표현할 때 〈have(has)＋been＋-ing〉의 형태로 쓴다.
It **has been raining** for 3 days.

2 현재완료진행형의 부정문과 의문문

부정문	have(has)＋not＋been＋-ing
의문문	Have(Has)＋주어＋been＋-ing …?

He **has not been working** for a while.
Have you **been sleeping** well?

Grammar Practice >>

Answer p. 8

A1 밑줄 친 부분의 용법을 〈보기〉에서 고르시오.

〈보기〉
ⓐ 완료   ⓑ 경험   ⓒ 계속   ⓓ 결과

(1) I have never seen the Statue of Liberty.

(2) I've lived here since I was a child.

(3) She has gone to her country.

(4) The orchestra has already finished playing.

(5) Have you ever watched a horror movie?

(6) The number of the homeless has increased for three years.

A2 두 문장이 같은 의미가 되도록 빈칸에 알맞은 말을 쓰시오.

(1) My father went to China and he is still there.

　= My father ＿＿＿＿＿ ＿＿＿＿＿ to China.

(2) I moved here 3 years ago and I still live here.

　= I ＿＿＿＿＿ ＿＿＿＿＿ here for 3 years.

A3 어법상 어색한 부분을 찾아 바르게 고쳐 쓰시오.

(1) When have you been to the new shopping mall?

　＿＿＿＿＿＿＿＿ → ＿＿＿＿＿＿＿＿

(2) I have experienced never hot weather like this.

　＿＿＿＿＿＿＿＿ → ＿＿＿＿＿＿＿＿

(3) I have be to Singapore three times.

　＿＿＿＿＿＿＿＿ → ＿＿＿＿＿＿＿＿

(4) I have not seeing Julia recently.

　＿＿＿＿＿＿＿＿ → ＿＿＿＿＿＿＿＿

B1 괄호 안에서 알맞은 것을 고르시오.

(1) How long have you (be, been) living here?

(2) I (have not, not have) been talking to him for a week.

(3) The movie (has showing, has been showing) for two months.

(4) I have been waiting for the shuttle bus (for, since) 30 minutes.

(5) Smith (has being worked, has been working) for the company since 2017.

(6) Sue has (being writing, been writing) a book about the origin of the universe since last month.

(7) Brian and Jim (has studied, have been studying) abroad for two years.

B2 우리말과 일치하도록 주어진 단어를 이용하여 빈칸에 알맞은 말을 쓰시오.

(1) Kevin은 두 시간 동안 영어를 공부하고 있는 중이다.

　→ Kevin ＿＿＿＿ ＿＿＿＿ ＿＿＿＿ English for two hours. (study)

(2) 그들이 얼마나 오랫동안 숨을 참고 있는 거니?

　→ How long ＿＿＿＿ they ＿＿＿＿ ＿＿＿＿ their breath? (hold)

(3) Cathy는 일주일 동안 약을 먹지 않고 있다.

　→ Cathy ＿＿＿＿ ＿＿＿＿ ＿＿＿＿ ＿＿＿＿ medicine for a week. (take)

교과서 어휘 🎧　**wallet** 지갑　**exhibition** 전시회　**lawyer** 변호사　**criminal** 범인　**statue** 조각상　**liberty** 자유　**breath** 숨　**hold** 유지하다　**medicine** 약

ⓒ 과거완료

1 과거완료: 과거의 어느 시점을 기준으로, 그 이전부터 기준 시점까지 일어난 일을 나타낼 때 쓰는 시제로 〈had + 과거분사〉의 형태로 쓴다.

부정문	had + not + 과거분사
의문문	Had + 주어 + 과거분사 …?

Semi **had cleaned** the house <u>before her mom came back.</u>
기준 시점

They **had not finished** dinner <u>when the doorbell sounded.</u>
기준 시점

Had he **left** his house <u>when you arrived?</u>
기준 시점

2 과거완료의 용법

용법	의미	용법	의미
완료	(그 전에) …했었다	계속	(그때까지 계속) …하고 있었다
경험	(그때까지) …해 본 적이 있었다	결과	…했었다 (그 결과 그때 …인 상태였다)

The show **had** just **ended** by the time I got there. 〈완료〉
I couldn't read the book because I **had** never **learned** Spanish. 〈경험〉
He **had worked** for the company for two years. 〈계속〉
He **had gone** abroad before I arrived at the airport. 〈결과〉

3 대과거: 과거에 일어났던 일의 순서를 나타낼 때 더 이전에 일어났던 일을 대과거라고 하며, 과거완료로 표현한다.

He <u>said</u> that the dog **had attacked** him before.
과거   대과거

> ◆ **Plus** Grammar
> **과거완료와 현재완료**
>
> 과거완료 → 현재완료
> 대과거   과거   현재
> 과거완료는 과거를 기준으로 더 이전의 과거(대과거)부터 과거 시점까지 일어난 일을, 현재완료는 현재까지 영향을 미치는 일을 나타낸다.

Ⓓ 과거완료진행

1 과거완료진행형: 어떤 동작이 대과거에서 시작되어 과거의 어느 시점까지 계속되었음을 강조할 때 〈had + been + -ing〉의 형태로 쓴다.
Lily **had been doing** her homework when her father came back.

2 과거완료진행형의 부정문과 의문문

부정문	had + not + been + -ing
의문문	Had + 주어 + been + -ing …?

I **had not been watching** TV for a long time.
Had Jack **been playing** computer games when you arrived there?

Grammar Practice >>

Answer p. 8

C1 괄호 안에서 알맞은 것을 고르시오.

(1) I (have, had) just finished the work when she asked me about it.

(2) I regretted that I (behave, had behaved) badly toward my parents.

(3) We (fix, had fixed) the machine before the repairman showed up.

(4) After he (has turned, had turned) off the TV, he began to study.

C2 밑줄 친 부분을 어법에 맞게 고쳐 쓰시오.

(1) Emily knew about Korea well because she has visited Korea before.

(2) Until then, she has never been abroad.

(3) I couldn't find the camera he had lend me.

C3 우리말과 일치하도록 주어진 단어를 이용하여 빈칸에 알맞은 말을 쓰시오.

(1) 그는 소라가 창문을 깼었다는 것을 알았다.

→ He knew that Sora _____ _____ the window. (break)

(2) 그녀는 3년간 프랑스어를 공부해 왔었다고 말했다.

→ She said that she _____ _____ French for 3 years. (study)

(3) Jimmy와 Ali가 도착했을 때, 버스는 이미 떠났었다.

→ The bus _____ already _____ when Jimmy and Ali arrived. (leave)

D1 괄호 안에서 알맞은 것을 고르시오.

(1) She (had, has) been cleaning the house until her mother came back.

(2) I didn't know that they (had, has) been playing games for two hours.

(3) When Sue opened the door, something (had, has) been burning in the kitchen.

(4) Richard didn't realize that his parents (had supporting, had been supporting) him all his life.

D2 주어진 단어들을 배열하여 문장을 완성하시오.

(1) Tom _____ for 30 minutes before it rained. (playing, had, basketball, been)

(2) I knew _____ for a long time. (she, been, that, had, crying)

(3) Jim _____ he was hired by the German company. (before, German, had, learning, been)

D3 우리말과 일치하도록 주어진 단어를 이용하여 빈칸에 알맞은 말을 쓰시오.

(1) 그들은 한 시간 동안 책을 읽고 있었다고 말했다.

→ They said that they _____ _____ _____ books for an hour. (read)

(2) 내가 그의 방에 들어갔을 때, 그는 계속 보고서를 쓰고 있었다.

→ He _____ _____ _____ a report when I entered his room. (write)

(3) 내가 태어났을 때, 부모님은 몇 년간 인천에 살고 있었다.

→ My parents _____ _____ _____ in Incheon for years when I was born. (live)

교과서 어휘 **doorbell** 초인종 **sound** 울리다 **behave** 행동하다 **repairman** 수리공 **show up** 나타나다 **lend** 빌려주다 **support** 지원하다

Grammar Test

01 빈칸에 알맞지 <u>않은</u> 것은?

> Have you heard about him _____?

① lately　　　　　② recently
③ last weekend　　④ before
⑤ since last spring

02 우리말을 영어로 바르게 옮긴 것은?

> 우리가 그곳에 도착했을 때, 그는 이미 떠났었다.

① When we arrive there, he has already left.
② When we were arriving there, he was leaving.
③ When we arrived there, he had already left.
④ When we arrived there, he has already left.
⑤ When we arrive there, he was leaving.

03 밑줄 친 부분의 용법이 〈보기〉와 같은 것은?

> ┌ 보기 ┐
> I've <u>known</u> Mr. Brown since I was a middle school student.

① I <u>have been</u> to China before.
② He <u>has</u> just <u>found</u> out the truth.
③ I <u>have</u> never <u>forgotten</u> her smile.
④ Someone <u>has broken</u> the window.
⑤ My brother <u>has worked</u> here for seven years.

서술형 평가

04 두 문장을 한 문장으로 바꿔 쓸 때 빈칸에 알맞은 말을 쓰시오.

> She went to Europe last month. She came back and she is in Korea now.

→ She _____ _____ to Europe.

서술형 평가

05 밑줄 친 부분을 어법에 맞게 고쳐 쓰시오.

> A Do you know Greg James?
> B Yes, we (1) <u>be</u> in the same class in 4th grade. So, I (2) <u>know</u> him since then.

(1) _____　　　　(2) _____

06 두 문장을 한 문장으로 바꿔 쓸 때 빈칸에 알맞은 것은?

> Jake began waiting for the subway 20 minutes ago. He is still waiting for the subway.
> → Jake _____ for the subway for 20 minutes.

① waited　　　　　② is to wait
③ was waiting　　　④ has been waiting
⑤ will wait

07 밑줄 친 부분의 용법이 나머지와 <u>다른</u> 것은?
① <u>Have</u> you ever <u>seen</u> elephants?
② We <u>haven't met</u> her before.
③ Roy <u>has</u> never <u>ridden</u> a camel before.
④ She <u>has lost</u> her new smartphone.
⑤ I <u>have been</u> to Prague several times.

[교과서　**truth** 진실, 사실　**come back** 돌아오다　**grade** 학년, 성적　**camel** 낙타　**several** 몇몇의
어휘]

서술형 평가

08 두 문장을 한 문장으로 바꿔 쓸 때 빈칸에 알맞은 말을 쓰시오.

> · My mom ate her dinner at 7 p.m.
> · I arrived home at 9 p.m.

→ My mom _____ _____ her dinner when I _____ home.

09 밑줄 친 부분을 바르게 고친 것은?

> Jimin was very upset because he <u>wait</u> for his friend for more than two hours.

① is waiting
② has waited
③ has been waiting
④ had waited
⑤ is going to wait

10 밑줄 친 부분이 어법상 어색한 것은?
① They've <u>bought</u> a new car.
② When <u>has</u> the girl <u>left</u> Seoul?
③ We <u>have</u> just <u>corrected</u> the errors.
④ I've <u>been</u> in Chicago since I was ten years old.
⑤ The newcomer <u>has</u> already <u>settled</u> down here.

서술형 평가

11 우리말과 일치하도록 어법상 어색한 부분을 찾아 바르게 고쳐 쓰시오.

> 나는 네가 이야기했던 그 교수님을 만났다.
> → I met the professor who you have talked about.

_____ → _____

서술형 평가

12 우리말과 일치하도록 주어진 단어들을 배열하시오.
(1) 우리는 그 음식점에 두 번 가 봤다.
   → We _____.
   (twice, have, the restaurant, been, to)
(2) 너희들은 얼마나 오랫동안 서로 알고 지냈니?
   → _____ each other?
   (how, you, have, known, long)

13 어법상 어색한 것은?
① She became a teacher at the school where I had been a student.
② I didn't know that she has been sleeping for a long time.
③ I didn't know him because I had never met him before.
④ Sumi borrowed the book that she had already read.
⑤ I got a poor grade because I had not studied hard.

14 밑줄 친 ①–⑤ 중 어법상 어색한 것은?

> A What ①<u>did</u> you do last Sunday?
> B I ②<u>went</u> shopping with my mom. How about you?
> A I ③<u>have studied</u> in the library.
> B ④<u>Did</u> you study English?
> A No, I studied math because I ⑤<u>had not studied</u> it for a long time.

교과서 **upset** 속상한 **correct** 고치다, 수정하다 **newcomer** 새로 온 사람, 신참자 **borrow** 빌리다
어휘

Reading

[1~2] 다음을 끊어 읽고 ☑, 해석을 쓰시오. ✎

The World Through My Eyes

Lin Wang, Ecologist

3 **Tsingy, the Stone Forest of Madagascar**

I've been ⓐ<u>visited</u> the stone forest of Madagascar to study plants and animals for over 20

years. The spiky stones of this place are true miracles of nature. This amazing shape has been

6 ⓑ<u>created</u> by rainfall. Rain has cut down the stones and ⓒ<u>made</u> them sharp and spiky over a

long period of time. The environment is harsh for animals ⓓ<u>to live in</u>, but they have found ways to

survive. For example, lemurs, ⓔ<u>which</u> only live in Madagascar, have

9 frog-like legs that help them jump from one stone tower to another. For

me, the stone forest is like a jack-in-the-box. It always surprises me and

keeps me on my toes!

*lemur 여우원숭이

---

1 밑줄 친 ⓐ–ⓔ 중 어법상 어색한 것은?

① ⓐ   ② ⓑ   ③ ⓒ   ④ ⓓ   ⑤ ⓔ

2 Tsingy에 관한 위 글의 내용과 일치하는 것은?

① 마다가스카르에 있는 산림이다.
② 오랜 기간 동안 바람에 의해 돌이 침식되었다.
③ 돌들의 모양이 뾰족하고 날카롭다.
④ 동물들이 살기에 좋은 환경이다.
⑤ 여우원숭이는 마다가스카르에서 멸종되었다.

교과서 **ecologist** 생태학자 **spiky** 뾰족한 **miracle** 기적 **shape** 모양 **rainfall** 강우 **sharp** 날카로운 **period** 기간 **harsh** 혹독한, 가혹한
어휘 🎧 **jack-in-the-box** 깜짝 장난감 상자(뚜껑을 열면 인형 등이 튀어나오는 상자) **keep ... on one's toes** …에게 정신을 바짝 차리게 하다

3 Tilly Smith에 관한 다음 글의 내용과 일치하지 <u>않는</u> 것은?

일화

Tilly Smith, a ten-year-old British schoolgirl, was relaxing on the beach in Thailand with her family. Suddenly, Tilly noticed something strange. The sea looked as though it was bubbling. Also, the water was going away from the shoreline. Many people walked onto the uncovered sand to collect fish and seashells. Yet, Tilly remembered something she **had learned** in school just two weeks earlier. She recognized the unusual events as warning signs of a tsunami. Tilly began screaming for her family to run to higher ground. She and her parents alerted others to leave the beach. The family raced to the hotel's third floor just as the tsunami struck. They watched from their window. A quick-thinking schoolgirl **had saved** about a hundred lives.

① 열 살짜리 영국 여학생이다.

② 태국의 해변에서 가족들과 휴식을 취하고 있었다.

③ 바다에서 거품이 이는 것을 보았다.

④ 쓰나미의 징조를 알아차렸다.

⑤ 가족의 목숨만을 간신히 구했다.

4 밑줄 친 ⓐ-ⓔ 중 글 전체의 흐름상 어색한 것은?

환경

Scientists **have been looking** at ways to substitute nonrenewable fossil fuels with renewable sources such as water, wind, and solar power. ⓐThese sources can be replaced or reused and so will not run out. ⓑHydroelectricity is one example of a renewable source. ⓒIt **has been produced** from the energy of falling or flowing water. ⓓOur research in solar energy is still in the beginning stages. ⓔHydroelectricity produces no direct waste and fewer greenhouse gases than energy plants powered by fossil fuels.

① ⓐ   ② ⓑ   ③ ⓒ   ④ ⓓ   ⑤ ⓔ

---

3   bubble 거품이 일다   alert 경고하다   strike 덮치다, 발생하다   quick-thinking 두뇌 회전이 빠른

4   substitute 대신하다   renewable 재생 가능한   replace 대체하다   run out 다 떨어지다   plant 공장

Expression

1 알고 있는지 묻기 / 알고 있음 표현하기

알고 있는지 묻기

- Do you know about ...?
- Have you heard about(of) ...?
- Are you aware of ...?
- Do you happen to know ...?

알고 있음 표현하기

- I know about ....
- I've heard about(of) ....
- I've been told about ....
- I'm aware of ....

2 기쁨이나 슬픔 표현하기

기쁨 표현하기

- I'm (so) glad(happy/excited) to hear that.
- That makes me happy.
- You did a good(great) job. / Good job.
- Great! / Terrific! / Nice!
- Well done!

슬픔 표현하기

- How sad.
- I'm (so) sad(unhappy).
- That makes me sad.

Expression Test

Answer p. 9

1 빈칸에 알맞은 것은?

> A I passed the math test.
> B That's great! _____

① That's all right.
② That's too bad.
③ I'm interested in it.
④ I'm with you on that.
⑤ I'm happy to hear that.

2 의도하는 바가 나머지와 <u>다른</u> 것은?

① I know about the story.
② I'm aware of the story.
③ I've heard about the story.
④ I nearly forgot about the story.
⑤ I've been told about the story.

3 빈칸에 알맞은 것은?

> A _____ the new library?
> B Yes, I have. They say it has about 100,000 books.

① Do you like
② Could you explain
③ Have you heard about
④ What do you think about
⑤ Are you looking forward to

서술형 평가

4 우리말과 일치하도록 빈칸에 알맞은 말을 쓰시오.

> A You look down today. What's the matter?
> B My best friend Jim moved to another school. That _____ me _____.
> (그것 때문에 슬퍼.)
> A Cheer up. Things will be better soon.

5 밑줄 친 부분과 바꿔 쓸 수 있는 것은?

> A <u>I've heard that</u> you can go inside the pyramids.
> B Sounds interesting!

① I wonder if
② I hope that
③ It is possible that
④ I've been told that
⑤ I'll never forget that

6 자연스러운 대화가 되도록 (A)–(D)를 바르게 배열한 것은?

> (A) I finally got on the school baseball team!
> (B) What's up, Michael?
> (C) Wow, that's great! I'm so happy to hear that!
> (D) Thank you.

① (A) – (C) – (B) – (D)
② (B) – (A) – (C) – (D)
③ (B) – (C) – (A) – (D)
④ (C) – (A) – (B) – (D)
⑤ (C) – (B) – (A) – (D)

1 주어진 단어들을 배열하여 밑줄 친 우리말을 영어로 옮기시오.

the shooting stars, I, around, have, will, heard, that, peak, 10 p.m.

A Mom, did you watch the weather report today? The night sky will be clear so we will be able to see hundreds of shooting stars tonight!

B Wow, fantastic! When is the best time to see them?

A 별똥별이 10시쯤 절정일 거라고 들었어요.

B Wow, it will be a special night!

2 밑줄 친 부분을 어법에 맞게 고쳐 쓰시오.

(1) She has already explained it before you came. → _____

(2) The student has found his textbook yesterday. → _____

(3) The sun has risen when we got to the beach. → _____

3 for 또는 since를 이용하여 두 문장을 한 문장으로 바꿔 쓰시오.

(1) Jeff was sick last weekend. He is still sick.
   → Jeff _____ last weekend.

(2) Lin started writing a novel two hours ago. She is still writing it.
   → Lin _____ two hours.

(3) Becky started working for a bank in 2017. She is still working there.
   → Becky _____ 2017.

4 일기 예보를 보고, 빈칸에 알맞은 말을 쓰시오.

Monday	Tuesday	Wednesday	Thursday

→ Today is Wednesday. It _____ _____ for three days.

5 민지는 친구들과 함께 선생님의 송별회를 준비하고 있다. 표를 보고, 〈조건〉에 맞게 대화를 완성하시오.

Name	Things to do	Done
Minji	order a cake	○
Jimin	decorate the classroom with balloons	○
Minho	write the thank you card	×
Sejin	clean the classroom	×

조건
(1) 현재완료형으로 쓸 것
(2) 주어진 단어를 포함할 것

Minji I (1) _____ a cake. (just) What about you, Jimin?

Jimin I've done my part, too.
   I (2) _____ with balloons. (already) Minho, how is it going?

Minho Sorry, I (3) _____. (yet)

Jimin That's okay. We can do it together.

Minji Sejin, (4) _____ the classroom?

Sejin Actually, I haven't started it yet.

Minji Oh, please, hurry. I'll help you.

난이도: 상 ★★★ 중 ★★ 하 ★

★
01 짝지어진 단어의 관계가 나머지와 <u>다른</u> 것은?

① fun – funny   ② spike – spiky
③ survive – survival   ④ nature – natural
⑤ stress – stressful

★★
02 영영풀이에 해당하는 것은?

a particular length of time with a beginning and an end

① class   ② rainfall   ③ miracle
④ start   ⑤ period

★
03 빈칸에 공통으로 들어갈 말로 알맞은 것은?

A Did you _____ that the sun never sets in Norway during summer?
B No, I didn't _____ that. How interesting!

① aware   ② heard   ③ know
④ happen   ⑤ feel

★ 서술형 평가
04 우리말과 일치하도록 빈칸에 알맞은 말을 쓰시오.

A How do you like the food?
B Mom, I like this pasta very much.
A Really? I'm _____ _____ _____ that. (그 말을 들으니 기쁘구나.)

★
05 빈칸에 알맞은 것은?

A Have you heard of the movie, *Me Before You*?
B Yes, _____. But I haven't had a chance to watch it.

① that's true
② I'm good at it
③ I have no idea
④ I've heard of it
⑤ I don't know what to say

★
06 빈칸에 알맞은 것은?

A I won first prize.
B That's wonderful! _____

① I wish I could hear that.
② That makes me sad.
③ I'm scared to hear that.
④ I'm delighted to hear that.
⑤ I don't know how to do that.

★★ 서술형 평가
07 자연스러운 대화가 되도록 (A)–(D)를 바르게 배열 하시오.

(A) Take it easy. Anyone can lose.
(B) But I made a big mistake. That makes me sad.
(C) Cheer up. Things will be better tomorrow.
(D) We lost the soccer match because of me.

_____ → _____ → _____ → _____

교과서 어휘🎧   **particular** 특정한   **length** 길이   **beginning** 시작   **end** 끝   **set** (해, 달이) 지다   **chance** 기회   **first prize** 1등상

08 밑줄 친 부분을 바르게 고친 것은?

> A I started learning English when I was 10 years old.
> B So, you <u>learn</u> it for six years, right?

① learn
② were learning
③ has learned
④ have learned
⑤ have been learned

시험에 잘 나오는 문제

09 빈칸에 알맞은 것은?

> I lost the book that Tony _____ for me.

① buys
② buying
③ has bought
④ had bought
⑤ has been buying

서술형 평가

10 어법상 어색한 부분을 찾아 바르게 고쳐 쓰시오.

> She has learned how to cook spaghetti yesterday.

_____ → _____

11 두 문장이 같은 의미가 되도록 할 때 빈칸에 알맞은 것은?

> He moved to California 10 years ago and he is still living there.
> = He _____ in California for 10 years.

① lived
② is to live
③ was living
④ has been living
⑤ had lived

12 짝지어진 문장의 우리말 해석이 <u>잘못된</u> 것은?

① I have never met him before.
   → 나는 전에 그를 만나 본 적이 없다.
② How have you been?
   → 어떻게 지내 왔니?
③ I have known him since he was a boy.
   → 나는 그가 소년이었을 때부터 그를 알아 왔다.
④ He has just come back home.
   → 그가 방금 집에 돌아왔다.
⑤ She has gone to Africa.
   → 그녀는 아프리카에 가 본 적이 있다.

시험에 잘 나오는 문제

13 밑줄 친 부분의 용법이 나머지와 <u>다른</u> 것은?

① David <u>has played</u> the cello for five years.
② I <u>have</u> never <u>had</u> such a cute pet.
③ He <u>has been</u> a teacher since 2000.
④ My sister <u>has slept</u> for twelve hours.
⑤ Chris <u>has practiced</u> dancing since 2018.

서술형 평가

14 밑줄 친 부분을 바르게 고쳐 쓰시오.

> Amy couldn't take a bath because she <u>break</u> her arm.

→ _____

서술형 평가

15 빈칸에 알맞은 말을 쓰시오.

> • Mina has painted the wall _____ an hour.
> • Smith has worked for the federal government _____ 2017.

교과서 어휘 **take a bath** 목욕하다　**arm** 팔　**paint** 페인트를 칠하다　**wall** 벽　**federal government** 연방 정부

[16~17] 빈칸에 알맞은 것을 고르시오.

★★
16

The train _____, so we couldn't get on the train.

① have already left
② has already left
③ is leaving
④ had already left
⑤ has been leaving

★★
17

Jason _____ for two hours when his cell phone rang.

① has slept
② was slept
③ is sleeping
④ has been sleeping
⑤ had been sleeping

★★ 서술형 평가
18 우리말과 일치하도록 주어진 단어를 이용하여 빈칸에 알맞은 말을 쓰시오.

Bob은 다음 주에 신혼여행을 가는데, 아직도 숙소를 예약하지 않았다. (book)
→ Bob will go on a honeymoon next week, but he _____ a hotel yet.

★★
19 밑줄 친 부분의 용법이 〈보기〉와 같은 것은?

보기
We <u>have worked</u> for three hours.

① I've already <u>eaten</u> my lunch.
② She <u>has cooked</u> for an hour.
③ I <u>have</u> never <u>been</u> to Jejudo.
④ He <u>hasn't finished</u> his homework yet.
⑤ They <u>have seen</u> the movie together before.

★★ 서술형 평가
20 두 문장을 한 문장으로 바꿔 쓸 때 빈칸에 알맞은 말을 쓰시오.

· Karen started talking on the phone an hour ago.
· She is still talking on the phone.

→ Karen _____ _____ _____ on the phone for an hour.

★★
21 우리말을 영어로 바르게 옮긴 것은?

Sally는 열 살이 될 때까지 바다를 본 적이 없었다.

① Sally didn't see the sea until she has been ten.
② Sally wasn't seeing the sea until she was ten.
③ Sally has never seen the sea until she was ten.
④ Sally had never seen the sea until she was ten.
⑤ Sally has never seen the sea until she had been ten.

교과서 **ring** 울리다　**book** 예약하다; 책　**honeymoon** 신혼여행
어휘

★★ 22 빈칸에 들어갈 말이 바르게 짝지어진 것은?

- Jenny _____ her cousin's birthday party last night.
- Tony and his sister _____ chess since two o'clock.

① attends – are playing
② attends – have been playing
③ attended – has played
④ attended – has been playing
⑤ attended – have been playing

★★ 23 밑줄 친 부분의 용법을 〈보기〉에서 고르시오.

보기
ⓐ 완료   ⓑ 경험   ⓒ 계속   ⓓ 결과

(1) I learned that he had been sick for a week.
(2) Emma had been to Prague once when she was young.
(3) When I arrived at the train station, the train had already left.

★★★ 24 어법상 어색한 것은?

① Kitty found that she has lost a doll.
② Sam has kept a diary since boyhood.
③ I have boiled the soup for 30 minutes.
④ Daniel has already had breakfast.
⑤ She has written many songs since the age of 15.

★ 25 다음 글의 주제로 알맞은 것은?

People have been eating foods that are sort of like pizza — bread baked with a topping for many centuries. But the pizza we see so often today with tomato sauce, mozzarella cheese, and basil has an official story. In 1899, Italian King Umberto and Queen Margherita visited a restaurant in Naples and were served three special pizzas. The queen said she liked the one that was red, white, and green best because it reminded her of the Italian flag. That is how Margherita pizza was born.

① 다양한 피자 토핑   ② 피자 만드는 방법
③ 피자가 인기 있는 이유   ④ 세계의 다양한 피자
⑤ 마르게리타피자의 탄생 배경

★★ 26 빈칸에 알맞은 것은?

More than 30,000 people die every year in traffic accidents, and many more suffer injuries. The good news is that since 1990, the number of people who die in car accidents has been falling by more than 20 percent. This is partly due to child safety seats, air bags, seat-belt laws and laws against talking on cell phones while driving. And new electronic innovations will make cars _____. Some car designers have been even talking about crashless cars.   *crashless 충돌 없는

① faster   ② safer   ③ funnier
④ cleaner   ⑤ bigger

교과서 **attend** 참석하다 **station** 정류장 **boyhood** (남자의) 어린 시절 **boil** 끓이다, 꿇다 **remind** 상기시키다 **suffer** 고통받다 **law** 법
어휘 **innovation** 혁신

[27~28] 다음을 읽고, 물음에 답하시오.

Throughout the history of the Olympic Games there have (A) been/to be many famous champions. But one of the most famous and successful Olympians was a strong Italian man named Milo. Milo won the wrestling event five times. That means he was the champion for more than 20 years! Milo's strength was famous. Sometimes he would hold out one hand and (B) challenge/to challenge someone to move his fingers. No one could move even his smallest finger. In one legend, he protected his friends by holding up the roof when the building was falling down. He did not let go until all of his friends (C) have gotten/had gotten out safely.

★★
27 위 글의 제목으로 알맞은 것은?

① The History of the Olympic Games
② A Strong Olympic Champion, Milo
③ Essential Techniques to Win the Wrestling
④ World-famous Olympic Champions
⑤ How Wrestlers Train Themselves to Be Strong

★★★
28 (A)–(C)에서 어법에 맞는 말이 바르게 짝지어진 것은?

	(A)	(B)	(C)
①	been	– challenge	– have gotten
②	been	– challenge	– had gotten
③	been	– to challenge	– had gotten
④	to be	– challenge	– have gotten
⑤	to be	– to challenge	– had gotten

[29~30] 다음을 읽고, 물음에 답하시오.

Getting fresh food from local farms can be difficult in big cities. There is a possible solution: Farm Up. Some architects and scientists have ⓐbe urging people to build vertical farms in multistory buildings. "Sky farms" are ideal for cities because they use a fraction of the land of traditional farms. Because they are indoors, these farms aren't harmed by hurricanes, droughts, and floods. Several vertical farms have already ⓑbe in operation in places like South Korea, U.S., and the Netherlands. Dickson Despommier, a professor at Columbia University, says "Agriculture in tall buildings will soon revolutionize the way we eat and live in cities."

★★ 서술형 평가
29 밑줄 친 Sky farms와 바꿔 쓸 수 있는 말을 위 글에서 찾아 쓰시오.

→ _____

★★ 서술형 평가
30 밑줄 친 ⓐ와 ⓑ를 알맞은 형태로 쓰시오.

ⓐ _____ ⓑ _____

교과서 **hold out** (손 등을) 내밀다 **let go** 놓다 **architect** 건축가 **urge** 권고하다, 설득하다 **vertical** 수직의 **multistory** 고층의, 다층의
어휘 **fraction** 부분, 일부 **harm** 해를 끼치다 **in operation** 운용 중인 **revolutionize** 혁신을 일으키다

······························· **>> Grammar**

A 현재완료

1 현재완료: 과거에 일어난 일이 현재까지 영향을 미치고 있을 때 쓰는 시제로 〈have〔has〕+과거분사〉의 형태로 쓴다.

부정문	have〔has〕+not+과거분사
의문문	Have〔Has〕+주어+과거분사 …?

I <u>lost</u> my wallet. 〈과거 – 현재 지갑을 찾았는지 알 수 없음〉
I **have lost** my wallet. 〈현재완료 – 현재에도 지갑을 잃어버린 상태임〉
James **hasn't arrived** yet.　　　　　　　　　**Have** you ever **heard** of the concert?

2 현재완료의 용법

용법	의미	함께 쓰이는 표현
완료	막 …했다	just, already, yet 등
경험	…해 본 적이 있다	ever, never, before, once 등
계속	(지금까지) …해 왔다	for, since, how long 등
결과	…해 버렸다 (그 결과 지금 …하다)	–

The singer **has** <u>just</u> **arrived** here.　　　We **have been** to the exhibition <u>once</u>.
The lawyer **has worked** here <u>for</u> 7 years.　I **have lost** my smartphone.

3 현재완료와 함께 쓸 수 없는 부사(구): 명백한 과거를 나타내는 부사(구)(ago, yesterday, last year 등)와 의문사 when은 현재완료와 함께 쓸 수 없다.
He has caught the criminal two weeks ago. (✕)
→ He **caught** the criminal two weeks **ago**. (○)

B 현재완료진행

현재완료진행형은 과거에 시작해서 현재에도 계속하고〔되고〕 있는 일을 표현할 때 〈have〔has〕+been+-ing〉의 형태로 쓴다.

부정문	have〔has〕+not+been+-ing
의문문	Have〔Has〕+주어+been+-ing …?

It **has been raining** for 3 days.
He **has not been working** for a while.
Have you **been sleeping** well?

68　Part I 실력 다지기

C 과거완료

1 과거완료: 과거의 어느 시점을 기준으로, 그 이전부터 기준 시점까지 일어난 일을 나타낼 때 쓰는 시제로 〈had + 과거분사〉의 형태로 쓴다.

용법	의미	용법	의미
완료	(그 전에) …했었다	계속	(그때까지 계속) …하고 있었다
경험	(그때까지) …해 본 적이 있었다	결과	…했었다 (그 결과 그때 …인 상태였다)

The show **had** just **ended** by the time I got there. 〈완료〉

I couldn't read the book because I **had** never **learned** Spanish. 〈경험〉

2 대과거: 과거에 일어났던 일의 순서를 나타낼 때 더 이전에 일어났던 일을 대과거라고 하며, 과거완료로 표현한다.

He <u>said</u> that the dog **had attacked** him before.

D 과거완료진행

과거완료진행형은 어떤 동작이 대과거에서 시작되어 과거의 어느 시점까지 계속되었음을 강조할 때 〈had + been + -ing〉의 형태로 쓴다.

부정문	had + not + been + -ing
의문문	Had + 주어 + been + -ing …?

Lily **had been doing** her homework when her father came back.

I **had not been watching** TV for a long time.

Had Jack **been playing** computer games when you arrived there?

·· >> Expression

1 알고 있는지 묻기 / 알고 있음 표현하기

🍎 알고 있는지 묻기
- Do you know about …?
- Have you heard about(of) …?
- Are you aware of …?
- Do you happen to know …?

🍎 알고 있음 표현하기
- I know about ….
- I've heard about(of) ….
- I've been told about ….
- I'm aware of ….

2 기쁨이나 슬픔 표현하기

🍎 기쁨 표현하기
- I'm (so) glad(happy/excited) to hear that.
- That makes me happy.
- You did a good(great) job. / Good job.
- Great! / Terrific! / Nice!
- Well done!

🍎 슬픔 표현하기
- How sad.
- I'm (so) sad(unhappy).
- That makes me sad.

Lesson 04

관계사

Grammar Preview

① 관계대명사

- 관계대명사: 〈접속사＋대명사〉의 역할을 하며, 관계사절을 이끌어 선행사를 꾸민다.

선행사 \ 격	주격	목적격	소유격
사람	who	who(m)	whose
사물, 동물	which	which	whose / of which
사람, 사물, 동물	that	that	–
선행사 포함	what	what	–

- 관계대명사의 계속적 용법: 계속적 용법은 〈콤마(,)＋관계대명사〉의 형태로, 관계대명사절이 선행사에 대해 추가 설명하는 것을 말한다. 관계대명사절이 선행사를 꾸밀 때는 제한적 용법이라고 한다.

She has two sons **who** became cooks.
〈제한적 용법 – 아들이 두 명 이상〉

She has two sons, **who** became cooks.
= and they 〈계속적 용법 – 아들이 두 명〉

② 관계부사, 복합관계사

- 관계부사: 〈접속사＋부사〉의 역할을 하며, 관계사절을 이끌어 장소, 때, 이유, 방법을 나타내는 선행사를 꾸민다.

선행사	관계부사	전치사+관계대명사
장소 (the place, city 등)	where	at(on, in) which
때 (the time, day 등)	when	at(on, in) which
이유 (the reason)	why	for which
방법 (the way)	how	in which

- 복합관계대명사: 〈관계대명사＋-ever〉의 형태로, 명사절 또는 양보의 부사절을 이끈다.

복합관계대명사	명사절	양보의 부사절
whoever	…하는 사람은 누구든지 (= anyone who)	누가 …할지라도 (= no matter who)
whatever	…하는 것은 무엇이든지 (= anything that)	무엇을 …할지라도 (= no matter what)
whichever	…하는 것은 어느 것이든지 (= anything that)	어느 것을 …할지라도 (= no matter which)

- 복합관계부사: 〈관계부사＋-ever〉의 형태로, 시간, 장소, 양보의 부사절을 이끈다.

복합관계부사	시간, 장소의 부사절	양보의 부사절
whenever	…할 때는 언제나 (= at any time when)	언제 …할지라도 (= no matter when)
wherever	…하는 곳은 어디든지 (= at any place where)	어디서 …할지라도 (= no matter where)
however	–	아무리 …할지라도 (= no matter how)

Ⓐ 관계대명사

1 관계대명사의 역할: 관계대명사는 〈접속사＋대명사〉의 역할을 하며, 관계사절을 이끌어 선행사를 꾸민다.

선행사＼격	주격	목적격	소유격
사람	who	who(m)	whose
사물, 동물	which	which	whose / of which
사람, 사물, 동물	that	that	–

Bill has three daughters **who** are students. 〈주격〉
　선행사(사람) ┗━ 관계대명사 who: three daughters를 대신하면서 절을 연결

Sam likes the book **which** I gave him. 〈목적격〉

I met a girl **whose** brother was a famous singer. 〈소유격〉

Look at the girl and her dog **that** are running there. 〈주격〉

2 관계대명사 what: 선행사를 포함하고 있으며, the thing(s) which(that)로 바꿔 쓸 수 있다. '…하는 것'이라는 뜻으로 명사절을 이끈다.

What I want to buy is this doll. 〈주어 역할〉
what: 선행사＋목적격 관계대명사

Remember **what** I said before. 〈목적어 역할〉

This is **what** he taught me. 〈보어 역할〉

◆ Plus Grammar
선행사에 〈사람＋사물(동물)〉, 최상급, 서수, the only, the same, the very, all, every, -thing 등이 포함된 경우 관계대명사 that이 주로 쓰인다.
Everything **that** he told me was false.

◆ Plus Grammar
관계대명사 **what** vs. 의문사 **what**
일반적으로 what을 '무엇'으로 해석해서 의미가 통하면 의문사, 그렇지 않으면 관계대명사로 볼 수 있다.
I don't know **what** his name is. 〈의문사〉 (나는 그의 이름이 뭔지 모른다.)
He gave me **what** I wanted. 〈관계대명사〉 (그는 내가 원했던 것을 내게 주었다.)

Ⓑ 관계대명사의 계속적 용법

계속적 용법은 〈콤마(,)＋관계대명사〉의 형태로, 관계대명사절이 선행사에 대해 추가 설명하는 것을 말한다. 관계대명사절이 선행사를 꾸밀 때는 제한적 용법이라고 한다.

She has two sons **who** became cooks. 〈제한적 용법 – 아들이 두 명 이상〉

She has two sons, **who** became cooks. 〈계속적 용법 – 아들이 두 명〉
　　　　　　　= and they (관계대명사를 〈접속사＋대명사〉로 바꿔 쓸 수 있음)

◆ Plus Grammar
• which는 앞 문장 전체를 선행사로 받기도 한다.
He said he was ill, **which**(but it) was a lie. (그는 아프다고 말했는데, 그것은 거짓말이었다.)
• 관계대명사 that과 what은 계속적 용법으로 쓸 수 없다.
He bought a bag, **that** was very expensive. (×)

Ⓒ 관계대명사의 생략

1 목적격 관계대명사의 생략: 제한적 용법에서 목적격 관계대명사를 생략할 수 있다. 단, what은 목적격으로 쓰여도 생략할 수 없다.

This is the T-shirt (**which**) I made for myself.

2 〈주격 관계대명사＋be동사〉 생략: 분사(형용사구) 앞의 〈주격 관계대명사＋be동사〉는 생략할 수 있다.

This woman (**who is**) smiling at us is my mother.

Grammar Practice >>

Answer p. 11

A1 괄호 안에서 알맞은 것을 고르시오.

(1) I saw a boy (who, which) was wearing jeans.

(2) This is the cake (whom, which) she made for me.

(3) Tell me (who, what) she likes.

(4) I spent all the money (that, whose) I had.

(5) That is the very movie (who, that) I want to see.

(6) I bought the book (that, whose) cover is yellow.

A2 두 문장을 한 문장으로 바꿔 쓸 때 빈칸에 알맞은 말을 쓰시오.

(1) Let's find the man. He sold us the camera.
→ Let's find the man _____ sold us the camera.

(2) He saw a girl. Her umbrella was pink.
→ He saw a girl _____ umbrella was pink.

(3) The store is over there. You are looking for it.
→ The store _____ you are looking for is over there.

B1 밑줄 친 부분에 주의하여 문장을 우리말로 옮기시오.

(1) She has a son, who studies in England.
→ _____

(2) She has a son who studies in England.
→ _____

B2 〈보기〉의 단어를 한 번씩만 이용하여 빈칸에 알맞은 말을 쓰시오.

┌─보기─────────────────────┐
│   for   and   but   │
└─────────────────────────┘

(1) I have a son, who takes after me.
= I have a son, _____ _____ takes after me.

(2) Clare invited Tom, who didn't come.
= Clare invited Tom, _____ _____ didn't come.

(3) I had to take care of a cat, which was sick.
= I had to take care of a cat, _____ _____ was sick.

C1 생략할 수 있는 부분을 찾아 밑줄을 그으시오.

(1) The bench which we were sitting on was hard.

(2) I live in a house which was built by Sam.

(3) That cup which was put on the table is mine.

(4) The counselor whom I met last Monday told me to exercise.

(5) The boy who is playing in the playground is my nephew.

C2 밑줄 친 부분을 생략할 수 있으면 ○표를 하고, 생략할 수 없으면 ×표 하시오.

(1) This is the middle school which I graduated from.

(2) She was the only person that was waiting for me.

(3) I read a novel which was written in English.

교과서 **cook** 요리사; 요리하다 **for oneself** 혼자 힘으로 **cover** 표지 **look for** …을 찾다 **take after** …을 닮다 **counselor** 상담원
어휘

D 관계부사

관계부사는 〈접속사＋부사〉의 역할을 하며, 관계사절을 이끌어 장소, 때, 이유, 방법을 나타내는 선행사를 꾸민다. 관계부사는 〈전치사＋관계대명사〉의 형태로 바꿔쓸 수 있다.

선행사	관계부사	전치사＋관계대명사
장소 (the place, city 등)	where	at(on, in) which
때 (the time, day 등)	when	at(on, in) which
이유 (the reason)	why	for which
방법 (the way)	how	in which

China is the country **where(in which)** I was born.
　　　　　선행사(장소) ←——— 관계부사 where: in the country를 대신하면서 절을 연결
I won't forget the day **when(on which)** I met you.
I don't know the reason **why(for which)** she didn't come to the meeting.

cf. 선행사 the way와 관계부사 how는 함께 쓰이지 않으며, 둘 중 하나만 쓴다.
　　Tell me **how(the way)** you could memorize all the words.
　　= Tell me **the way in which** you could memorize all the words.

> **◆ Plus Grammar**
> • 선행사의 생략
> time, place, reason 등 일반적인 선행사이면 생략하는 경우가 많다.
> I know (**the reason**) why he went there. (나는 그가 그곳에 간 이유를 안다.)
> • 관계부사의 생략 및 대체
> 일반적인 선행사 뒤에 오는 관계부사는 that으로 대신하거나 생략할 수 있다.
> Summer is the time (**when/ that**) we can enjoy swimming.

E 복합관계사

1 복합관계대명사: 〈관계대명사＋-ever〉의 형태로 선행사를 포함하고 있고, 명사절 또는 양보의 부사절을 이끈다.

복합관계대명사	명사절	양보의 부사절
whoever	…하는 사람은 누구든지 (= anyone who)	누가 …할지라도 (= no matter who)
whatever	…하는 것은 무엇이든지 (= anything that)	무엇을 …할지라도 (= no matter what)
whichever	…하는 것은 어느 것이든지 (= anything that)	어느 것을 …할지라도 (= no matter which)

Whoever(Anyone who) likes comics can join our club.
Whatever(No matter what) you do, it is important to do your best.

2 복합관계부사: 〈관계부사＋-ever〉의 형태로 선행사를 포함하고 있고, 시간, 장소, 양보의 부사절을 이끈다.

복합관계부사	시간, 장소의 부사절	양보의 부사절
whenever	…할 때는 언제나 (= at any time when)	언제 …할지라도 (= no matter when)
wherever	…하는 곳은 어디든지 (= at any place where)	어디서 …할지라도 (= no matter where)
however	–	아무리 …할지라도 (= no matter how)

└ 뒤에 형용사나 부사가 옴

Please ask me **whenever(at any time when)** you have a question.
However(No matter how) fast you run, you can't catch him.

Grammar Practice >>

(Answer p. 11)

D1 괄호 안에서 알맞은 것을 고르시오.

(1) This is the park (when, where) my brother plays basketball.

(2) I don't know the reason (why, how) I came here.

(3) It's the season (when, where) birds move.

(4) Busan is the city (when, where) an international film festival is held.

(5) Kathy is very kind to others. That is (why, how) everybody likes her.

D2 두 문장이 같은 의미가 되도록 빈칸에 알맞은 말을 쓰시오.

(1) This is the shop at which we bought the present for Mina.
= This is the shop _____ we bought the present for Mina.

(2) The teacher wonders the reason for which the students didn't come.
= The teacher wonders the reason _____ the students didn't come.

(3) It's the time at which the dinner show starts.
= It's the time _____ the dinner show starts.

D3 밑줄 친 부분을 바르게 고쳐 쓰시오.

(1) Can you tell me the way how I can get better at English?

(2) I will visit the house which the actor lived.

E1 두 문장이 같은 의미가 되도록 빈칸에 알맞은 말을 쓰시오.

(1) She is busy at any time when I visit her.
= She is busy _____ I visit her.

(2) No matter where you go, I will follow you.
= _____ you go, I will follow you.

(3) No matter when I come, he'll wait for me.
= _____ I come, he'll wait for me.

(4) He'll answer anything that you ask him.
= He'll answer _____ you ask him.

(5) Be positive no matter how hard your life is.
= Be positive _____ hard your life is.

E2 우리말과 일치하도록 빈칸에 알맞은 말을 쓰시오.

(1) 그가 만든 것은 무엇이든지 항상 훌륭했다.
→ _____ he made was always excellent.

(2) 누가 그렇게 말할지라도, 나는 그것을 믿지 않을 것이다.
→ _____ may say so, I will not believe it.

(3) 그가 가는 곳이 어디든지 그는 좋은 친구를 사귈 것이다.
→ _____ he goes, he will make good friends.

(4) 네가 아무리 빨리 달린다 할지라도, 너는 정시에 도착할 수 없다.
→ _____ fast you run, you can't arrive on time.

교과서 **memorize** 암기하다 **season** 계절 **international** 국제적인 **film** 영화 **wonder** 궁금해하다 **get better** 좋아지다
어휘 **follow** 따라가다 **positive** 긍정적인 **excellent** 훌륭한 **on time** 정시에

Grammar Test

01 괄호 안에서 알맞은 것을 고르시오.

(1) I like the girls (who, whose) are kind.

(2) Do you remember the day (when, what) we met?

(3) Look at the mountain (which, whose) top is covered with snow.

[02~03] 빈칸에 알맞은 것을 고르시오.

02

> She is a singer _____ everyone knows in Korea.

① whose
② whom
③ what
④ which
⑤ where

03

> He donated all the money _____ he had in his wallet.

① who
② whose
③ what
④ that
⑤ of which

서술형 평가

04 우리말과 일치하도록 빈칸에 알맞은 말을 쓰시오.

> 디자인이 멋진 저 휴대전화를 보세요.

→ Look at that cell phone _____ design is great.

05 밑줄 친 ①–⑤ 중 생략할 수 있는 것은?

> This ①is ②the cake ③which Joan ④made ⑤for her grandmother.

06 두 문장이 같은 의미가 되도록 할 때 빈칸에 알맞은 것은?

> Tim has a dog, and it is faithful.
> = Tim has a dog, _____ is faithful.

① what
② who
③ whose
④ which
⑤ that

07 밑줄 친 부분이 어법상 어색한 것은?

① Whoever comes first wins the race.
② My parents do for me whatever I request.
③ Whichever they choose, we will accept it.
④ Wherever you make will be delicious.
⑤ We welcome whoever wants to join the club.

08 빈칸에 들어갈 말이 바르게 짝지어진 것은?

> · You should not want to have _____ is not yours.
> · Tell me the reason _____ you gave up the opportunity.

① whose – on which
② what – on which
③ what – for which
④ that – for which
⑤ that – in which

교과서 어휘 🎧 **be covered with** …으로 덮이다　**donate** 기부하다　**faithful** 충직한　**request** 요청하다　**accept** 받아들이다　**join** 가입하다
give up 포기하다　**opportunity** 기회

09 우리말을 영어로 바르게 옮긴 것은?

> 이것이 내가 입어 보고 싶은 스웨터이다.

① This is the sweater I want to try on.
② This is the sweater of which I want to try.
③ This is the sweater which I want to try.
④ This is the sweater what I want to try.
⑤ This is the sweater what I want to try on.

10 밑줄 친 부분의 쓰임이 〈보기〉와 같은 것은?

보기
> That's exactly <u>what</u> I wanted.

① <u>What</u> animal is this?
② <u>What</u>'s your favorite song?
③ <u>What</u> he told me was exciting.
④ I asked him <u>what</u> color he liked.
⑤ <u>What</u> makes you happy all the time?

서술형 평가

11 우리말과 일치하도록 주어진 단어들을 바르게 배열하시오.

> Jia가 가장 좋아하는 그 기타리스트는 나의 삼촌이다.
> (the most, my uncle, Jia, whom, is, likes)

→ The guitarist ＿＿＿＿＿＿＿＿＿＿＿＿＿＿＿.

서술형 평가

12 두 문장이 같은 의미가 되도록 빈칸에 알맞은 말을 쓰시오.

(1) However cold it is outside, she always goes jogging.
　= ＿＿＿＿ ＿＿＿＿ ＿＿＿＿ ＿＿＿＿ it is outside, she always goes jogging.

(2) I will marry anyone who brings me golden apples.
　= I will marry ＿＿＿＿ ＿＿＿＿ ＿＿＿＿ golden apples.

13 어법상 옳은 것은?

① Tell me the way how you did it.
② The day when she left was Sunday.
③ This is the house which my uncle lives.
④ I can't tell you the reason in which I am afraid of the dark.
⑤ This is the drawer when Brian found the key yesterday.

14 밑줄 친 부분 중 생략할 수 <u>없는</u> 것은?

① The bus <u>which</u> I got on was very crowded.
② Anyone <u>that</u> sees an accident should call the police.
③ The dictionary <u>which</u> I used yesterday was hers.
④ Yumi fell in love with the man <u>who was</u> dressed in black.
⑤ She cleaned the pieces of the glass <u>which was</u> broken by me.

교과서 **try on** …을 입어 보다　**exactly** 정확히　**marry** …와 결혼하다　**afraid** 두려워하는　**drawer** 서랍　**accident** 사고　**dictionary** 사전
어휘 **fall in love** 사랑에 빠지다

Reading

[1~2] 다음을 끊어 읽고 ☑, 해석을 쓰시오. ✏

Speak Your Mind Effectively!

Today, we're going to talk about using good communication skills to express ourselves effectively.

3

> You lost my earphones again. Why are you so careless?

Let's start with the clip about Brian. When he tries to talk to his brother, he always ends up arguing with his brother. Let's find out the reason ___(A)___ he has this problem.

6 Brian is starting a sentence with "you" to express his feelings. _____, he should use the "I-message." Starting with "I" can help him focus on ___(B)___ he feels or thinks rather than point the finger at his brother. A small

> I'm really upset because my favorite earphones are lost.

9 change in the way we express ourselves can solve or even prevent communication problems.

---

1 빈칸 (A), (B)에 들어갈 말이 바르게 짝지어진 것은?
① when – that ② how – what ③ why – what
④ why – that ⑤ why – which

2 빈칸에 알맞은 것은?
① Thus ② So ③ Nevertheless ④ Instead ⑤ Therefore

교과서 **effectively** 효과적으로 **communication** 의사소통 **express** 표현하다 **argue** 언쟁을 하다, 다투다 **focus on** …에 집중하다
어휘 🎧 **point the finger at** …을 비난하다 **prevent** 막다, 예방하다

3 다음 글의 제목으로 알맞은 것은?

자연

Volcanoes have extraordinary power. They can cause massive destruction and death. Yet volcanoes can be helpful in many ways. Volcanic ash contains many minerals **that** help plants grow. The ash mixes with soil to make fertile land for plants. Also, under volcanoes the Earth's heat make underground water boil. The hot water and steam rise up to ground. This creates hot springs. The hot water and steam can also be used to heat homes and produce electricity. Steam from under the ground is used to turn huge turbines. This produces a small but growing portion of the world's electricity with very little pollution.

*mineral 무기질

① What Causes a Volcano?　　　　② What Are the Benefits of Volcanoes?
③ How Do Scientists Predict Volcanoes?　　④ What Are the Different Types of Volcanoes?
⑤ How Many Active Volcanoes Are There?

4 밑줄 친 부분의 이유로 알맞은 것은?

동물

We don't think much about eyelids, but eyelids have many functions. They keep our eyes wet and push away dust and dirt. Some animals, like fish and snakes, don't have eyelids at all. That's fine for fish **whose** eyes stay watery all the time. But how do snakes sleep with no eyelids? They sleep with their eyes open. Their brains can still switch off to sleep. Meanwhile, camels totally lucked out: each eye has three eyelids. One of them is clear so the camel can see through it during desert sandstorms. But <u>in a staring contest, the snakes and fish will win</u>.

① They have good eyesight.　　　　② They have no eyelids at all.
③ They lay a lot of eggs at a time.　　④ They hold their breath for a long time.
⑤ They can do something else while sleeping.

3　volcano 화산　extraordinary 엄청난　destruction 파괴　ash 재　fertile 비옥한　portion 일부, 부분
4　eyelid 눈꺼풀　function 기능　watery 물기가 많은　switch off 끄다　clear 투명한　stare 빤히 쳐다보다

Expression

1 이해 점검하기 / 오해 지적해 주기

💙 **이해 점검하기**

- Do you understand?
- Do you get it?
- Do you see(know) what I mean?
- Is this(everything) clear?
- Do you follow me?

💙 **오해 지적해 주기**

- (No,) I mean ... (not ...).
- I'm afraid that's wrong(not right).
- That's not what I meant to say.

2 의견 묻고 답하기

💙 **의견 묻기**

- What do you think of(about) ...?
- How do you like ...?
- How do you feel about ...?
- What is your view(opinion)?

💙 **의견 표현하기**

- (Well,) I think(feel / believe) ....
- It seems to me (that) ....
- In my view(opinion), ...

Expression Test

Answer p. 12

1 의도하는 바가 나머지와 <u>다른</u> 것은?

① Do you get it?

② Do you understand?

③ Is that clear to you?

④ Do you remember it?

⑤ Have you understood its meaning?

2 빈칸에 알맞은 것은?

A It _____ to me that you really like drawing pictures.

B Yes, I love drawing pictures! My dream is to be a painter someday.

① is

② seems

③ appears

④ looks

⑤ thinks

3 밑줄 친 부분과 바꿔 쓸 수 <u>없는</u> 것은?

A Creativity is the key to invention. <u>Do you know what I mean?</u>

B No, I don't. Could you explain it to me in detail?

① Is that clear to you?

② Are you with me?

③ Do you follow me?

④ Do you see that?

⑤ Do you understand?

4 밑줄 친 부분의 의도로 알맞은 것은?

A What do you think about bringing cell phones to school?

B <u>In my opinion, it is helpful in case of an emergency.</u>

① 오해 지적해 주기

② 이해 점검하기

③ 확인하기

④ 의견 표현하기

⑤ 능력 표현하기

5 빈칸에 알맞은 것은?

A Don't let the cat out of the bag about Peter's surprise party.

B A cat? I don't have a cat.

A _____ Keep his party a secret.

① That's true.

② That's a good idea.

③ I haven't got a clue.

④ That's not what I meant.

⑤ There is a cat on the corner.

6 자연스러운 대화가 되도록 (A)–(D)를 바르게 배열한 것은?

(A) What did you think of the movie?

(B) Of course, I did. I saw it last week.

(C) Did you see the movie *Little Prince*?

(D) Well, for me, it was a little boring.

① (A) – (B) – (C) – (D)

② (A) – (D) – (C) – (B)

③ (B) – (A) – (D) – (C)

④ (C) – (A) – (B) – (D)

⑤ (C) – (B) – (A) – (D)

1 빈칸에 알맞은 말을 〈보기〉에서 골라 쓰시오.

┌─보기─
That's correct.
That makes me sad.
That's not what I meant.
└─

A Nick, how was your diving trip yesterday?
B Well... I got cold feet.
A That's too bad. Why were your feet so cold?
B _____ I mean that I got scared, so I couldn't dive.
A I see. Then, why don't you listen to music before you dive?
B Listen to music? Does it help?
A Yeah, it helps me a lot when I feel nervous.

2 그림을 보고, 주어진 단어들과 관계대명사를 이용하여 문장을 완성하시오.

(1) The girl _____ is Mina. (sitting, on, the bench)
(2) Mina is wearing a pink dress _____. (beautiful)
(3) Mina is reading a book _____ to her. (her teacher, recommended)

3 빈칸에 알맞은 말을 〈보기〉에서 골라 쓰시오.

┌─보기─
when   where   how
└─

(1) A library is a place _____ many books are kept.
(2) Tell me _____ you unlocked the car.
(3) I know the time _____ she will arrive.

4 우리말과 일치하도록 주어진 단어들을 이용하여 빈칸에 알맞은 말을 쓰시오.

(1) 네가 나와 이야기하고 싶을 때는 언제든지 전화해.
   → Call me _____.
   (whenever, want, talk to)
(2) 나는 네가 있는 곳은 어디든지 갈 수 있다.
   → I can go _____.
   (wherever, be)
(3) 나는 열심히 연습하는 사람은 누구든지 선택하고 싶다.
   → I want to _____.
   (whoever, choose, practice, hard)

5 관계대명사를 이용하여 두 문장을 한 문장으로 바꿔 쓰시오.

(1) The girl is my sister. You met her at the party.
   → The girl _____ is my sister.
(2) I have a friend. His uncle was a famous singer in the late 1990s.
   → I have _____ in the late 1990s.
(3) This is the cartoon character. I like it best.
   → This is _____.

★★
01 영영풀이에 해당하는 것은?

to tell or show what you are feeling or thinking by using words, looks, or actions

① welcome ② argue ③ invite
④ focus ⑤ express

★★ 서술형 평가
02 빈칸에 알맞은 단어를 〈보기〉에서 골라 쓰시오.

보기
prevent   communication   effectively

(1) You should spend your time _____.
(2) Regular exercise helps _____ weight gain.
(3) Jake is trying to improve his _____ skills.

★★
03 자연스러운 대화가 되도록 (A)–(D)를 바르게 배열한 것은?

(A) Why did you hit your books?
(B) Sorry. I really had to hit the books yesterday.
(C) Oh no, that's not what I meant. I had to study yesterday because I had an exam this morning.
(D) How come you didn't come to my birthday party yesterday?

① (A) – (B) – (C) – (D)
② (A) – (C) – (B) – (D)
③ (D) – (B) – (A) – (C)
④ (D) – (B) – (C) – (A)
⑤ (D) – (C) – (B) – (A)

★ 서술형 평가
04 우리말과 일치하도록 빈칸에 알맞은 말을 쓰시오.

A "A healthy mind in a healthy body." Do you know what I _____?
(내 말이 무슨 뜻인지 알겠니?)
B All right. I'll try to exercise.

★ 서술형 평가
05 그림을 보고, 주어진 단어들을 배열하여 문장을 완성하시오.

A What _____?
(you, think, that, do, yellow, about, backpack)
B Well, I don't like it. I think it's too big.

★
06 밑줄 친 부분과 바꿔 쓸 수 없는 것은?

A Do you like shopping at a local market?
B Yeah, I think it's great. The prices are low, and it's always lively.

① I feel ② I believe
③ I heard ④ in my opinion
⑤ it seems to me that

교과서   **spend** 쓰다, 소비하다 **gain** 증가; 얻다 **hit the books** 열심히 공부하다 **local** 지역의 **lively** 생기 넘치는
어휘

07 빈칸에 알맞지 <u>않은</u> 것은?

A _____

B Sorry, but can you show me one more time?

① Is that clear?
② Do you understand?
③ Is everything clear?
④ Why are you disappointed?
⑤ Do you know what I mean?

08 빈칸에 알맞은 것은?

This is the man _____ can help you right now.

① who   ② whose   ③ which
④ whom   ⑤ what

시험에 잘 나오는 문제

09 빈칸에 공통으로 들어갈 말로 알맞은 것은?

• Do you know _____ I'm talking about?
• That's exactly _____ I wanted.

① who   ② whose   ③ what
④ which   ⑤ whom

10 빈칸에 알맞지 <u>않은</u> 것은? (2개)

Peter is the man _____ I've been looking forward to meeting.

① who   ② whose   ③ whom
④ which   ⑤ that

서술형 평가

11 밑줄 친 부분을 한 단어로 바꿔 쓰시오.

Here is the store <u>at which</u> I bought the sandwich.

→ _____

12 빈칸에 들어갈 말이 바르게 짝지어진 것은?

I will be right here waiting for you _____ you go and _____ you do.

① whoever – whatever
② whoever – whichever
③ wherever – whenever
④ wherever – whatever
⑤ whenever – whoever

서술형 평가

13 두 문장을 한 문장으로 바꿔 쓸 때 빈칸에 알맞은 관계부사를 쓰시오.

• This is the shop.
• I bought a bag in the shop.

→ This is the shop _____ I bought a bag.

서술형 평가

14 우리말과 일치하도록 빈칸에 알맞은 말을 쓰시오.

네가 아무리 부자일지라도, 너는 너무 많은 돈을 써서는 안 된다.

→ _____ rich you may be, you shouldn't spend too much money.

교과서
어휘 **disappointed** 실망한   **right now** 지금 당장   **rich** 부유한

★★
15 어법상 옳은 것끼리 짝지어진 것은?

ⓐ He has two brothers, whom are doctors.

ⓑ The man that repaired my bike is very kind.

ⓒ Look at the girl and the cat who are running over there.

ⓓ Harry Potter is a young magician whose magic is very powerful.

① ⓐ
② ⓐ, ⓑ
③ ⓑ, ⓒ
④ ⓑ, ⓓ
⑤ ⓒ, ⓓ

★★
16 밑줄 친 부분 중 생략할 수 있는 것은?

① Remember <u>what</u> I said before.

② Have you found the keys <u>that</u> you lost?

③ The woman <u>who</u> wears a hat is a doctor.

④ Do you still remember <u>when</u> we first met?

⑤ Where is the cheese <u>that</u> was in the refrigerator?

★★
17 빈칸에 공통으로 들어갈 말로 알맞은 것은?

• I don't know the children _____ are playing hide-and-seek there.

• This is something _____ I want to know about.

① which
② who
③ whom
④ what
⑤ that

★★
18 밑줄 친 부분과 바꿔 쓸 수 있는 것이 바르게 짝지어진 것은?

• No one knows the reason <u>for which</u> I did so.

• This is the house <u>in which</u> Michael lives.

① where – when
② why – when
③ why – how
④ why – where
⑤ when – that

★★★
19 어법상 <u>어색한</u> 것은?

① This is a car which was made in Korea.

② She can't hear which you say at all.

③ I saw a boy whose life was in danger.

④ This is Mr. Carter whom I have told you about.

⑤ Do you know the chairman who is giving a speech now?

시험에 잘 나오는 문제
★★
20 밑줄 친 부분의 쓰임이 나머지와 <u>다른</u> 것은?

① <u>What</u> is your favorite song?

② That is <u>what</u> I intended to order.

③ <u>What</u> you need to prepare is nothing.

④ <u>What</u> he said made me mad at him.

⑤ <u>What</u> happened to me yesterday was terrible.

서술형 평가
★★
21 두 문장이 같은 의미가 되도록 빈칸에 알맞은 말을 쓰시오.

We stayed at the Grand Hotel, and it had many special rooms.

= We stayed at the Grand Hotel, _____ had many special rooms.

교과서 **magician** 마법사, 마술사 **powerful** 강력한 **refrigerator** 냉장고 **hide-and-seek** 숨바꼭질 **chairman** 의장, 회장
어휘 **intend** 의도하다 **mad** 몹시 화가 난

★★
22 빈칸에 들어갈 말이 바르게 짝지어진 것은?

- I ate all the food _____ was made by Peter.
- Spring is the season _____ new life begins.

① which – where
② which – why
③ that – when
④ that – where
⑤ for which – in which

★★★ 시험에 잘 나오는 문제
23 빈칸에 which가 들어갈 수 <u>없는</u> 것은?

① This is the movie _____ I like.
② This is the doll _____ I used to play with.
③ I will clean the room _____ Semi will stay.
④ She showed me a skirt _____ has a ribbon on it.
⑤ My dad bought me a cell phone _____ was brand new.

★★★
24 어법상 <u>어색한</u> 것은?

① The nurse treats patients, who have burns.
② This is the reason why I'm here.
③ I met a girl whose eyes are blue.
④ He gave me shoes, that were made in Italy.
⑤ Tell me the reason for which you went there.

★★
25 글의 흐름으로 보아, 주어진 문장이 들어가기에 알맞은 곳은?

In cities where earthquakes occur often, some buildings are constructed with quake safety in mind. (①) They are designed to absorb vibrations. (②) Engineers are now also developing "smart buildings." (③) These structures have sensors that will automatically activate special systems during an earthquake. (④) Engineers are developing more systems to reduce damage. (⑤)

One of the systems uses a kind of shock absorber similar to those in a car.

①　　②　　③　　④　　⑤

★★
26 빈칸에 알맞은 것은?

Scarecrows are funny stick figures that wear plaid shirts stuffed with hay. They don't stand around in the field just to decorate the place. Farmers build scarecrows to scare away crows, since crows eat crops. But scarecrows scare the birds not by looking like people, but by _____ like people. By wearing our clothes, scarecrows smell like us, and birds apparently don't think we smell good. Is it the ketchup we spilled on ourselves, or the apple juice? It doesn't matter. Either way, scarecrows protect crops from birds.

① smiling
② hearing
③ smelling
④ touching
⑤ sounding

교과서 **brand new** 완전 새것인 **burn** 화상 **occur** 발생하다 **absorb** 흡수하다 **vibration** 진동 **activate** 활성화하다 **plaid** 격자무늬의
어휘 **hay** 건초 **apparently** 분명히 **spill** 흘리다, 쏟다 **matter** 중요하다

[27~28] 다음을 읽고, 물음에 답하시오.

Meat and fish are an important part of most people's diets. They contain protein, ⓐ which our bodies need. Our muscles and organs ⓑ are mainly made of protein. Protein helps the body to grow and repair itself. Some sources of protein are better for our bodies than others. White meat and fish have a much lower fat content than red meat. Because of this, it is better ⓒ to eat white meat than to eat red meat. As with all foods, ⓓ the way how we cook meat can affect how healthy it is. Food that is fried is not ⓔ as good for us as food that is grilled.

★★
27 위 글의 내용과 일치하지 <u>않는</u> 것은?
① 근육과 기관들은 주로 단백질로 이루어져 있다.
② 단백질은 몸이 스스로 치료할 수 있게 도와준다.
③ 흰색 고기는 지방 함유량이 적다.
④ 붉은색 고기가 흰색 고기보다 몸에 더 좋다.
⑤ 구운 음식이 튀긴 음식보다 몸에 더 좋다.

★★
28 밑줄 친 ⓐ-ⓔ 중 어법상 <u>어색한</u> 것은?
① ⓐ ② ⓑ ③ ⓒ ④ ⓓ ⑤ ⓔ

[29~30] 다음을 읽고, 물음에 답하시오.

The desert is not the easiest place for animals to live. They must deal with extreme temperatures. Many animals in the desert simply stay out of the sunlight. They may spend much of their time underground, only coming out at night to look for food. Some animals have adaptations <u>that</u> help them deal with the heat. Camels have long legs that keep their body away from the heat of the sand. Fennec foxes and jackrabbits have large ears that lose heat. Many desert animals have paler fur or lighter skin than their relatives living in other climates. Lighter colors absorb less heat than darker ones.

*Fennec fox 사막여우   *jackrabbit 산토끼

★★
29 위 글의 제목으로 알맞은 것은?
① What Causes Serious Desertification?
② Which Is the Hottest Desert on Earth?
③ How Do Animals Keep Cool in the Desert?
④ Why Is Desert Cold at Night?
⑤ What Kinds of Animals Live in the Desert?

★★
30 밑줄 친 that과 쓰임이 같은 것은?
① He spoke so well that everybody was pleased.
② Jason won't forget the day that he won the prize.
③ The suitcase didn't seem that heavy at the time.
④ I think that is the best way to solve the problem.
⑤ He found the book that was written in 1989.

교과서   **protein** 단백질   **organ** 장기, 기관   **content** 함유량, 함량   **grill** 석쇠에 굽다   **extreme** 극도의   **adaptation** 적응
어휘   **deal with** …을 처리하다, 다루다   **pale** 옅은   **climate** 기후

.... **>> Grammar**

A 관계대명사

관계대명사는 〈접속사＋대명사〉의 역할을 하며, 관계사절을 이끌어 선행사를 꾸민다.

선행사 ＼ 격	주격	목적격	소유격
사람	who	who(m)	whose
사물, 동물	which	which	whose / of which
사람, 사물, 동물	that	that	–
선행사 포함	what	what	–

B 관계대명사의 계속적 용법

계속적 용법은 〈콤마(,)＋관계대명사〉의 형태로, 관계대명사절이 선행사에 대해 추가 설명하는 것을 말한다. 관계대명사절이 선행사를 꾸밀 때는 제한적 용법이라고 한다.

She has two sons **who** became cooks. 〈제한적 용법 – 아들이 두 명 이상〉

She has two sons, **who** became cooks. 〈계속적 용법 – 아들이 두 명〉
　　　　　　　　 ＝ and they (관계대명사를 〈접속사＋대명사〉로 바꿔 쓸 수 있음)

C 관계대명사의 생략

1 목적격 관계대명사의 생략: 제한적 용법에서 목적격 관계대명사를 생략할 수 있다.
This is the T-shirt (**which**) I made for myself.

2 〈주격 관계대명사＋be동사〉 생략: 분사(형용사구) 앞의 〈주격 관계대명사＋be동사〉는 생략할 수 있다.
This woman (**who is**) smiling at us is my mother.

D 관계부사

관계부사는 〈접속사＋부사〉의 역할을 하며, 관계사절을 이끌어 장소, 때, 이유, 방법을 나타내는 선행사를 꾸민다.

선행사	관계부사	전치사＋관계대명사
장소 (the place, city 등)	where	at(on, in) which
때 (the time, day 등)	when	at(on, in) which
이유 (the reason)	why	for which
방법 (the way)	how	in which

E 복합관계사

1 복합관계대명사: 〈관계대명사+-ever〉의 형태로 선행사를 포함하고 있고, 명사절 또는 양보의 부사절을 이끈다.

복합관계대명사	명사절	양보의 부사절
whoever	…하는 사람은 누구든지 (= anyone who)	누가 …할지라도 (= no matter who)
whatever	…하는 것은 무엇이든지 (= anything that)	무엇을 …할지라도 (= no matter what)
whichever	…하는 것은 어느 것이든지 (= anything that)	어느 것을 …할지라도 (= no matter which)

2 복합관계부사: 〈관계부사+-ever〉의 형태로 선행사를 포함하고 있고, 시간, 장소, 양보의 부사절을 이끈다.

복합관계부사	시간, 장소의 부사절	양보의 부사절
whenever	…할 때는 언제나 (= at any time when)	언제 …할지라도 (= no matter when)
wherever	…하는 곳은 어디든지 (= at any place where)	어디서 …할지라도 (= no matter where)
however	–	아무리 …할지라도 (= no matter how)

·· **>> Expression**

1 이해 점검하기 / 오해 지적해 주기

🍎 이해 점검하기
- Do you understand?
- Do you get it?
- Do you see(know) what I mean?
- Is this(everything) clear?
- Do you follow me?

🍎 오해 지적해 주기
- (No,) I mean … (not …).
- I'm afraid that's wrong(not right).
- That's not what I meant to say.

2 의견 묻고 답하기

🍎 의견 묻기
- What do you think of(about) …?
- How do you like …?
- How do you feel about …?
- What is your view(opinion)?

🍎 의견 표현하기
- (Well,) I think(feel / believe) ….
- It seems to me (that) ….
- In my view(opinion), ….

Lesson 05

수동태

Grammar Preview

1 수동태

• **수동태**: 수동태는 주어가 동작의 영향을 받거나 당하는 것을 나타내는 동사의 형태로 〈be동사＋과거분사 ＋by＋목적격(행위자)〉으로 나타내며, be동사를 통해 시제를 표현한다.

〈능동〉 Ryan cleaned the stairs yesterday.

〈수동〉 The stairs were cleaned by Ryan yesterday.

• **수동태의 시제**

과거시제 수동태	was(were)＋과거분사	미래시제 수동태	will be＋과거분사
진행시제 수동태	be동사＋being＋과거분사	완료시제 수동태	have(has, had)＋been＋과거분사

Her computer **will be fixed** by the repairman. 〈미래시제 수동태〉

The lecture **was being delivered** by my brother. 〈진행시제 수동태〉

The bakery **has been run** by them since last year. 〈완료시제 수동태〉

• **조동사가 있는 수동태**: 〈조동사＋be＋과거분사〉의 형태로 나타낸다.

Every kind of food **can be delivered** by them.   The rules **should be followed** (by people).

2 다양한 형태의 수동태

• **4형식 문장의 수동태**

He showed her a lot of photos.

→ She **was shown** a lot of photos by him. 〈간접목적어 주어〉

→ A lot of photos **were shown** to her by him. 〈직접목적어 주어〉

• **5형식 문장의 수동태**

I call my brother "teddy bear." → My brother **is called** "teddy bear" by me. 〈목적격보어가 변하지 않는 경우〉

They saw him enter the room. → He **was seen** to enter the room (by them). 〈목적격보어가 변하는 경우〉

• **by 이외의 전치사를 쓰는 수동태 표현**

be interested in …에 관심이 있다	be surprised at …에 놀라다
be worried about …에 대해 걱정하다	be covered with …으로 덮이다
be satisfied with …에 만족하다	be known to …에게 알려져 있다

1 수동태

A 수동태

1 수동태: 수동태는 주어가 동작의 영향을 받거나 당하는 것을 나타내는 동사의 형태로 〈be동사＋과거분사＋by＋목적격(행위자)〉으로 나타내며, be동사를 통해 시제를 표현한다.

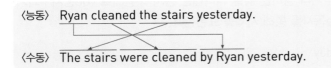

〈능동〉 Ryan cleaned the stairs yesterday.

〈수동〉 The stairs were cleaned by Ryan yesterday.

2 수동태의 부정문과 의문문

부정문	주어＋be동사＋not＋과거분사 ….
의문문	be동사＋주어＋과거분사 …? － Yes, 주어＋be동사. / No, 주어＋be동사＋not.

This article **was not(wasn't) written** by Kate.

Was he **scolded** by Jane? — Yes, he was. / No, he wasn't.

When **was** the picture **taken** by you?

> **Plus** Grammar
>
> • 〈by＋목적격(행위자)〉의 생략
> 행위자가 일반인이거나 알 수 없거나 행위자를 밝힐 필요가 없을 경우에는 〈by＋목적격(행위자)〉을 생략할 수 있다.
> English is spoken in America (**by the Americans**).
>
> • 수동태로 쓰지 않는 동사
> have(가지다), resemble(닮다), like(좋아하다) 등 상태를 나타내는 동사는 수동태로 쓰지 않는다.

B 수동태의 시제

	형태	의미
과거시제 수동태	was(were)＋과거분사	…되었다, …당했다
미래시제 수동태	will be＋과거분사	…될 것이다, …당할 것이다
진행시제 수동태	be동사＋being＋과거분사	…받는(되는) 중이다
완료시제 수동태	have(has, had)＋been＋과거분사	…되었다, …당해 왔다

Her computer **will be fixed** by the repairman. 〈미래시제 수동태〉

The lecture **was being delivered** by my brother. 〈진행시제 수동태〉

The bakery **has been run** by them since last year. 〈완료시제 수동태〉

C 조동사가 있는 수동태

조동사 뒤에는 동사원형이 오므로 〈조동사＋be＋과거분사〉의 형태로 나타내고, 부정문은 조동사 뒤에 not을 붙인다.

Every kind of food **can be delivered** by them.

The rules **should be followed** (by people).

These drugs **should not be used** in the elderly.

Grammar Practice >>

Answer p. 15

A1 괄호 안에서 알맞은 것을 고르시오.

(1) This play (wrote, was written) by Shakespeare.

(2) When (did, was) the vase broken into pieces by Mary?

(3) She (trusted, was trusted) because she was honest.

(4) The tree (is, was) hit by a car yesterday.

(5) When was this novel (writing, written)?

(6) The island (is located, located) in the northwest part of the Indian Ocean.

A2 밑줄 친 부분을 알맞은 형태로 고쳐 쓰시오.

(1) A glass was broken by he.

(2) History is make by ordinary people.

(3) Was the contract sign by him?

(4) Cake is make from flour, milk, and eggs.

(5) The tea was not drink by me.

(6) Where was the criminal catch yesterday?

(7) Why was the Statue of Liberty build?

B1 주어진 문장을 우리말로 옮기시오.

(1) The restaurant was being built.

→ _____

(2) The thief will be punished by the police officer.

→ _____

(3) He will be praised by the teacher tomorrow.

→ _____

B2 주어진 문장을 수동태로 바꿔 쓰시오.

(1) She will finish the work.

→ _____

(2) We were building a new hospital here.

→ _____

(3) I had solved the problem.

→ _____

(4) They have sold the house on the corner.

→ _____

(5) Technology has changed our lives.

→ _____

C1 우리말과 일치하도록 괄호 안에서 알맞은 것을 고르시오.

(1) 기차 일정은 내일 바뀔 것이다.

→ The train schedule (will change, will be changed) tomorrow.

(2) Jason이 우리의 리더로 선출될지도 모른다.

→ Jason (may be electing, may be elected) as our leader.

(3) 그 나무는 잘려야만 한다.

→ The tree (must is cut, must be cut) down.

C2 어법상 어색한 부분을 찾아 바르게 고쳐 쓰시오.

(1) All kinds of cookies can bake by this famous chef.

_____ → _____

(2) The novel should be reading by many teenagers.

_____ → _____

(3) Can these brown shoes is exchanged?

_____ → _____

교과서 **stair** 계단 **scold** 꾸짖다, 야단치다 **deliver** (연설·강연 등을) 하다, 배달하다 **run** 운영하다 **drug** 약물 **ordinary** 평범한
어휘 🎧 **contract** 계약 **flour** 밀가루 **criminal** 범죄자 **punish** 처벌하다 **exchange** 교환하다

2 다양한 형태의 수동태

D 4형식 문장의 수동태

간접목적어와 직접목적어를 각각 주어로 하는 두 개의 수동태 문장을 만들 수 있다. 직접목적어를 주어로 할 때에는 동사에 따라 간접목적어 앞에 전치사를 써야 한다.

He showed her a lot of photos.
　　　　　간접목적어　　직접목적어
→ She **was shown** a lot of photos by him. 〈간접목적어 주어〉
→ A lot of photos **were shown** to her by him. 〈직접목적어 주어〉

cf. read, write, make, buy, sell, send 등은 직접목적어만을 주어로 쓴다.
　He sent me a birthday card.
　　→ A birthday card **was sent** to me by him.

> **Plus Grammar**
> 간접목적어 앞에 쓰는 전치사
>
> | | |
> |---|---|
> | to | write, send, give, teach, tell, show 등 |
> | for | get, make, buy 등 |
> | of | ask, require 등 |
>
> Some candies **were made for** him. (약간의 사탕이 그를 위해 만들어졌다.)

E 5형식 문장의 수동태

1 목적격보어가 변하지 않는 경우: 목적격보어로 쓰인 명사, 형용사, 분사, to부정사는 수동태로 전환할 때 〈be동사＋과거분사〉 뒤에 그대로 온다.
I call my brother "teddy bear."
　→ My brother **is called** "teddy bear" by me.
He advised me to exercise regularly.
　→ I **was advised** to exercise regularly by him.

2 목적격보어가 변하는 경우: 지각동사, 사역동사의 목적격보어로 쓰인 동사원형은 수동태로 전환할 때 to부정사로 쓴다.
They saw him enter the room.
　→ He **was seen** to enter the room (by them).

F 주의해야 할 수동태

1 by 이외의 전치사를 쓰는 수동태 표현

be interested in …에 관심이 있다	be surprised at …에 놀라다
be worried about …에 대해 걱정하다	be covered with …으로 덮이다
be satisfied with …에 만족하다	be known to …에게 알려져 있다

I **am worried about** this math test. 　The field **is covered with** flowers.

2 목적어가 that절인 문장의 수동태: that절이 수동태 문장의 주어가 되는 경우, 주어 자리에 가주어 It을 쓰고 that절(진주어)은 문장 맨 뒤로 보낸다. that절의 주어를 문장의 주어로 쓸 때는 that절의 동사가 to부정사로 바뀐다.
People say that fruits are good for the body.
　→ **It is said that** fruits are good for the body (by people).
　→ Fruits **are said to be** good for the body (by people).

> **Plus Grammar**
> 동사구 수동태
> 동사구는 하나의 동사로 취급하여 수동태를 만들 때에도 한 덩어리로 움직인다.
> • take care of: …을 돌보다
> • run over: (차가) …을 치다
> • look up to: …을 존경하다
> • speak well(ill) of: …을 칭찬하다(나쁘게 말하다)
> Mina **is spoken well of** by all the teachers. (Mina는 모든 선생님들에게 칭찬받는다.)

Grammar Practice >>

Answer p. 15

D1 빈칸에 알맞은 말을 〈보기〉에서 골라 쓰시오.

┌─보기─────────────────────┐
│   to   for   of   │
└────────────────────────┘

(1) A special prize was given _____ my brother by them.

(2) This toy house was made _____ kids.

(3) No questions were asked _____ us.

D2 주어진 문장을 수동태로 바꿔 쓸 때 빈칸에 알맞은 말을 쓰시오.

(1) He gave her a pretty doll.

→ She _____ _____ a pretty doll by him.

→ A pretty doll _____ _____ _____ _____ by him.

(2) Tom buys me the pumpkin cookies.

→ The pumpkin cookies _____ _____ _____ _____ by Tom.

(3) He told me a horrible story.

→ A horrible story _____ _____ _____ _____ by him.

E1 어법상 어색한 부분을 찾아 바르게 고쳐 쓰시오.

(1) Mike was seen walk his dog.

_____ → _____

(2) The pretty girl is calling "princess" by me.

_____ → _____

(3) They were made coming inside.

_____ → _____

E2 우리말과 일치하도록 주어진 단어들을 바르게 배열 하시오.

(1) 나는 그들에 의해 행복해졌다.

→ I was _____ by them. (happy, made)

(2) 그는 어제 대통령으로 선출되었다.

→ He _____ yesterday. (elected, President, was)

(3) 그가 소파에서 쉬고 있는 것이 목격되었다.

→ He was _____ on the sofa. (relax, to, seen)

F1 빈칸에 알맞은 전치사를 쓰시오.

(1) The famous singer is known _____ everybody.

(2) The mountain is covered _____ snow.

(3) She was surprised _____ the score.

(4) Jenny is interested _____ playing tennis.

F2 우리말과 일치하도록 주어진 단어들을 이용하여 빈칸에 알맞은 말을 쓰시오.

(1) 내 강아지가 트럭에 치였다.

→ My dog _____ _____ _____ _____ a truck. (run over)

(2) Peter는 그의 친구들에게 평판이 좋다.

→ Peter _____ _____ _____ _____ _____ his friends. (speak well of)

(3) 정직이 최선의 방책이라고 말해진다.

→ It _____ _____ _____ honesty is the best policy. (say)

교과서   **regularly** 규칙적으로   **field** 들판   **pumpkin** 호박   **horrible** 무서운, 끔찍한   **score** 점수, 득점   **honesty** 정직
어휘   **policy** 방책, 정책

Grammar Test

01 빈칸에 알맞은 것은?

The thief _____ by the police yesterday.

① arrested
② be arrested
③ was arrested
④ will be arrested
⑤ has been arrested

서술형 평가

02 빈칸에 알맞은 말을 쓰시오.

A Who wrote *Romeo and Juliet*?
B It _____ _____ by Shakespeare.

03 주어진 문장을 수동태로 바꿔 쓸 때 알맞은 것은?

My mother made me clean the floor.

① I made to clean the floor by my mother.
② I was made clean the floor by my mother.
③ The floor was made to clean by my mother.
④ I was made to clean the floor by my mother.
⑤ The floor was made to be cleaned by my mother.

04 밑줄 친 ①-⑤ 중 어법상 어색한 것은?

①The children ②will care for ③by Jane ④while their parents ⑤attend the meeting.

05 빈칸에 공통으로 들어갈 말로 알맞은 것은?

• The child's face is filled _____ happiness.
• She was satisfied _____ her life in London.

① by
② to
③ with
④ at
⑤ of

서술형 평가

06 그림을 보고, 주어진 단어를 이용하여 문장을 완성하시오.

The papers are being _____ into pieces by him. (tear)

서술형 평가

07 주어진 단어를 이용하여 빈칸에 알맞은 말을 쓰시오.

(1) His jacket has never _____ _____ before. (wash)
(2) Why were you _____ by the math teacher? (scold)

교과서 **arrest** 체포하다 **clean** 닦다, 청소하다 **floor** 바닥 **care for** …을 돌보다 **tear** 찢다
어휘 🎧

08 빈칸에 at이 들어갈 수 있는 것은?

① Jim was married _____ Lisa.

② They were surprised _____ the news.

③ I was satisfied _____ my friend's answer.

④ The letter was shown _____ me by him.

⑤ The desk is covered _____ a lot of books.

서술형 평가

09 우리말과 일치하도록 주어진 단어들을 이용하여 문장을 완성하시오.

그 축구공들은 아프리카의 가난한 아이들을 위해 구입되었다. (be, buy, the poor children)

→ The soccer balls _____ in Africa.

10 주어진 문장을 수동태로 바꿔 쓸 때 알맞은 것은?

Why did he write his poem in English?

① Why his poem wrote in English by him?

② Why he did write his poem in English by him?

③ Why his poem was written in English by him?

④ Why was his poem wrote in English by him?

⑤ Why was his poem written in English by him?

서술형 평가

11 어법상 어색한 부분을 찾아 바르게 고쳐 쓰시오.

This region should protect by the people.

_____ → _____

서술형 평가

12 두 문장이 같은 의미가 되도록 빈칸에 알맞은 말을 쓰시오.

People said that the soccer player was full of confidence.

= _____ _____ said _____ the soccer player was full of confidence.

13 어법상 옳은 것은?

① He is worried about his appearance.

② This animal should protected from danger.

③ The dress was bought to her by her sister.

④ As time went by, more postcards were send to me.

⑤ She was surprised for something white in the darkness.

14 어법상 어색한 것은?

① The trees are been cut by my uncle.

② The game was canceled because of the storm.

③ My dog is being given water by my friend.

④ They were made to carry boxes.

⑤ He was seen to steal some bread by the police.

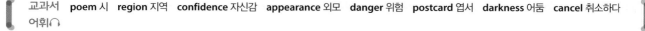

교과서 **poem** 시 **region** 지역 **confidence** 자신감 **appearance** 외모 **danger** 위험 **postcard** 엽서 **darkness** 어둠 **cancel** 취소하다
어휘

Reading

[1~2] 다음을 끊어 읽고 ☑, 해석을 쓰시오. ✎

Can You Spot Fake News? _____

Let's look into an article✓thinking about the hidden motives✓behind it.

3 **SLAV SHOOTS A FRIEND IN ARGUMENT** _____

Mejk Swenekafew,✓a Slav worker at the Columbia Coal Mine,✓

was shot and wounded✓by John Pecitello✓near the mining camp✓

6 Thursday evening. The two men had an argument. The argument led

to a fight,✓and Pecitello shot Swenekafew twice,✓in the chest and leg.

He is now at the hospital. Pecitello ran away✓after the shooting. The police are searching for him.

9 Is there anything strange✓about the article? Read the Slav's name✓backwards;✓it spells "we-

fake-news." *The Daily Telegram* published this _____ article✓so that they could prove✓if *The*

Daily News,✓their competitor,✓was stealing their articles. *The Daily News* published the same

12 article✓about "Swenekafew"✓and thus got caught stealing. (A)The public harshly criticized✓the

people at *The Daily News*.

_____

1 빈칸에 알맞은 것은?

① impressive   ② serious   ③ fake   ④ featured   ⑤ leading

2 밑줄 친 (A)를 수동태 문장으로 바꿔 쓰시오.

_____

교과서 **motive** 동기 **coal** 석탄 **mine** 광산 **wound** 부상을 입히다 **run away** 달아나다 **backwards** 거꾸로 **spell** 철자를 쓰다
어휘 🎧 **competitor** 경쟁 상대 **steal** 훔치다 **criticize** 비난하다

Answer p. 15

3 다음 글의 내용과 일치하지 <u>않는</u> 것은?

건축

In 1989, the French government was looking for a way to solve the traffic problem in the Tarn Valley. Officials wanted to build a new bridge to stop cars from getting stuck in the valley. But they **were worried about** building something that might destroy the scenery or upset the people who lived in the valley. In December 2004, the Millau Viaduct opened. The bridge is so beautiful that it almost looks like a natural part of the valley. With some parts of the bridge taller than the Eiffel Tower, tourists who drive on the bridge will feel like they are flying over the valley. Below the bridge, the valley's people are enjoying life with fewer cars and less pollution.

① Tarn Valley 주변은 교통 체증이 심했다.　② 2004년에 미요 대교가 개통되었다.
③ 미요 대교의 일부는 에펠탑보다 높다.　④ 미요 대교는 너무 아름다워서 계곡의 일부처럼 보인다.
⑤ Tarn Valley 주민들은 많은 관광객 때문에 고통받고 있다.

4 다음 글에서 언급되지 <u>않은</u> 것은?

동물

For years, dinosaurs **were thought** to be big, dumb, and cold-blooded. But many were about the size of modern-day birds or dogs. Of course, no dinosaur was as smart as a human, but some smaller dinosaurs like the two-meter Troodon had fairly large brains. It **is known** that Tyrannosaurus rex was a powerful predator. In the movies, T. rex is often a speedy giant, but in fact, this dinosaur could not run very fast. Physically, it was too large. In reality, T. rex probably moved as fast as an elephant. Also, T. rex had very small arms. Without strong arms, this dinosaur probably wasn't a powerful hunter.

① 공룡에 대한 통념　② 인간만큼 똑똑했던 공룡
③ 영화 속 티라노사우루스의 모습　④ 티라노사우루스가 빠르지 못했던 이유
⑤ 티라노사우루스의 팔의 길이

3　**valley** 계곡　**destroy** 파괴하다　**scenery** 경치, 풍경　**upset** 속상하게 만들다　**pollution** 오염
4　**dumb** 멍청한, 바보 같은　**cold-blooded** 냉혈의　**predator** 포식자　**physically** 신체적으로

Expression

1 허락 요청하고 답하기

I'm going to the National Museum this Saturday. Could you give me directions on how to get there?

Sure. I can show you the way there. Is it okay if I go to the museum with you?

Oh! I'm totally okay with that!

National Museum

💬 허락 요청하기

- May(Can) I ...?
- Let me ....
- Do you mind if I ...?
- Is it okay if I ...?
- Would it be possible ...?

💬 허락 요청에 답하기

- Yes. / Okay. / All right.
- Sure. / Of course.
- (Yes,) You can.
- (No,) You can't.
- Not at all.
- (I'm afraid) That's(It's) not possible.

2 설명 요청하기 / 반복 요청하기

I usually drink a glass of milk before I go to bed, but I still have trouble falling asleep.

Well, I've heard that drinking a glass of milk doesn't actually help you fall asleep.

Milk has special chemicals that make people sleepy. But the amount in a glass is too small to have any effect.

Oh, really? Could you explain to me why that is?

Milk

💬 설명 요청하기

- What is ... exactly?
- What do you mean by ...?
- Could you explain ...?
- Can you tell me more about ...?

💬 반복 요청하기

- (I'm) Sorry?
- What did you say?
- I beg your pardon?
- I don't know what you mean(meant).
- Would you say that again?

Expression Test

Answer p. 16

1 빈칸에 알맞은 말을 주어진 철자를 이용하여 쓰시오.

> A Do you m_____ if I borrow your bike?
> B No, I don't. I can lend it.

2 밑줄 친 부분과 바꿔 쓸 수 있는 것은?

> A <u>Can you tell me about this movie?</u>
> B Yes. It's about self-esteem and love.

① Can you explain this movie?
② Would you like to see this movie?
③ How about going to see this movie?
④ Can I talk about this movie with you?
⑤ Are you wondering who made this movie?

3 의도하는 바가 나머지와 <u>다른</u> 것은?
① May I use your computer?
② Is it okay if I use your computer?
③ Could you use your computer?
④ Do you mind if I use your computer?
⑤ Can I use your computer?

4 짝지어진 대화가 <u>어색한</u> 것은?
① A Do you mind turning off your cell phone?
   B Of course. I don't mind at all.
② A Is it okay if I play computer games now?
   B I'm afraid you can't.
③ A Can you explain this picture?
   B It's a snake which ate an elephant.
④ A May I ask you some questions?
   B Sure.
⑤ A Can you explain how to solve this puzzle?
   B Sure. Let me show how to do it.

5 빈칸에 알맞지 <u>않은</u> 것은?

> A Mom, I've just finished my homework. Is it okay if I go out and play soccer?
> B _____ Go ahead.

① Sure.
② Why not?
③ Okay.
④ Of course not.
⑤ No problem.

6 우리말과 일치하도록 빈칸에 알맞은 말을 쓰시오.

> A She is a night owl.
> B I don't know _____ you mean.
>   (네 말이 무슨 뜻인지 모르겠어.)
> A She likes to work at night.

1 빈칸에 공통으로 들어갈 말을 〈보기〉에서 골라 쓰시오.

┌─보기─
Do you know how to
Is it okay if I
Are you planning to
└─

A Welcome to the National Museum. How can I help you?
B Hi. _____ take pictures in the museum?
A Yes, but please don't use flash. By the way, you can't take your backpack inside the museum.
B Oh, I didn't know that. _____ bring my water bottle?
A Yes, that's fine. You can leave your bag in the locker.
B Okay, thank you.

2 그림을 보고, 주어진 단어를 이용하여 빈칸에 알맞은 말을 쓰시오.

The towers _____ many trees. (surround)

3 주어진 문장을 수동태로 바꿔 쓰시오.

(1) The members must keep the secret.
  → _____

(2) The doctor has treated all the patients.
  → _____

4 우리말과 일치하도록 주어진 단어를 이용하여 빈칸에 알맞은 말을 쓰시오.

(1) 우리는 호텔 서비스에 만족한다.
  → We _____ _____ _____ the hotel service. (satisfy)

(2) 이 사진은 어제 Judy에 의해 찍혔다.
  → This photo _____ _____ by Judy yesterday. (take)

(3) 도로가 눈으로 덮여 있다.
  → The road _____ _____ _____ snow. (cover)

5 그림을 보고, 〈보기〉의 단어들을 이용하여 대화를 완성하시오. (형태 변화 가능)

┌─보기─
return   put   take out
└─

A Mike. Your room is so dirty and your grandmother is coming today!
B Oh, I forgot.
A Let's clean up your room.
B Okay.
A All the clothes should (1)_____ in the drawers. The garbage should (2)_____, too.
B I'll do it right away. By the way, can you return these books to the library? They should (3)_____ today.
A Okay, I'll take them.

Final Test

Answer p. 17

난이도: 상 ★★★ 중 ★★ 하 ★

★★
01 영영풀이에 해당하는 것은?

the reason that makes someone do something, especially when this reason is kept hidden

① wound
② spell
③ mine
④ motive
⑤ clue

★★
02 빈칸에 알맞은 단어를 〈보기〉에서 골라 쓰시오.

보기
backwards   fake   spell

(1) I gave a _____ name.
(2) How do you _____ your name?
(3) In the movie they take a journey _____ through time.

★
03 빈칸에 알맞은 것은?

A Do you mind _____ I put my seat back?
B Certainly not.

① if
② where
③ when
④ what
⑤ and

서술형 평가
★
04 우리말과 일치하도록 빈칸에 알맞은 말을 쓰시오.

A Can you _____ how to cook spaghetti?
(스파게티 만드는 방법을 설명해 줄 수 있니?)
B Sure. It's easy.

★
05 밑줄 친 부분과 바꿔 쓸 수 없는 것은?

A Can I use your pen?
B Sure. Go ahead.

① May I use your pen?
② Let me use your pen.
③ Could I use your pen?
④ You can use your pen.
⑤ Do you mind if I use your pen?

★★
06 빈칸에 알맞은 것은?

A Why the long face, Jimin?
B I'm sorry? _____ My face is not long.
A I mean, you look unhappy.

① I feel sad.
② That's true.
③ I agree with you.
④ Things will be better soon.
⑤ I don't know what you mean.

서술형 평가
★★
07 자연스러운 대화가 되도록 (A)–(D)를 바르게 배열하시오.

(A) It means that something is easy to do.
(B) A piece of cake? What do you mean by that?
(C) How did you solve the puzzle?
(D) It was a piece of cake.

_____ → _____ → _____ → _____

교과서   **reason** 이유   **especially** 특히   **journey** 여행, 여정
어휘 🎧

08 ★ 빈칸에 알맞은 것은?

The room has not _____ for two months.

① cleaned
② to clean
③ cleaning
④ be cleaned
⑤ been cleaned

09 ★★ 시험에 잘 나오는 문제
빈칸에 들어갈 말이 바르게 짝지어진 것은?

· Mary was pleased _____ the birthday gift.
· His name is known _____ all the students.

① of – to
② with – at
③ at – with
④ with – to
⑤ by – with

10 ★★ 우리말과 일치하도록 할 때 빈칸에 알맞은 것은?

이 꽃은 중국어로 무엇이라고 불리니?
→ What _____ in Chinese?

① is called this flower
② is this flower called
③ do this flower call
④ does this flower call
⑤ does this flower be called

11 ★★ 괄호 안에서 알맞은 것을 고르시오.

(1) I (asked, was asked) some personal questions by him.
(2) The king (was built, built) the castle 100 years ago.
(3) Medicine should (be kept, keep) out of reach of children.

12 ★★ 서술형 평가
밑줄 친 부분을 어법에 맞게 고쳐 쓰시오.

(1) The magazine will publish next month.
→ _____

(2) My wallet has stolen by someone.
→ _____

13 ★★ 빈칸에 알맞은 것은?

A Who will teach us math?
B We _____ math by Mr. Lee.

① teach
② are taught
③ have been taught
④ will be taught
⑤ is being taught

14 ★★ 주어진 문장을 수동태로 바꿔 쓸 때 알맞은 것은?

They are constructing a large shopping mall.

① A large shopping mall is been constructed by them.
② A large shopping mall is being constructed by them.
③ A large shopping mall is been constructing by them.
④ A large shopping mall are been constructed by them.
⑤ A large shopping mall are being constructed by them.

교과서 **personal** 개인적인 **castle** 성 **medicine** 약, 약물 **out of reach** 손이 닿지 않는 곳에 **publish** 발행하다 **construct** 건설하다
어휘

15 ★★ 서술형 평가
빈칸에 공통으로 들어갈 말을 쓰시오.

• French was taught _____ us by Ms. Scott.
• The letters will be sent _____ my mother by my brother.

16 ★★ 서술형 평가
두 문장이 같은 의미가 되도록 빈칸에 알맞은 말을 쓰시오.

Jerry made her a wooden bowl.

= A wooden bowl _____ _____ _____ _____ by Jerry.

17 ★★ 어법상 어색한 것은?
① Is the room used by Sujin?
② The car washed by my brother.
③ A bag was bought for her by me.
④ The bus was crowded with people.
⑤ The boy was looked after by his sister.

18 ★★ 서술형 평가
우리말과 일치하도록 주어진 단어들을 배열하시오.
(1) 그 남자는 모든 사람의 존경을 받는다.
   (by, up, everyone, is, the man, looked, to)
   → _____
(2) 나는 반장으로 선출되었다.
   (my class, I, was, president, of, elected)
   → _____

19 ★★ 시험에 잘 나오는 문제
주어진 문장을 수동태로 바꿔 쓸 때 어색한 것은?
① Jim made his son leave at once.
   → His son was made to leave at once by Jim.
② When did she send the picture?
   → When was the picture sent by her?
③ They were building the apartment.
   → The apartment was been built by them.
④ He gave a photo to me.
   → A photo was given to me by him.
⑤ You should bring your ID card.
   → Your ID card should be brought by you.

20 ★★★ 밑줄 친 부분 중 생략할 수 있는 것은?
① The nest was built by that white bird.
② Spanish is spoken in Mexico by them.
③ This window was broken by your little son.
④ The light was not turned on by my father.
⑤ The event is sponsored by these companies.

21 ★★★ 어법상 어색한 것은?
① It can be seen from a great distance.
② The park is kept clean by the volunteers.
③ The play *Hamlet* was written by Shakespeare.
④ I was made wash the dishes by my mother.
⑤ Andy was asked a difficult question by her.

교과서 **bowl** 그릇 **at once** 즉시 **ID card** 신분증 **nest** 둥지 **sponsor** 후원하다 **distance** 거리
어휘⌒

★★ <u>서술형 평가</u>
22 두 문장이 같은 의미가 되도록 빈칸에 알맞은 말을 쓰시오.

I saw him enter the stadium.

= He was _____ _____ _____ the stadium by me.

★★★ <u>서술형 평가</u>
23 주어진 문장과 같은 의미가 되도록 빈칸에 알맞은 말을 쓰시오.

People say that the Earth is getting warmer and warmer.

= _____ is said _____ the Earth is getting warmer and warmer.

= The Earth is _____ _____ _____ _____ warmer and warmer.

★★★
24 어법상 옳은 것은?
① She was made go there by me.
② Many soldiers were killed in the war.
③ Your daughter was resembled by you.
④ This car was made in Germany by they.
⑤ The same texts can is read in different ways.

★
25 글쓴이가 주장하는 바로 알맞은 것은?

Sometimes people are so busy that they actually need some time to sit around and be bored. In a 2014 study in the UK, 80 subjects were given boring tasks, such as reading and copying down stuff from the dictionary. When they were asked to come up with creative ways to use plastic cups, they tended to come up with more creative ways than those who weren't given a boring task.

① 장시간 앉아 있는 것은 건강에 해롭다.
② 지루한 시간을 보내는 것이 필요하다.
③ 우선순위를 정해 일을 하는 것이 좋다.
④ 여러 가지 일을 한꺼번에 하는 것이 효율적이다.
⑤ 지루한 일을 할 때는 중간에 휴식을 취해야 한다.

★★
26 Machu Picchu에 관해 언급되지 <u>않은</u> 것은?

For nearly 450 years, the Incan city of Machu Picchu was hidden from the world. The city was located up high in the mountains of Peru. Machu Picchu was built by the Inca and was a religious center. The people of the great Incan city seemed to disappear. Why? That remains a mystery. One theory is that disease killed the people of Machu Picchu. Today, Machu Picchu is one of the most important tourist sites because the lost city is so remarkable and beautiful.

① 위치   ② 건설한 사람들
③ 주요 농작물   ④ 관련 이론
⑤ 관광객들에게 사랑받는 이유

교과서 **task** 과업 **come up with** …을 생각해 내다 **tend to** …하는 경향이 있다 **hide** 숨기다 **disappear** 사라지다 **theory** 이론
어휘 **remarkable** 놀라운

[27~28] 다음을 읽고, 물음에 답하시오.

In 1974, local farmers in the Shaanxi Province of China made an amazing discovery: a huge army of buried warriors. (①) The soldiers, which were life-size statues, had been hidden for more than 2,200 years, silently protecting their leader's tomb. (②) When uncovered, the statues were standing in the exact position of a real army. (③) Today, this fearless army also stands as a world-famous artistic wonder. (④) Each statue <u>made</u> by hand and had a unique face. (⑤) The entire structure, 57 square kilometers, is still being unearthed.   *unearth (땅속에서) 파내다, 발굴하다

★★
27 글의 흐름으로 보아, 주어진 문장이 들어가기에 알맞은 곳은?

Experts have learned much from this position about the fighting strategies of ancient China.

①   ②   ③   ④   ⑤

★★ 서술형 평가
28 밑줄 친 부분을 알맞은 형태로 고쳐 쓰시오.

→ _____

[29~30] 다음을 읽고, 물음에 답하시오.

On August 24, 2006, the world's astronomers decided that Pluto was ⓐ<u>no longer</u> a planet. Now our solar system only has eight planets, not nine. Scientists argued about ⓑ<u>whether or not</u> Pluto is really a planet. Questions about Pluto increased with the discovery of Eris, an icy object very far from the Sun. Eventually, scientists decided that for an object ⓒ<u>to classify</u> as a planet, it must meet three criteria: (1) It must circle the Sun. (2) It must be large and round. (3) Its orbit must be free of other objects.

Both Pluto and Eris circle the Sun and are round. But their orbits are strange and ⓓ<u>are shared</u> with other objects. For those reasons, they cannot ⓔ<u>be called</u> planets. Instead, they are now called "dwarf planets."   *dwarf planet 왜행성

★★
29 위 글의 내용과 일치하지 <u>않는</u> 것은?
① 태양계 행성은 9개에서 8개가 되었다.
② 에리스가 발견되면서 명왕성에 대한 의문이 증가되었다.
③ 행성으로 분류되려면 세 가지 기준을 충족해야 한다.
④ 명왕성과 에리스는 태양을 돌지 않는다.
⑤ 명왕성과 에리스는 왜행성으로 불린다.

★★★
30 밑줄 친 ⓐ-ⓔ 중 어법상 <u>어색한</u> 것은?
① ⓐ   ② ⓑ   ③ ⓒ   ④ ⓓ   ⑤ ⓔ

교과서 **army** 군대 **warrior** 전사 **statue** 조각상 **tomb** 무덤 **fearless** 용감한 **wonder** 경이로움 **expert** 전문가 **strategy** 전략
어휘 **classify** 분류하다 **criterion** 기준 (*pl.* criteria) **circle** …의 둘레를 돌다 **orbit** 궤도

··· >> **Grammar**

Ⓐ **수동태**

1 수동태: 수동태는 주어가 동작의 영향을 받거나 당하는 것을 나타내는 동사의 형태로 〈be동사＋ 과거분사＋by＋목적격(행위자)〉으로 나타내며, be동사를 통해 시제를 표현한다.

〈능동〉 Ryan cleaned the stairs yesterday.

〈수동〉 The stairs were cleaned by Ryan yesterday.

2 수동태의 부정문과 의문문

부정문	주어＋be동사＋not＋과거분사 ….
의문문	be동사＋주어＋과거분사 …? – Yes, 주어＋be동사. / No, 주어＋be동사＋not.

This article **was not(wasn't) written** by Kate.
Was he **scolded** by Jane? — Yes, he was. / No, he wasn't.

Ⓑ **수동태의 시제**

	형태	의미
과거시제 수동태	was(were)＋과거분사	…되었다, …당했다
미래시제 수동태	will be＋과거분사	…될 것이다, …당할 것이다
진행시제 수동태	be동사＋being＋과거분사	…받는(되는) 중이다
완료시제 수동태	have(has, had)＋been＋과거분사	…되었다, …당해 왔다

Ⓒ **조동사가 있는 수동태**

조동사 뒤에는 동사원형이 오므로 〈조동사＋be＋과거분사〉의 형태로 나타내고, 부정문은 조동사 뒤에 not을 붙인다.

Every kind of food **can be delivered** by them.
These drugs **should not be used** in the elderly.

Ⓓ **4형식 문장의 수동태**

간접목적어와 직접목적어를 각각 주어로 하는 두 개의 수동태 문장을 만들 수 있다.

He showed her a lot of photos.
　　　　간접목적어　직접목적어

→ She **was shown** a lot of photos by him. 〈간접목적어 주어〉
→ A lot of photos **were shown** to her by him. 〈직접목적어 주어〉

E 5형식 문장의 수동태

1 목적격보어가 변하지 않는 경우: 목적격보어로 쓰인 명사, 형용사, 분사, to부정사는 수동태로 전환할 때 〈be동사＋과거분사〉 뒤에 그대로 온다.
I call my brother "teddy bear." → My brother **is called** <u>teddy bear</u> by me.

2 목적격보어가 변하는 경우: 지각동사, 사역동사의 목적격보어로 쓰인 동사원형은 수동태로 전환할 때 to부정사로 쓴다.
They saw him enter the room. → He **was seen** <u>to enter</u> the room (by them).

F 주의해야 할 수동태

1 by 이외의 전치사를 쓰는 수동태 표현

be interested in …에 관심이 있다	be surprised at …에 놀라다
be worried about …에 대해 걱정하다	be covered with …으로 덮이다
be satisfied with …에 만족하다	be known to …에게 알려져 있다

2 목적어가 that절인 문장의 수동태: that절이 수동태 문장의 주어가 되는 경우, 주어 자리에 가주어 It을 쓰고 that절(진주어)은 문장 맨 뒤로 보낸다.
People say that fruits are good for the body.
→ **It is said that** fruits are good for the body (by people).

·· **≫ Expression**

1 허락 요청하고 답하기

🐾 허락 요청하기
- May〔Can〕I …?
- Let me ….
- Do you mind if I …?
- Is it okay if I …?
- Would it be possible …?

🐾 허락 요청에 답하기
- Yes. / Okay. / All right.
- Sure. / Of course.
- (Yes,) You can.
- (No,) You can't.
- Not at all.
- (I'm afraid) That's〔It's〕not possible.

2 설명 요청하기 / 반복 요청하기

🐾 설명 요청하기
- What is … exactly?
- What do you mean by …?
- Could you explain …?
- Can you tell me more about …?

🐾 반복 요청하기
- (I'm) Sorry?
- What did you say?
- I beg your pardon?
- I don't know what you mean〔meant〕.
- Would you say that again?

**I love those who yearn
for the impossible.**

Johann Wolfgang von Goethe

II

듣기 실전
모의고사

01회 » 듣기 실전 모의고사

01 대화를 듣고, 남자가 고른 머그컵을 고르시오.

02 대화를 듣고, 여자가 지불할 금액을 고르시오.

① \$6 　　　② \$25 　　　③ \$30
④ \$50 　　　⑤ \$60

03 대화를 듣고, 여자가 남자에게 전화한 목적으로 가장 적절한 것을 고르시오.

① 구급차를 부르려고
② 진료를 예약하려고
③ 심폐소생술을 배우려고
④ 응급 환자를 치료하려고
⑤ 화상 치료 방법을 물어보려고

04 대화를 듣고, 두 사람이 만나기로 한 날짜를 고르시오.

① September 10th
② September 11th
③ September 12th
④ September 14th
⑤ September 17th

05 대화를 듣고, 두 사람이 대화하는 장소로 가장 적절한 곳을 고르시오.

① art gallery 　　　② bank
③ bookstore 　　　④ photo studio
⑤ computer repair shop

06 다음 그림의 상황에 가장 적절한 대화를 고르시오.

① 　　② 　　③ 　　④ 　　⑤

07 대화를 듣고, 남자가 여자에게 부탁한 일로 가장 적절한 것을 고르시오.

① 불 켜기 　　　　② 창문 열기
③ 선풍기 켜기 　　④ 선풍기 청소하기
⑤ 나사돌리개 가져오기

08 다음을 듣고, 생존 수영에 관해 언급되지 <u>않은</u> 것을 고르시오.

① 정의 　　　② 목표 　　　③ 자세
④ 준비물 　　⑤ 유의 사항

09 다음을 듣고, 무엇에 관한 설명인지 고르시오.

① 반지 　　　② 장갑 　　　③ 팔찌
④ 손목시계 　⑤ 네일아트

10 다음을 듣고, 두 사람의 대화가 <u>어색한</u> 것을 고르시오.

① 　　② 　　③ 　　④ 　　⑤

11 대화를 듣고, 남자가 대화 직후에 할 일로 가장 적절한 것을 고르시오.

① 식물에 물 주기 　　② 학교로 출발하기
③ 학교에 갈 준비하기 　④ 잠자리에서 일어나기
⑤ 아버지께 전화 드리기

12 다음 표를 보면서 대화를 듣고, 두 사람이 구입할 쌀을 고르시오.

	Weight (kg)	Price (won)	Place of Origin
①	10	30,000	Korea
②	10	25,000	China
③	5	18,000	Korea
④	5	16,000	China
⑤	20	57,000	Korea

13 다음을 듣고, 무엇에 관한 내용인지 고르시오.

① 분리수거 방법
② 분리수거의 중요성
③ 업사이클링의 필요성
④ 업사이클링에 드는 비용
⑤ 일회용품 이용의 위험성

14 대화를 듣고, 여자가 할 일로 가장 적절한 것을 고르시오.

① 자기 전에 가벼운 운동하기
② 자기 전에 따뜻한 우유 마시기
③ 잠이 올 때까지 인터넷 검색하기
④ 좀 더 이른 시각에 잠자리에 들기
⑤ 자기 전에 전자 기기 이용하지 않기

15 다음을 듣고, 방송의 목적으로 가장 적절한 것을 고르시오.

① 비둘기의 생태를 소개하려고
② 공원 폐장 시간을 안내하려고
③ 비둘기에 의한 전염병 예방법을 알리려고
④ 비둘기에게 줄 수 있는 먹이를 판매하려고
⑤ 비둘기에게 먹이를 주지 말라고 당부하려고

16 대화를 듣고, 남자가 지난 주말에 한 일로 가장 적절한 것을 고르시오.

① 삼촌과 여행 가기 ② 제초제 구매하기
③ 농장의 잡초 뽑기 ④ 아버지의 농사일 돕기
⑤ 조부모님 댁 방문하기

17 대화를 듣고, 여자의 마지막 말에 대한 남자의 응답으로 가장 적절한 것을 고르시오.

Man: _____

① I haven't made the tea myself yet.
② You should first go to the hospital.
③ They are very good for your health.
④ Just mix them and then add warm water.
⑤ Do you need cinnamon powder?

18 대화를 듣고, 남자의 마지막 말에 대한 여자의 응답으로 가장 적절한 것을 고르시오.

Woman: _____

① Did you have lunch already?
② Where are you going?
③ I hope it won't rain tomorrow.
④ I want to have burgers and fries for lunch.
⑤ Sure. Meet me at the library after lunch.

19 대화를 듣고, 여자의 마지막 말에 대한 남자의 응답으로 가장 적절한 것을 고르시오.

Man: _____

① There is no more vacant room.
② Tell me how to improve my writing.
③ It isn't a good idea to write it again.
④ You can't improve your grades.
⑤ Well, I think the first part needs more detail.

20 다음 상황 설명을 듣고, Rebecca가 Isaac에게 할 말로 가장 적절한 것을 고르시오.

Rebecca: _____

① Have you seen my wallet?
② I just found my wallet.
③ Thank you for your help.
④ What are you doing with my wallet?
⑤ I wasn't suspecting you. I was just asking for your help.

01 대화를 듣고, 남자가 고른 머그컵을 고르시오.

①②③④⑤

M Rachel, you have a nice _____ _____ _____.
W All of these are my creation. You may have one if you wish.
M Wow, really? Can I have that white mug with the black circle?
W You mean the one with _____ _____ around the circle?
M That one's nice too but I meant the one with the word "MUG" _____ _____ _____.
W I got it. There you go.
M I owe you one. Thanks a lot.

02 대화를 듣고, 여자가 지불할 금액을 고르시오.

① $6   ② $25   ③ $30
④ $50   ⑤ $60

M Good morning, ma'am.
W Good morning. _____ _____ are the strawberries?
M They are 6 dollars _____ _____. But the strawberries are on sale this week. They are 25 dollars for 5 kilograms.
W That is good. I would like 10 kilograms of strawberries.
M Here you are. Do you need _____ _____?
W No, it's okay.

03 대화를 듣고, 여자가 남자에게 전화한 목적으로 가장 적절한 것을 고르시오.

① 구급차를 부르려고
② 진료를 예약하려고
④ 응급 환자를 치료하려고
③ 심폐소생술을 배우려고
⑤ 화상 치료 방법을 물어보려고

[Telephone rings.]
M Rose Clinic, how may I help you?
W I'm calling because I just _____ _____ from boiling water.
M So would you like to come to the clinic?
W No, I don't think it is that serious.
M Then, what do you need?
W I just want to know how to _____ _____ _____.
M Okay. _____ _____ the burned area with cool running water until the pain goes away.
W Thanks a lot.

>> **WORDS** circle 원   clinic 병원   boil 끓다   go away 없어지다

04 대화를 듣고, 두 사람이 만나기로 한 날짜를 고르시오.

① September 10th
② September 11th
③ September 12th
④ September 14th
⑤ September 17th

M Jiwon, can we finish writing the script for the English presentation tomorrow after school?

W I'm sorry I can't. I have to go to the piano lesson.

M It's September 10th already and we have _____ _____ _____ from now, you know.

W Why don't we _____ _____ on Friday?

M You mean the 14th? It's only three days before the presentation and I don't think it's a good idea.

W How about the 12th then? School _____ _____ that day.

M Okay. I have an appointment with the dentist, but I think I can reschedule it.

05 대화를 듣고, 두 사람이 대화하는 장소로 가장 적절한 곳을 고르시오.

① art gallery
② bank
③ bookstore
④ photo studio
⑤ computer repair shop

W Hello, can I have _____ _____ _____ today?

M Yes, we can. Did you bring the memory card?

W Here it is. How long does it take?

M Let me see _____ _____. Oh, it's more than 100 photos!

W I took many photos during the holidays.

M It will take _____ _____ _____.

W I see. I'll stop by a bank and come back after two hours.

06 다음 그림의 상황에 가장 적절한 대화를 고르시오.

① W Can I borrow your umbrella?
  M Yeah, I have _____ _____ in my car.
② W It's raining _____ _____ _____.
  M You had better wear a raincoat and boots.
③ W Wasn't it supposed to rain all day long today?
  M I thought so too.
④ W Did you buy a new raincoat?
  M Yes, I bought it yesterday.
⑤ W I didn't know that it was going to rain.
  M Maybe you can _____ _____ _____.

① ② ③ ④ ⑤

>> **WORDS** **presentation** 발표, 프레젠테이션 **appointment** 약속 **holiday** 휴가 **stop by** …에 들르다

07 대화를 듣고, 남자가 여자에게 부탁한 일로 가장 적절한 것을 고르시오.

① 불 켜기　② 창문 열기
③ 선풍기 켜기　④ 선풍기 청소하기
⑤ 나사돌리개 가져오기

M It's gotten really hot recently. Can we turn on the fan?
W We have to clean it first unless you want _____ _____ _____ everywhere.
M Okay. I'll _____ _____ _____.
W It's so nice of you. Do you need a screwdriver?
M No, I don't. Just _____ _____ _____ _____ for me, please? It's getting dark.
W Okay. Do you need anything else?
M Not really. Thanks.

08 다음을 듣고, 생존 수영에 관해 언급되지 않은 것을 고르시오.

① 정의　② 목표　③ 자세
④ 준비물　⑤ 유의 사항

M Let me tell you about survival swimming. It is a _____ _____ you can apply when you fall into water by accident. The _____ _____ of survival swimming is to float on the surface of the water until you _____ _____. To swim for survival, float on the water as if you're lying down on your bed. Remember, you should _____ _____ _____ so that it doesn't sink and try not to move a lot to save your energy.

09 다음을 듣고, 무엇에 관한 설명인지 고르시오.

① 반지　② 장갑
③ 팔찌　④ 손목시계
⑤ 네일아트

W This is something you wear _____ _____ _____. Some people wear this to make their hands more beautiful or to look nice, and other people exchange this when they get married or engaged. Still others wear this to show that they _____ _____ a certain group. It can be designed in all kinds of shapes and its size may vary depending _____ _____ _____ of your finger.

10 다음을 듣고, 두 사람의 대화가 어색한 것을 고르시오.

①　②　③　④　⑤

① W Have you seen the movie, *Parasite*?
　M Yes, it was really great.
② W Can I get some water?
　M Of course. You can use the cup _____ _____ _____.
③ W How do you _____ your last name, sir?
　M It's D-A-R-S-Y.
④ W How much are these carrots?
　M They are 1,000 won _____.
⑤ W Did you finish _____ _____ _____?
　M Yeah. I'm going to write about the global warming.

>> **WORDS**　fan 선풍기　screwdriver 나사돌리개　survival 생존　apply 적용하다　fall into …에 빠지다　by accident 우연히　float 뜨다
sink 가라앉다

11 대화를 듣고, 남자가 대화 직후에 할 일로 가장 적절한 것을 고르시오.

① 식물에 물 주기
② 학교로 출발하기
③ 학교에 갈 준비하기
④ 잠자리에서 일어나기
⑤ 아버지께 전화 드리기

[Telephone rings.]
W Hi, Mark. Did you get up already?
M Sure, I'm _____ _____ go to school now. How was your trip to France, Mom?
W It was such a beautiful place. By the way, have you been watering the plants _____ _____ _____?
M Oops, I totally _____ _____ it.
W I knew it. Make sure you water them before you leave for school.
M Yes, Mom.

12 다음 표를 보면서 대화를 듣고, 두 사람이 구입할 쌀을 고르시오.

	Weight (kg)	Price (won)	Place of Origin
①	10	30,000	Korea
②	10	25,000	China
③	5	18,000	Korea
④	5	16,000	China
⑤	20	57,000	Korea

W Oh, no. There's no more rice at home. Let's order it online.
M Okay. I think we'd better buy a large sack since we _____ _____ a lot. There's a 10-kilogram sack and it's 30,000 won.
W We don't need that much. A 5-kilogram sack _____ _____ _____.
M Okay. Rice from China is _____ than domestic rice.
W I do prefer _____ _____.
M Good. Then, let's buy this one.

13 다음을 듣고, 무엇에 관한 내용인지 고르시오.

① 분리수거 방법
② 분리수거의 중요성
③ 업사이클링의 필요성
④ 업사이클링에 드는 비용
⑤ 일회용품 이용의 위험성

W You just drank a bottle of coke. What do you do with the _____ _____? Well, you can recycle it, but not a lot of used materials can actually _____ _____. Besides, recycling can sometimes be _____ _____. So some innovators have come up with reusing those old materials in a _____ _____. This is what upcycling is.

14 대화를 듣고, 여자가 할 일로 가장 적절한 것을 고르시오.

① 자기 전에 가벼운 운동하기
② 자기 전에 따뜻한 우유 마시기
③ 잠이 올 때까지 인터넷 검색하기
④ 좀 더 이른 시각에 잠자리에 들기
⑤ 자기 전에 전자 기기 이용하지 않기

M You look tired. What's wrong?
W I can't _____ _____ at night.
M What time do you usually go to bed?
W I go to bed at around 10 but it's _____ _____ 12 that I actually fall asleep.
M So do you just lie on your bed with _____ _____ _____ for two hours?
W No, I surf on the Internet until I get drowsy.
M I think that's the problem. You should _____ _____ electronic devices one hour before you sleep.
W Okay, I'll try that.

15 다음을 듣고, 방송의 목적으로 가장 적절한 것을 고르시오.

① 비둘기의 생태를 소개하려고
② 공원 폐장 시간을 안내하려고
③ 비둘기에 의한 전염병 예방법을 알리려고
④ 비둘기에게 줄 수 있는 먹이를 판매하려고
⑤ 비둘기에게 먹이를 주지 말라고 당부하려고

W Good afternoon. I have an announcement for visitors of our park. Please _____ _____ the pigeons. The number of pigeons has _____ _____ because of the food that have been continually given by visitors. This causes _____ _____ _____ _____ to the other visitors. So please don't give food to the pigeons. We hope you enjoy your visit.

16 대화를 듣고, 남자가 지난 주말에 한 일로 가장 적절한 것을 고르시오.

① 삼촌과 여행 가기
② 제초제 구매하기
③ 농장의 잡초 뽑기
④ 아버지의 농사일 돕기
⑤ 조부모님 댁 방문하기

W Paul, how can you sleep at school all day?
M Well, I _____ _____ from working all weekend long.
W You said that you were going to visit your uncle during the weekend, right?
M Yeah. My uncle runs a farm so my Dad and I went to _____ _____ pull out all the weeds.
W Couldn't he just use some chemicals to _____ _____ _____?
M It's an organic farm and he never uses weed killers.
W So you went there as a human weed killer.
M That's right. I was so tired that I couldn't help but get sleepy in class.

17 대화를 듣고, 여자의 마지막 말에 대한 남자의 응답으로 가장 적절한 것을 고르시오.

① I haven't made the tea myself yet.
② You should first go to the hospital.
③ They are very good for your health.
④ Just mix them and then add warm water.
⑤ Do you need cinnamon powder?

W Could you turn off the air conditioner? I _____ _____.
M Are you sure? The current room temperature is 26 degrees Celsius.
W Oh, yeah? I didn't know that.
M Are you feeling okay? Maybe you _____ _____ _____.
W I guess you're right. I've also had a sore throat since this morning.
M Try some honey cinnamon tea before you go to bed tonight. It helps improve your _____ _____.
W I don't know how to make it.
M Do you have _____ _____ and some honey at home?
W Yes, I do. What do I do with them?

>> WORDS announcement 알림, 공고, 발표 **cause** 야기하다 **pull out** 뽑다 **weed** 잡초 **organic** 유기농의 **weed killer** 제초제
temperature 온도, 기온 **cinnamon** 계피

18 대화를 듣고, 남자의 마지막 말에 대한 여자의 응답으로 가장 적절한 것을 고르시오.

① Did you have lunch already?
② Where are you going?
③ I hope it won't rain tomorrow.
④ I want to have burgers and fries for lunch.
⑤ Sure. Meet me at the library after lunch.

M   I hope there's an earthquake or blizzard this week.
W   What do you mean?
M   I was hoping our final exams would _____ _____ if there was a disaster.
W   Haha! I never thought of it that way.
M   Forget it. I'm just being silly. So are you _____ _____ for the exams?
W   Well, I've been studying harder for it than for the midterms but I'm not sure if I'm doing it right.
M   Me too. Do you want to go to the library and _____ _____?

19 대화를 듣고, 여자의 마지막 말에 대한 남자의 응답으로 가장 적절한 것을 고르시오.

① There is no more vacant room.
② Tell me how to improve my writing.
③ It isn't a good idea to write it again.
④ You can't improve your grades.
⑤ Well, I think the first part needs more detail.

W   Fred, did you go over _____ _____ _____?
M   Yes, I did.
W   Please give me _____ _____.
M   Overall, I think you wrote it very well.
W   Could you be more specific?
M   It's informative and well-organized with good examples.
W   Is there any room _____ _____?

20 다음 상황 설명을 듣고, Rebecca가 Isaac에게 할 말로 가장 적절한 것을 고르시오.

① Have you seen my wallet?
② I just found my wallet.
③ Thank you for your help.
④ What are you doing with my wallet?
⑤ I wasn't suspecting you. I was just asking for your help.

M   Rebecca has _____ _____ _____ earlier today. She remembers that Isaac was with her _____ _____ _____ she took money from her wallet. So Rebecca asks if Isaac has seen her wallet. However, Isaac _____ _____ because he thinks that Rebecca is suspecting him of stealing the wallet. She wants to _____ _____ the misunderstanding. In this situation, what would Rebecca most likely say to Isaac?

>> **WORDS**   blizzard 눈보라   go over …을 검토하다   specific 구체적인   informative 유익한   well-organized 정리가 잘 된   suspect 의심하다   misunderstanding 오해

02회 » 듣기 실전 모의고사

01 대화를 듣고, 두 사람이 구입할 시계를 고르시오.

①   ②   ③

④   ⑤

02 대화를 듣고, 남자가 하고 있는 아르바이트에 관해 언급되지 <u>않은</u> 것을 고르시오.

① 가게 이름 ② 가게 위치 ③ 급여
④ 업무 ⑤ 근무 요일

03 대화를 듣고, 남자가 여자에게 전화한 목적으로 가장 적절한 것을 고르시오.

① 홈페이지 주소를 물어보려고
② 집 주소 변경을 알리려고
③ 프로그램 내용에 대해 항의하려고
④ 라디오 프로그램 주파수를 물어보려고
⑤ 사연과 신청곡 보내는 방법을 물어보려고

04 대화를 듣고, 현재 시각으로 가장 적절한 것을 고르시오.

① 4:35 p.m. ② 4:45 p.m. ③ 4:55 p.m.
④ 5 p.m. ⑤ 5:10 p.m.

05 대화를 듣고, 두 사람이 대화하는 장소로 가장 적절한 곳을 고르시오.

① 빨래방 ② 옷 가게 ③ 헬스장
④ 세탁소 ⑤ 원단 가게

06 다음 그림의 상황에 가장 적절한 대화를 고르시오.

① ② ③ ④ ⑤

07 대화를 듣고, 여자가 남자에게 부탁한 일로 가장 적절한 것을 고르시오.

① 족발 주문하기 ② 소고깃국 데우기
③ 밥솥에 밥 안치기 ④ 저녁 메뉴 결정하기
⑤ 족발 만드는 법 검색하기

08 다음을 듣고, 무엇에 관한 내용인지 고르시오.

① 커피의 유래 ② 커피 맛의 차이
③ 커피 제조 방법 ④ 커피 용어의 의미
⑤ 커피콩 제배 지역

09 다음을 듣고, 무엇에 관한 설명인지 고르시오.

① 우표 ② 현금 ③ 동전
④ 기념주화 ⑤ 신용카드

10 다음을 듣고, 두 사람의 대화가 <u>어색한</u> 것을 고르시오.

① ② ③ ④ ⑤

11 대화를 듣고, 여자가 할 일로 가장 적절한 것을 고르시오.

① 식초 사러 가기
② 다큐멘터리 보기
③ 식초로 머리 헹구기
④ 식초의 효능 검색하기
⑤ 환경 보호 캠페인 참여하기

12 다음 표를 보면서 대화를 듣고, 두 사람이 구입할 식물을 고르시오.

	Plant	Price	Feature
①	Rose geranium	₩15,000	Keeps away mosquitos
②	Coral wood	₩20,000	Purifies air
③	Banyan tree	₩30,000	Purifies air
④	Areca palm	₩50,000	Purifies air
⑤	Apple mint	₩10,000	Has a sweet smell

13 대화를 듣고, 생일 파티를 하기로 한 날짜를 고르시오.

① June 13th   ② June 14th
③ June 15th   ④ June 17th
⑤ June 18th

14 대화를 듣고, 남자가 어제 한 일로 가장 적절한 것을 고르시오.

① 콘서트 관람하기   ② 친구들과 축구하기
③ 축구 경기 관람하기   ④ 병원에서 진료 받기
⑤ 해변에서 일광욕하기

15 다음을 듣고, 방송의 목적으로 가장 적절한 것을 고르시오.

① 관람 규칙을 설명하려고
② 미아의 보호자를 찾으려고
③ 아동복 할인을 광고하려고
④ 감기 예방법을 설명하려고
⑤ 실종 아동 찾기 캠페인을 홍보하려고

16 대화를 듣고, 두 사람이 하이킹을 가기로 한 날짜를 고르시오.

① April 7th   ② April 10th
③ April 17th   ④ April 24th
⑤ April 30th

17 대화를 듣고, 남자의 마지막 말에 대한 여자의 응답으로 가장 적절한 것을 고르시오.

Woman: _____

① I'm sorry I'm late.
② Well, it was due on Wednesday.
③ I think they'll change their minds.
④ Of course. You have nothing to lose.
⑤ You're lucky that you weren't seriously hurt.

18 대화를 듣고, 여자의 마지막 말에 대한 남자의 응답으로 가장 적절한 것을 고르시오.

Man: _____

① I'm sorry to hear that.
② I love reading as much as you do.
③ You could have read books to her.
④ I love my grandmother so much.
⑤ Why don't you spend some time with your grandparents?

19 대화를 듣고, 남자의 마지막 말에 대한 여자의 응답으로 가장 적절한 것을 고르시오.

Woman: _____

① Where is the nearest hospital?
② Yes, let me take you to the hospital.
③ No. I study Chinese day and night.
④ No. I didn't eat those fries.
⑤ Yes, I did. I wouldn't be able to come to school the next day if I didn't.

20 다음 상황 설명을 듣고, Tim이 Esther에게 할 말로 가장 적절한 것을 고르시오.

Tim: _____

① It's not your fault.
② What is your personal color?
③ You just found your personal color.
④ The problem is the design, not the color.
⑤ Why don't you try a different color? I think blue will look better on you.

01 대화를 듣고, 두 사람이 구입할 시계를 고르시오.

① ② ③ ④ ⑤

W Now let's choose a clock for our bedroom.

M Since the interior of our bedroom is _____ _____, let's pick a clock that isn't round.

W I agree. How about a clock with a _____ _____?

M Well, it definitely looks better than the round one.

W Yeah. It's decorated _____ _____ _____. Do you like this design better?

M I don't know. What do you think?

W I prefer a clock without _____ _____.

M Okay, let's buy that one then.

02 대화를 듣고, 남자가 하고 있는 아르바이트에 관해 언급되지 <u>않은</u> 것을 고르시오.

① 가게 이름 ② 가게 위치
③ 급여 ④ 업무
⑤ 근무 요일

W How have you been doing these days, Jacob?

M I've started a part-time job at a coffee shop and I've been quite busy lately.

W Which coffee shop do you work at?

M I work at Roast Coffee. It's _____ _____ our apartment complex.

W Oh yeah. I've been there once and it was really nice. What do you do there?

M I mostly _____ _____ from the customers and clean up the desks after the customers leave.

W I see. Do you _____ _____ _____?

M No, I just work on Wednesdays and Fridays.

W I see.

03 대화를 듣고, 남자가 여자에게 전화한 목적으로 가장 적절한 것을 고르시오.

① 홈페이지 주소를 물어보려고
② 집 주소 변경을 알리려고
③ 프로그램 내용에 대해 항의하려고
④ 라디오 프로그램 주파수를 물어보려고
⑤ 사연과 신청곡 보내는 방법을 물어보려고

[Telephone rings.]

W ABC Radio Station. How can I help you?

M Hello, I'm a listener of ABC Radio and I _____ _____ _____.

W Okay, please go on.

M I want to send my story and song request to the radio program, *With You* and I don't know _____ _____ _____ _____.

W You can either _____ _____ to the webpage of the program or download ABC Radio application.

M I see. Thank you for your help.

W You're welcome.

>> **WORDS** **definitely** 확실히 **decorate** 장식하다 **customer** 손님

Answer p. 24

04 대화를 듣고, 현재 시각으로 가장 적절한 것을 고르시오.

① 4:35 p.m.　② 4:45 p.m.
③ 4:55 p.m.　④ 5 p.m.
⑤ 5:10 p.m.

W　Oh, my God. I'm late for my swimming class.

M　When does class start?

W　Class starts at 5 p.m. I _____ _____ _____ at 4:45 at the latest.

M　You can go now, then.

W　But the clock says it's already 4:55.

M　Oh, I've adjusted the clock 10 minutes _____ _____ the actual time.

W　Why would anybody do that?

M　I do it so that I won't be late. Since it's 4:45 _____, you won't be late for your class if you get going now.

05 대화를 듣고, 두 사람이 대화하는 장소로 가장 적절한 곳을 고르시오.

① 빨래방　② 옷 가게　③ 헬스장
④ 세탁소　⑤ 원단 가게

M　Hello, how may I help you?

W　I've lost some weight recently and so I want to _____ _____ _____ of this skirt.

M　Okay. How much would you like to reduce the size?

W　I'm not so sure. Could you please _____ my waist?

M　Sure. Let me see.... I guess a half an inch would be enough.

W　Okay. I also want these coats to _____ _____.

M　All right. They will be ready by Thursday.

W　Great.

06 다음 그림의 상황에 가장 적절한 대화를 고르시오.

① ② ③ ④ ⑤

① M　Stay away from there.
　 W　All right. The oven looks very hot.
② M　This vending machine ate my coins again.
　 W　Really? It must be _____ _____ _____.
③ M　How about drinking _____ _____?
　 W　Good idea. I'd love to have warm milk.
④ M　It's so cold and windy today.
　 W　Yeah. We'd better not go out today.
⑤ M　It's really nice to _____ _____.
　 W　Yes. This is the perfect place in this hot weather.

>> **WORDS**　**adjust** 조절하다　**reduce** 줄이다　**vending machine** 자판기

07 대화를 듣고, 여자가 남자에게 부탁한 일로 가장 적절한 것을 고르시오.

① 족발 주문하기
② 소고깃국 데우기
③ 밥솥에 밥 안치기
④ 저녁 메뉴 결정하기
⑤ 족발 만드는 법 검색하기

W What do you want to have for dinner, Jason?
M What do we have in the fridge, Mom?
W We've got some beef stew and some side dishes.
M Can we please _____ _____ today?
W No way. I've already prepared the rice for cooking.
M But I'm _____ _____ eating the beef stew for three days in a row.
W I've got an idea. Why don't you _____ some *jokbal*? We can have it with cooked rice.
M Yay, I'll order it right away.

08 다음을 듣고, 무엇에 관한 내용인지 고르시오.

① 커피의 유래　② 커피 맛의 차이
③ 커피 제조 방법　④ 커피 용어의 의미
⑤ 커피콩 재배 지역

W Let me explain some coffee-related _____ _____ _____. The first term is *café latte*. In French, *café* means coffee, and *latte* _____ _____. So *café latte* means coffee with milk. The second term is caramel *macchiato*. *Macchiato* is an Italian word which means "_____ or marked." So caramel *macchiato* refers to coffee stained with caramel syrup.

09 다음을 듣고, 무엇에 관한 설명인지 고르시오.

① 우표　② 현금　③ 동전
④ 기념주화　⑤ 신용카드

M It is something you need when you _____ _____. It has two main kinds: coins and paper. Every country has its own design. These days, credit cards and other _____ _____ _____ have been replacing it. As a result, people don't bring it in their wallets as often as they _____ _____.

10 다음을 듣고, 두 사람의 대화가 <u>어색한</u> 것을 고르시오.

①　②　③　④　⑤

① W I feel so small these days.
　 M I sometimes feel that way too. Cheer up.
② W I'm afraid I won't be able to do well on final exams.
　 M You've been studying really hard. I'm sure you'll do great.
③ W I think I look ugly.
　 M Come on. You have the _____ _____ _____ in the world.
④ W Nobody cares for me. In fact, everybody hates me.
　 M I _____ _____ people like her.
⑤ W I _____ _____ when people ask me about my dream.
　 M Don't worry. You've got plenty of time to think about it.

>> **WORDS**　**in a row** 계속해서, 연이어　**term** 용어　**stain** 얼룩지게 하다　**feel small** 초라한 기분이 들다　**care for** …을 좋아하다

11 대화를 듣고, 여자가 할 일로 가장 적절한 것을 고르시오.

① 식초 사러 가기
② 다큐멘터리 보기
③ 식초로 머리 헹구기
④ 식초의 효능 검색하기
⑤ 환경 보호 캠페인 참여하기

M I saw a documentary about water pollution yesterday and I made ＿＿＿＿ ＿＿＿＿ ＿＿＿＿.
W Oh, yeah? What is it?
M I decided not to use hair conditioner from now on.
W Won't your hair be too stiff if you don't use it?
M The documentary suggested that we use vinegar ＿＿＿＿.
W Vinegar? I wouldn't want to use vinegar for my hair.
M Not only is it good for the environment, it is good for your health too. It's really effective at ＿＿＿＿ ＿＿＿＿ ＿＿＿＿ of shampoo.
W Hmm, let me watch the documentary before I decide ＿＿＿＿ ＿＿＿＿ ＿＿＿＿ it or not.

12 다음 표를 보면서 대화를 듣고, 두 사람이 구입할 식물을 고르시오.

	Plant	Price	Feature
①	Rose geranium	₩15,000	Keeps away mosquitos
②	Coral wood	₩20,000	Purifies air
③	Banyan tree	₩30,000	Purifies air
④	Areca palm	₩50,000	Purifies air
⑤	Apple mint	₩10,000	Has a sweet smell

M Honey, this is the list of the plants I selected. I think you can choose one for our living room from the list.
W Awesome. Oh, does the Rose geranium keep away mosquitos?
M Yes, it has a smell that ＿＿＿＿ ＿＿＿＿.
W That's interesting but I prefer the ones that purify the air.
M That leaves us three options.
W The Areca palm seems gorgeous but I'm not willing to ＿＿＿＿ ＿＿＿＿ ＿＿＿＿ 30,000 won on plants.
M How about the Coral wood then? It has shiny red fruits which ＿＿＿＿ ＿＿＿＿ coral.
W That's nice. Let's buy it.

13 대화를 듣고, 생일 파티를 하기로 한 날짜를 고르시오.

① June 13th ② June 14th
③ June 15th ④ June 17th
⑤ June 18th

M Judy, what's the date today?
W It's June 13th.
M Isn't your birthday ＿＿＿＿ ＿＿＿＿ ＿＿＿＿?
W Right. My birthday is June 18th. Why?
M I want to throw a party for you on that day.
W Thank you. But it's a Wednesday. I think ＿＿＿＿ ＿＿＿＿ ＿＿＿＿ my birthday will be better for having a party.
M Right. Then how about June 14th?
W It's Saturday, right? I'm ＿＿＿＿ ＿＿＿＿ with my family on that day.
M I see. Then let's have the party on the next day, the 15th.
W Okay. How sweet you are!

>> **WORDS** **vinegar** 식초 **effective** 효과적인 **awesome** 기막히게 좋은, 굉장한 **purify** 정화하다 **gorgeous** 아주 멋진
throw a party 파티를 열다

Dictation Test >> 02회

14 대화를 듣고, 남자가 어제 한 일로 가장 적절한 것을 고르시오.

① 콘서트 관람하기
② 친구들과 축구하기
③ 축구 경기 관람하기
④ 병원에서 진료 받기
⑤ 해변에서 일광욕하기

W Hi, David.
M Hey, Becky. What happened to your voice? Did you catch a cold?
W No, I went to the K-pop concert yesterday. I _____ _____ throughout the concert. It was a fantastic night.
M I can imagine.
W How was your weekend?
M I _____ _____ with my friends all day yesterday.
W So that's why you _____ _____. I thought you've been to the beach or something.
M You don't have to go to the beach to get a sun burn.

15 다음을 듣고, 방송의 목적으로 가장 적절한 것을 고르시오.

① 관람 규칙을 설명하려고
② 미아의 보호자를 찾으려고
③ 아동복 할인을 광고하려고
④ 감기 예방법을 설명하려고
⑤ 실종 아동 찾기 캠페인을 홍보하려고

W Hello, here's a quick announcement from the management booth. We _____ _____ a 4-year-old boy. He _____ _____ a black jumper, blue jeans and white sneakers. He was found crying alone near the water fountain. If you are his parent or guardian, please come to the management booth and _____ _____. Thank you.

16 대화를 듣고, 두 사람이 하이킹을 가기로 한 날짜를 고르시오.

① April 7th   ② April 10th
③ April 17th   ④ April 24th
⑤ April 30th

M Jane, let's go hiking this Saturday.
W This Saturday is April 10th, right?
M Right. Are you _____ on that day?
W Well, I'll have to _____ _____ _____ in the country. That day is my grandfather's birthday.
M Then how about making it _____ _____ _____?
W You mean on the 17th?   M Yes.
W I don't have any plans on that day. Let's go hiking on that day.

17 대화를 듣고, 남자의 마지막 말에 대한 여자의 응답으로 가장 적절한 것을 고르시오.

① I'm sorry I'm late.
② Well, it was due on Wednesday.
③ I think they'll change their minds.
④ Of course. You have nothing to lose.
⑤ You're lucky that you weren't seriously hurt.

M Oh, no.
W What's the matter?
M The application for the musical audition _____ _____ on Monday. I totally forgot to submit it and it's already Wednesday.
W Oh... why don't you call the office and ask if you can _____ _____ _____ late?
M I don't think they will _____ _____ _____ it late.
W If I were you, I would try it. You know, trying wouldn't hurt.
M Do you really think so?

>> **WORDS** guardian 보호자 application 지원(서) submit 제출하다

18 대화를 듣고, 여자의 마지막 말에 대한 남자의 응답으로 가장 적절한 것을 고르시오.

① I'm sorry to hear that.
② I love reading as much as you do.
③ You could have read books to her.
④ I love my grandmother so much.
⑤ Why don't you spend some time with your grandparents?

W Mark, why are you always _____ _____?
M Well, I love reading books. I think it is because of my Grandma.
W What did she do to you? Did she force you to read books?
M Not at all. She _____ _____ _____ books to me before I went to bed when I was little.
W I see.
M They are my favorite memories when I was little.
W I wish I had such great memories with my own Grandma too. However, both of my grandmothers _____ _____ before I was born.

19 대화를 듣고, 남자의 마지막 말에 대한 여자의 응답으로 가장 적절한 것을 고르시오.

① Where is the nearest hospital?
② Yes, let me take you to the hospital.
③ No. I study Chinese day and night.
④ No. I didn't eat those fries.
⑤ Yes, I did. I wouldn't be able to come to school the next day if I didn't.

W Paul, can I borrow your notes for the Chinese class?
M Here you go. But why do you need it?
W I _____ _____ yesterday, and I didn't want to miss anything important.
M Oh, right. I was about to ask you why you didn't come to class.
W You know how I'm _____ _____ shrimps, right?
M Yeah, of course.
W I didn't know that the fries we ate for lunch yesterday were _____ _____ shrimp. So I just ate them.
M Oh, no. Did you have to go to the hospital?

20 다음 상황 설명을 듣고, Tim이 Esther 에게 할 말로 가장 적절한 것을 고르시오.

① It's not your fault.
② What is your personal color?
③ You just found your personal color.
④ The problem is the design, not the color.
⑤ Why don't you try a different color? I think blue will look better on you.

M Esther and Tim just _____ _____ _____ about personal color on their English textbook. The article said that everyone has a personal color that _____ _____ _____. Esther asked Tim if the color of her shirt suited her but Tim _____ _____ the color was her personal color. In this situation, what would Tim most likely say to Esther?

>> WORDS **force** 강요하다 **miss** 놓치다 **personal** 개인의 **suit** 어울리다 **fault** 잘못

01 대화를 듣고, 여자가 원하는 담요를 고르시오.

02 대화를 듣고, 여자가 지난 주말에 한 일로 가장 적절한 것을 고르시오.

① 병문안 가기　　② 수학 숙제 끝내기
③ 숙제 도와주기　　④ 진료 받기
⑤ 아파서 누워 있기

03 대화를 듣고, 여자가 남자에게 전화한 목적으로 가장 적절한 것을 고르시오.

① 진료 예약을 하려고
② 점심시간을 물어보려고
③ 약의 성분을 물어보려고
④ 진료 예약 일자를 변경하려고
⑤ 학교 제출용 서류를 발급받으려고

04 대화를 듣고, Grandma Moses가 화가로서 활동하기 시작한 나이를 고르시오.

① 26세　　② 50세　　③ 76세
④ 92세　　⑤ 102세

05 대화를 듣고, 두 사람이 대화하는 장소로 가장 적절한 곳을 고르시오.

① 놀이동산　　② 패스트푸드점
③ 자동차 수리점　　④ 자동차 전시장
⑤ 롤러스케이트장

06 다음 그림의 상황에 가장 적절한 대화를 고르시오.

①　　②　　③　　④　　⑤

07 대화를 듣고, 남자가 여자에게 부탁한 일로 가장 적절한 것을 고르시오.

① 운동화 빨기
② 연고 가져다주기
③ 베이킹 소다 사 오기
④ 베이킹 소다 가져다주기
⑤ 세탁소에 운동화 맡기기

08 다음을 듣고, 무엇에 관한 내용인지 고르시오.

① 불고기 양념 만드는 방법
② 불고기에 쓰이는 고기의 부위
③ 고기를 타지 않게 굽는 방법
④ 불고기와 곁들여 먹으면 좋은 음식
⑤ 훈제한 맛이 나는 불고기 만드는 방법

09 다음을 듣고, 무엇에 관한 설명인지 고르시오.

① 치실　　② 칫솔　　③ 미백 치약
④ 구강 청정제　　⑤ 치아 교정기

10 다음을 듣고, 두 사람의 대화가 <u>어색한</u> 것을 고르시오.

①　　②　　③　　④　　⑤

11 대화를 듣고, 여자가 할 일로 가장 적절한 것을 고르시오.

① 마사지 받기
② 병원에서 진찰 받기
③ 사진 관찰하기
④ 통증을 줄이는 운동하기
⑤ 바른 자세를 위해 노력하기

12 다음 표를 보면서 대화를 듣고, 두 사람이 함께 수강할 수업을 고르시오.

	Class	Period	Time
①	Korean	1	08:00-09:30
②	English		
③	Korean	2	09:40-11:10
④	Math	3	11:20-12:50
⑤	English		

13 대화를 듣고, 남자가 대화 직후에 할 일로 가장 적절한 것을 고르시오.

① 영화 감상하기
② 영어 교재 구입하기
③ 영어 학원에 등록하기
④ 드라마 대사를 따라 말하기
⑤ 미국 텔레비전 쇼 다운받기

14 대화를 듣고, 남자가 지불할 금액을 고르시오.

① $5   ② $6   ③ $10
④ $12   ⑤ $13

15 다음을 듣고, 방송의 목적으로 가장 적절한 것을 고르시오.

① 캠페인 참여를 독려하려고
② 환경 보호 운동을 알리려고
③ 기금 마련 콘서트를 홍보하려고
④ 기아가 발생하는 원인을 설명하려고
⑤ 음식물 쓰레기 줄이는 방법을 안내하려고

16 다음을 듣고, Friday Evening Movie Club에 관해 언급되지 <u>않은</u> 것을 고르시오.

① 역사   ② 모임 횟수   ③ 활동 내용
④ 참가비   ⑤ 가입 혜택

17 대화를 듣고, 여자의 마지막 말에 대한 남자의 응답으로 가장 적절한 것을 고르시오.

Man: _____

① I've already had enough. I'm so full.
② Of course. Pepper is my favorite spice.
③ I need to drop by my office after lunch.
④ Sure. You can change it.
⑤ Oh, can I have a cup of lemon tea instead of coffee?

18 대화를 듣고, 남자의 마지막 말에 대한 여자의 응답으로 가장 적절한 것을 고르시오.

Woman: _____

① I wonder if you would like it.
② It will stop raining sooner or later.
③ What is the title of the song?
④ No. My favorite musician is Chopin.
⑤ Be my guest. I can replay it for you over and over.

19 대화를 듣고, 여자의 마지막 말에 대한 남자의 응답으로 가장 적절한 것을 고르시오.

Man: _____

① No, I just got a haircut.
② Do you like boys with short hair too?
③ I didn't know that she liked short hair.
④ You look better than before.
⑤ Yeah, this is the first time I got my hair permed.

20 다음 상황 설명을 듣고, Paul이 Ruth에게 할 말로 가장 적절한 것을 고르시오.

Paul: _____

① There is no reason for delay.
② I'm worried about your health.
③ Shall we stop and take a look?
④ You can be more effective when you don't have enough time.
⑤ I feel secure when I do things in advance.

01 대화를 듣고, 여자가 원하는 담요를 고르시오.

M Is there anything you want for Christmas?

W I would like to have _____ _____ _____.

M What kind of blanket do you want?

W I usually prefer something simple without any patterns but I'd like to have _____ _____ this time.

M Like what?

W I don't have anything specific in mind.

M I once saw Cindy using a blanket that had an image of a big rabbit on it. Everybody thought it was cute. How about that?

W That'll be nice but please buy me one that has _____ _____ on it if you can find one.

02 대화를 듣고, 여자가 지난 주말에 한 일로 가장 적절한 것을 고르시오.

① 병문안 가기 ② 수학 숙제 끝내기
③ 숙제 도와주기 ④ 진료 받기
⑤ 아파서 누워 있기

M Did you finish your math assignment?

W I've only solved two problems and I still have eight left.

M You had the whole weekend to finish it. Was there _____ _____?

W Well, I've been _____ _____ _____. So I've slept for almost 30 hours during the weekend.

M Wow. Are you feeling any better?

W Yeah, but I think I should go to the hospital after school.

M Yes, you should. By the way, do you want me to help you with the math assignment?

W I _____ _____ but I would like to do it myself.

03 대화를 듣고, 여자가 남자에게 전화한 목적으로 가장 적절한 것을 고르시오.

① 진료 예약을 하려고
② 점심시간을 물어보려고
③ 약의 성분을 물어보려고
④ 진료 예약 일자를 변경하려고
⑤ 학교 제출용 서류를 발급받으려고

[Telephone rings.]

M Grace Pediatrics. How may I be of assistance?

W Hello, I visited the hospital an hour ago and I just realized that I had forgotten to _____ _____ a doctor's note. I have to submit it to my school.

M Your name and birthday, please.

W It's Sophia Hong and I was born in November 17, 2005.

M Okay. We'll have the documents ready for you. When would you like to _____ _____ _____?

W I'll be right there in 30 minutes.

M It's lunch time soon and if you can't come in 10 minutes, I suggest that you _____ _____ 1 o'clock.

W I see.

》 WORDS **specific** 구체적인 **pediatrics** 소아과 **doctor's note** 진단서

04 대화를 듣고, Grandma Moses가 화가로서 활동하기 시작한 나이를 고르시오.

① 26세　② 50세　③ 76세
④ 92세　⑤ 102세

W What are you reading, David?
M I'm reading a book called "My Life's History" written by Grandma Moses.
W Who's Grandma Moses?
M She is one of the most _____ _____ in America.
W And why is she called Grandma Moses?
M She got her nickname from the fact that she _____ _____ _____ as a painter when she was 76.
W That's unbelievable.
M Indeed. Grandma Moses _____ _____ for 26 years until she died at the age of 102. She published this book when she was 92.

05 대화를 듣고, 두 사람이 대화하는 장소로 가장 적절한 곳을 고르시오.

① 놀이동산　② 패스트푸드점
③ 자동차 수리점　④ 자동차 전시장
⑤ 롤러스케이트장

W Which ride do you want to _____ _____ next?
M Why don't we try the roller coaster one more time?
W No way. It was scary. How about bumper cars?
M That'll be fun too. Where is it?
W Right over there. Oh, my. Look at the line.
M I'm sure we'll have to wait for _____ _____ two hours.
W Let's grab a bite before we get on the line.
M Or we can buy some burgers and fries and eat _____ _____ for our turn.
W Great idea.

06 다음 그림의 상황에 가장 적절한 대화를 고르시오.

①　②　③　④　⑤

① W Make sure you _____ your passport.
　M No worries. I already put it in my backpack.
② W I don't remember where I put my passport.
　M _____ _____ and try to search for it again.
③ W May I see your passport?
　M Can I show you another ID card instead?
④ W I forgot my password for the website.
　M Just tap the blue button and try to set a _____ _____.
⑤ W What do I need to bring to reissue my passport?
　M You need two pictures and your ID card.

>> **WORDS**　**unbelievable** 믿을 수 없는　**grab a bite** 간단히 먹다　**turn** 차례　**reissue** 재발급하다, 재발행하다

07 대화를 듣고, 남자가 여자에게 부탁한 일로 가장 적절한 것을 고르시오.

① 운동화 빨기
② 연고 가져다주기
③ 베이킹 소다 사 오기
④ 베이킹 소다 가져다주기
⑤ 세탁소에 운동화 맡기기

W Tim, what happened to your sneakers? There are stains _____ _____ _____.
M I accidentally spilt coffee on them in the morning.
W Oh, no. Were you burned?
M Fortunately, it was iced coffee.
W That's a relief.
M Yeah. Anyway, is there a way I can _____ _____ all of the stains?
W I _____ _____ baking soda when you brush sneakers.
M Can you give me some if you have it at home?
W Of course. I can give it to you tomorrow.

08 다음을 듣고, 무엇에 관한 내용인지 고르시오.

① 불고기 양념 만드는 방법
② 불고기에 쓰이는 고기의 부위
③ 고기를 타지 않게 굽는 방법
④ 불고기와 곁들여 먹으면 좋은 음식
⑤ 훈제한 맛이 나는 불고기 만드는 방법

W Here's how you can add a _____ _____ to your *bulgogi*. First, add oil to a hot pan and fry some scallions which are called "pa" in Korean. Then put the *bulgogi* into the pan and cook them until the meat _____ _____. Now, here's the most important part. Don't pour soy sauce _____ _____ the *bulgogi* but around it. This way, you'll have a tasty *bulgogi* dish that has a mouth-watering smoky flavor.

09 다음을 듣고, 무엇에 관한 설명인지 고르시오.

① 치실   ② 칫솔
③ 미백 치약   ④ 구강 청정제
⑤ 치아 교정기

M It is something that you can use before or after you _____ _____ _____. It is basically a piece of _____ that you can use to remove any remaining food between your teeth. You should be careful when using it because your gums _____ _____ if you push it in too hard. Dentists recommend using it two to three times a week.

10 다음을 듣고, 두 사람의 대화가 <u>어색한</u> 것을 고르시오.

①   ②   ③   ④   ⑤

① W Can you go get me some coffee?
  M Sure. What kind of coffee would you like?
② W Look, there must have been a traffic accident.
  M That's why there's a traffic jam. I hope _____ _____ _____.
③ W What time can you pick me up?
  M Sorry, I didn't mean to _____ _____.
④ W Where have you been during lunch time?
  M I talked with my _____ _____.
⑤ W Why don't we have chicken soup for dinner?
  M Sorry but we don't have the ingredients in the fridge.

>> WORDS **accidentally** 우연히, 뜻하지 않게 **scallion** 파 **soy sauce** 간장 **mouth-watering** 군침이 돌게 하는 **smoky** 훈제한 맛이 나는 **gum** 잇몸

11 대화를 듣고, 여자가 할 일로 가장 적절한 것을 고르시오.

① 마사지 받기
② 병원에서 진찰 받기
③ 사진 관찰하기
④ 통증을 줄이는 운동하기
⑤ 바른 자세를 위해 노력하기

W I've been suffering from severe _____ _____.
M Come here. Let me massage your neck a little bit.
W Thanks. Ouch, it really hurts.
M Why don't you do some neck exercises from time to time?
W Well, I do it all the time but the pain won't _____ _____.
M Then I think you need to fix your posture.
W Do you think so?
M Yeah. Let me take a picture of you _____ _____ and show you. Here, look.
W Wow, seriously, I look like a turtle. I guess I should try really hard to _____ _____ _____.

12 다음 표를 보면서 대화를 듣고, 두 사람이 함께 수강할 수업을 고르시오.

	Class	Period	Time
①	Korean	1	08:00-09:30
②	English		
③	Korean	2	09:40-11:10
④	Math	3	11:20-12:50
⑤	English		

W Brian, did you decide on which classes to take during the summer?
M Not yet. Shall we take the English class _____ _____ at 8 o'clock together?
W Hey, I can't wake up that early during vacation. Why not take the 11:20 English class with me?
M I want to take the math class in the _____ _____.
W How about this then? You take English and math on the first and the third period, and we take the _____ _____ _____ in the second period.
M That schedule looks exhausting to me. I want to enjoy my summer vacation.
W Come on, buddy.   M All right.

13 대화를 듣고, 남자가 대화 직후에 할 일로 가장 적절한 것을 고르시오.

① 영화 감상하기
② 영어 교재 구입하기
③ 영어 학원에 등록하기
④ 드라마 대사를 따라 말하기
⑤ 미국 텔레비전 쇼 다운받기

M Olivia, I think your English pronunciation is really good.
W Thanks. I've been practicing _____ _____ while watching American television shows.
M Do you repeat after the actors?
W Yeah. When there's a line I want to memorize, I pause and _____ _____ the line is said.
M How many times do you repeat each line?
W I go over again and again until I am satisfied.
M I want to _____ _____ _____. Can you recommend any television shows to me?
W Since you like thrillers, how about "Grimm?"
M Awesome. I'm going to download the show right now.

>> WORDS suffer 고통받다 posture 자세 pronunciation 발음 repeat 반복하다

14 대화를 듣고, 남자가 지불할 금액을 고르시오.

① $5   ② $6   ③ $10
④ $12   ⑤ $13

W May I help you?
M Yes. I want some cookies. How much is this pack?
W It's 6 dollars. But if you _____ _____, we'll sell them to you for 10 dollars.
M Sounds good. I'll take _____ _____ of them. And I need an orange juice.
W A _____ _____ is 3 dollars and a medium-sized one is 2 dollars.
M One medium-sized orange juice, please.
W Anything else?
M That's all.

15 다음을 듣고, 방송의 목적으로 가장 적절한 것을 고르시오.

① 캠페인 참여를 독려하려고
② 환경 보호 운동을 알리려고
③ 기금 마련 콘서트를 홍보하려고
④ 기아가 발생하는 원인을 설명하려고
⑤ 음식물 쓰레기 줄이는 방법을 안내하려고

W Isn't it sad to think that children are _____ _____ hunger in some parts of the world when people have been throwing so much food away? In response to this situation, the world-famous rock band, BYS, has been _____ _____ a fundraising concert. The tickets will be sold from Monday 7 p.m. and all profit will be used to _____ _____ _____.

16 다음을 듣고, Friday Evening Movie Club에 관해 언급되지 <u>않은</u> 것을 고르시오.

① 역사   ② 모임 횟수
③ 활동 내용   ④ 참가비
⑤ 가입 혜택

M Hello, students. Today, I'm going to introduce our Friday Evening Movie Club to you. We gather _____ _____ _____ at school and watch a movie. Then we discuss the movie while _____ _____ together. You have to pay 10 dollars for every meeting. But if you join us, you don't need to _____ _____ _____ for the first month.

17 대화를 듣고, 여자의 마지막 말에 대한 남자의 응답으로 가장 적절한 것을 고르시오.

① I've already had enough. I'm so full.
② Of course. Pepper is my favorite spice.
③ I need to drop by my office after lunch.
④ Sure. You can change it.
⑤ Oh, can I have a cup of lemon tea instead of coffee?

W Hi, Mr. Williams. What would you like to have for today?
M I'd like to have a hot americano and a ham cheese bagel.
W Great. Is it for here or _____ _____?
M I want to have it for here. By the way, could you not _____ _____ on the bagel?
W Really? It would probably taste better with it.
M Yeah, but I personally don't like the smell of pepper.
W No problem. Is there _____ _____ you need?

>> **WORDS** hunger 굶주림, 기아   in response to …에 응하여   fundraising 모금   profit 이익, 수익   discuss 논의하다

Answer p. 29

18 대화를 듣고, 남자의 마지막 말에 대한 여자의 응답으로 가장 적절한 것을 고르시오.

① I wonder if you would like it.
② It will stop raining sooner or later.
③ What is the title of the song?
④ No. My favorite musician is Chopin.
⑤ Be my guest. I can replay it for you over and over.

M What is the title of this piano piece on the computer?
W It's "Raindrop" by Chopin.
M Oh, yeah? I thought it was a _____ _____ for today's rainy weather.
W You can say that again. This part sounds _____ _____ _____.
M Indeed. Sometimes it's softer, and other times it's louder.
W Yeah, this part sounds just like pouring rain.
M It's so beautiful. Can we listen to the _____ _____ one more time?

19 대화를 듣고, 여자의 마지막 말에 대한 남자의 응답으로 가장 적절한 것을 고르시오.

① No, I just got a haircut.
② Do you like boys with short hair too?
③ I didn't know that she liked short hair.
④ You look better than before.
⑤ Yeah, this is the first time I got my hair permed.

W Chris, I like your new hair style.
M I'm glad you like it but there's a long story _____ _____.
W I'd like to hear about it.
M Well, I heard the girl I like talking to a friend. She said that she liked boys with short hair. So, I _____ _____ _____ and showed it to her.
W What happened then?
M It was a disaster. She _____ _____ my hair. She said that it made me look like a chestnut.
W Oh, no. So that's why you permed your hair.

20 다음 상황 설명을 듣고, Paul이 Ruth에게 할 말로 가장 적절한 것을 고르시오.

① There is no reason for delay.
② I'm worried about your health.
③ Shall we stop and take a look?
④ You can be more effective when you don't have enough time.
⑤ I feel secure when I do things in advance.

M Ruth is very upset because she has only _____ _____ _____ until her science report is due. Meanwhile, Paul, who hasn't even started doing it, seems very relaxed. Ruth asks why he doesn't seem to _____ _____ at all. Paul wants to explain that he sometimes _____ _____ the last moment on purpose and thinks it is not bad. In this situation, what would Paul most likely say to Ruth?

>> **WORDS** **piece** 한 편의 악곡, 작품 **chestnut** 밤 **perm** (머리를) 파마하다 **due** …하기로 되어 있는 **meanwhile** 한편

01 대화를 듣고, 여자가 구입할 넥타이를 고르시오.

① ② ③ ④ ⑤

02 대화를 듣고, 새 지하철에 관해 언급되지 <u>않은</u> 것을 고르시오.

① 학교까지 소요 시간　② 배차 간격
③ 일반 요금　④ 학생 할인 여부
⑤ 할인율

03 대화를 듣고, 남자가 여자에게 전화한 목적으로 가장 적절한 것을 고르시오.

① 일자리를 구하려고
② 예약을 확인하려고
③ 잃어버린 물건을 찾으려고
④ 재킷의 환불을 요청하려고
⑤ 제품의 가격을 문의하려고

04 대화를 듣고, 두 사람이 만날 시각을 고르시오.

① 7:00 p.m.　② 7:20 p.m.
③ 7:50 p.m.　④ 8:00 p.m.
⑤ 8:10 p.m.

05 대화를 듣고, 두 사람이 대화하는 장소로 가장 적절한 곳을 고르시오.

① club room　② photo studio
③ camera shop　④ movie theater
⑤ television studio

06 다음 그림의 상황에 가장 적절한 대화를 고르시오.

① ② ③ ④ ⑤

07 대화를 듣고, 여자가 남자에게 부탁한 일로 가장 적절한 것을 고르시오.

① 자명종 빌려주기　② 전화로 깨워 주기
③ 기차표 예매해 주기　④ 함께 아침 운동하기
⑤ 기차역까지 배웅해 주기

08 다음을 듣고, 여자가 환경 보호 방법으로 언급하지 <u>않은</u> 것을 고르시오.

① 양치할 때 컵 이용하기
② 자기 전에 컴퓨터 끄기
③ 중고 물건 구입하기
④ 분리수거 철저히 하기
⑤ 비닐봉지 덜 쓰기

09 다음을 듣고, 무엇에 관한 설명인지 고르시오.

① clock　② letter　③ present
④ calendar　⑤ newspaper

10 다음을 듣고, 두 사람의 대화가 <u>어색한</u> 것을 고르시오.

① ② ③ ④ ⑤

11 대화를 듣고, 남자가 지불할 금액을 고르시오.

① $50　② $80　③ $130
④ $160　⑤ $180

12 다음 표를 보면서 대화를 듣고, 두 사람이 관람할 쇼를 고르시오.

Ice Show		
	Date	Performers
①	July 21	Linda Joe, Brian Gwen
②	July 22	East Hunt, Steven Foster
③	July 23	Helen Shaw, Jim Bell
④	July 24	Amy Gray, Michael Owen
⑤	July 25	Mary White, Jim Carter

13 대화를 듣고, 남자가 치과에 가기로 한 요일과 시각을 고르시오.

① 금요일 오전 11시
② 토요일 오전 9시 30분
③ 토요일 오후 1시 30분
④ 월요일 오전 9시 30분
⑤ 월요일 오후 1시 30분

14 대화를 듣고, 여자가 한 일이 아닌 것을 고르시오.

① 오페라 감상하기　② 박물관 가기
③ 호주 음식 먹기　④ 농장 방문하기
⑤ 펭귄 구경하기

15 다음을 듣고, 무엇에 관한 내용인지 고르시오.

① 숙면의 중요성　② 졸음운전 예방법
③ 불면증 해소 방법　④ 음주 운전의 위험성
⑤ 방어 운전의 중요성

16 대화를 듣고, 남자가 할 일로 가장 적절한 것을 고르시오.

① 아들 마중가기　② 캠핑 장소 알아보기
③ 캠핑 장비 준비하기　④ 아들에게 전화하기
⑤ 새 휴대전화 구입하기

17 대화를 듣고, 남자의 마지막 말에 대한 여자의 응답으로 가장 적절한 것을 고르시오.

Woman: _____

① I'd better stay at home.
② That shirt looks good, too.
③ No, I can't pick you up there.
④ Yes. You are good at painting.
⑤ Sure. How about the green one?

18 대화를 듣고, 여자의 마지막 말에 대한 남자의 응답으로 가장 적절한 것을 고르시오.

Man: _____

① I'll take the black one.
② The sooner, the better.
③ Sorry for keeping you waiting.
④ I just bought it five months ago.
⑤ It usually takes about three hours.

19 대화를 듣고, 남자의 마지막 말에 대한 여자의 응답으로 가장 적절한 것을 고르시오.

Woman: _____

① It's just three dollars.
② A paperback with 100 pages.
③ About two or three months ago.
④ It was written by a famous writer.
⑤ It's about the information revolution.

20 다음 상황 설명을 듣고, Tony가 학생들에게 할 말로 가장 적절한 것을 고르시오.

Tony: _____

① Do you want to help me?
② Is there anything else you want?
③ You should not listen to music in the library.
④ Did you do well on your test?
⑤ Would you mind being quiet?

01 대화를 듣고, 여자가 구입할 넥타이를 고르시오.

① ② ③ ④ ⑤

M May I help you?

W Yes, I'm looking to _____ _____ for my father.

M How about a tie? These are our _____ _____.

W Wow! They all look very great.

M What about the one with a lot of _____? It sells very well.

W Umm.... My father doesn't like stripes.

M Then how about the one with a lot of big and small _____?

W Oh, I like that one. I'll take it.

02 대화를 듣고, 새 지하철에 관해 언급 되지 <u>않은</u> 것을 고르시오.

① 학교까지 소요 시간
② 배차 간격
③ 일반 요금
④ 학생 할인 여부
⑤ 할인율

M Mom, I'm always late to school because it takes over forty minutes to _____ _____ _____ by bus.

W Oh, that's too bad. But I heard that the new subway line stops near your school.

M I didn't know that. That's good news. But is it fast enough?

W Sure. From here it will take only about fifteen minutes. The subway train _____ _____ ten minutes. There is also a special discount for students.

M Really? How much is the discount rate?

W Students can take the train at _____ _____.

M That's good.

03 대화를 듣고, 남자가 여자에게 전화한 목적으로 가장 적절한 것을 고르시오.

① 일자리를 구하려고
② 예약을 확인하려고
③ 잃어버린 물건을 찾으려고
④ 재킷의 환불을 요청하려고
⑤ 제품의 가격을 문의하려고

[Telephone rings.]

W Hello. Phil's clothing. What can I do for you?

M I _____ _____ _____ at your store about an hour ago.

W Oh, is there any problem with your jacket?

M No. I think I _____ _____ _____ at your store. Have you seen it?

W I'm sorry but I haven't. You _____ _____ _____ it just before I started work.

M Oh, really? Then what should I do?

W If you _____ _____ _____ your phone number, I'll ask the manager and then I'll call you.

M Oh, I see. My phone number is 234-5678. Thanks.

>> **WORDS** **sell** 팔리다; 팔다 **stripe** 줄무늬 **discount** 할인 **rate** 비율

04 대화를 듣고, 두 사람이 만날 시각을 고르시오.

① 7:00 p.m. ② 7:20 p.m.
③ 7:50 p.m. ④ 8:00 p.m.
⑤ 8:10 p.m.

M The film festival is _____ _____ at Central Park. They are showing *New Moon* tonight. Can you watch it with me?

W I'd love to. What time does the movie start?

M Eight, but how about _____ _____ and having dinner together?

W I don't think I have time for dinner because I have piano lesson until seven in the evening.

M Then I will bring some sandwiches and we can eat them _____ _____ the movie.

W That's a good idea. We can meet at the main gate of the park at _____ _____ _____.

M Okay.

05 대화를 듣고, 두 사람이 대화하는 장소로 가장 적절한 곳을 고르시오.

① club room
② photo studio
③ camera shop
④ movie theater
⑤ television studio

M Hi, Lisa. Come in.

W Oh, Tom! Thank you for _____ me here! Wow! I can't believe you work here.

M Yes, it's a great job. I've always been interested in _____.

W So, is this where they _____ _____?

M Some of them. I can show you where they film *Sweet Princess*, if you'd like.

W That would be great! That's one of my favorite dramas.

M Follow me then. It's right down this hall. Please try _____ _____ _____ anything while you are here. The cameras they use are very expensive.

06 다음 그림의 상황에 가장 적절한 대화를 고르시오.

① W What can I do for you?
  M Can you _____ a nice TV?
② W Do you mind if I _____ _____ the TV now?
  M Sorry, but I don't want to watch the TV now.
③ W Do you know where the remote control is?
  M No. I was _____ _____ it to turn on the TV, too.
④ W How about buying a new TV?
  M I don't think we need a new one now.
⑤ W You'd better _____ _____ the TV while you're studying.
  M Mom, I'll turn it off after watching this show.

① ② ③ ④ ⑤

>> WORDS **film** 영화; 촬영하다, 찍다 **show** 상영하다, 보여주다 **main gate** 정문 **remote control** 리모컨

07 대화를 듣고, 여자가 남자에게 부탁한 일로 가장 적절한 것을 고르시오.

① 자명종 빌려주기
② 전화로 깨워 주기
③ 기차표 예매해 주기
④ 함께 아침 운동하기
⑤ 기차역까지 배웅해 주기

W David, do you still _____ _____ _____ in the morning?

M Yes, I usually get up about 5:30.

W Wow! Amazing! Then, can you give me _____ _____ _____ tomorrow morning? I'm supposed to catch the first train at 6:30.

M Sure. No problem. But why don't you set your alarm clock?

W Of course, I will do that. But sometimes it doesn't help me at all. I _____ _____ it.

M I see. Then, what time do you want me to call?

W 5:30 will be fine.

08 다음을 듣고, 여자가 환경 보호 방법으로 언급하지 <u>않은</u> 것을 고르시오.

① 양치할 때 컵 이용하기
② 자기 전에 컴퓨터 끄기
③ 중고 물건 구입하기
④ 분리수거 철저히 하기
⑤ 비닐봉지 덜 쓰기

W "Going green" is not difficult. Here are some simple ways to help the environment. First, use a cup when you _____ your teeth. Second, _____ your computers _____ at night before you go to bed. It can help save 40 watt-hours a day. Third, buy things from a second-hand store to _____ _____ _____ to make them. Lastly, try to use less _____ _____ each day. It is an easy way to protect the environment.

09 다음을 듣고, 무엇에 관한 설명인지 고르시오.

① clock   ② letter
③ present   ④ calendar
⑤ newspaper

M This helps you remember special days. You _____ things like your friend's birthday and your parents' _____ _____ on it. This also tells you what day of the week it is today. In the old days, it was mostly _____ _____ paper. By the way, these days even your smartphone has it.

10 다음을 듣고, 두 사람의 대화가 <u>어색한</u> 것을 고르시오.

①   ②   ③   ④   ⑤

① M I think health is the most important.
   W You can say that again.
② M I won the _____ _____ in the marathon.
   W I can't believe that!
③ M What does it _____ _____?
   W It's used for playing games.
④ M Do you mind _____ down the volume? It's too loud.
   W Not at all. I'm sorry.
⑤ M Where was the picture taken?
   W I think it _____ _____ in Paris.

>> **WORDS**   **be supposed to** …하기로 되어 있다   **save** 절약하다   **watt-hour** 와트시(時) (1시간 1와트의 전기량)   **second-hand** 중고의

11 대화를 듣고, 남자가 지불할 금액을 고르시오.

① $50   ② $80   ③ $130
④ $160   ⑤ $180

W May I help you?

M Yes, please. I'd like to _____ _____ _____ this art class here. How much is it?

W It's 80 dollars a month.

M I'll take the class.

W All right. And do you have your brushes, paints, pencils and erasers?

M No. I _____ _____ them. Oh, do you sell them here?

W Yes. They cost 50 dollars _____ _____.

M Okay. I'll take them.

12 다음 표를 보면서 대화를 듣고, 두 사람이 관람할 쇼를 고르시오.

Ice Show		
	Date	Performers
①	July 21	Linda Joe, Brian Gwen
②	July 22	East Hunt, Steven Foster
③	July 23	Helen Shaw, Jim Bell
④	July 24	Amy Gray, Michael Owen
⑤	July 25	Mary White, Jim Carter

W Have you _____ _____ for the ice show?

M I was just about to. Look at this schedule and tell me when is good for you.

W Any day is fine with me _____ Sunday.

M Sunday is the 24th, right? Then we won't be able to see Amy Gray's performance.

W The performers on the 23rd are also great.

M Sorry, but I already have plans for that day.

W Then, let's see the one with Brian Gwen. He beat Steven Foster and won the _____ _____ at the Winter Olympics.

M Okay. I'll make a reservation online.

13 대화를 듣고, 남자가 치과에 가기로 한 요일과 시각을 고르시오.

① 금요일 오전 11시
② 토요일 오전 9시 30분
③ 토요일 오후 1시 30분
④ 월요일 오전 9시 30분
⑤ 월요일 오후 1시 30분

[Telephone rings.]

W Dr. Kim's Dental Clinic. May I help you?

M Can I _____ _____ _____? I have a toothache.

W Oh, I see. How about Friday at 11 o'clock?

M Sorry, but I'm quite busy on that day. Are you open on Saturday morning?

W I'm afraid we are _____ on Saturdays.

M Then, can I visit on Monday?

W You can come at _____ 9:30 a.m. _____ 1:30 p.m. next Monday, sir.

M 9:30 is too early for me. Please _____ _____ at 1:30 in the afternoon next Monday. My name is Kevin Peterson.

W All right, Mr. Peterson. We'll see you then.

>> **WORDS**   **brush** 붓   **paint** 그림물감   **reservation** 예약   **toothache** 치통

14 대화를 듣고, 여자가 한 일이 <u>아닌</u> 것을 고르시오.

① 오페라 감상하기
② 박물관 가기
③ 호주 음식 먹기
④ 농장 방문하기
⑤ 펭귄 구경하기

M　Hi, Cathy. Long time no see. How was your summer vacation?

W　I _____ _____ Australia.

M　Australia? What did you do there?

W　I enjoyed an opera at the Sydney Opera House and visited lots of _____ and parks in Sydney. I also _____ _____ Australian food.

M　Fantastic! What else did you do?

W　I went to see the _____ on Philip Island near Melbourne. They were so cute.

M　That sounds fun.

15 다음을 듣고, 무엇에 관한 내용인지 고르시오.

① 숙면의 중요성
② 졸음운전 예방법
③ 불면증 해소 방법
④ 음주 운전의 위험성
⑤ 방어 운전의 중요성

W　I'd like to talk about a dangerous _____ _____. If you drive for many hours, it is very easy to _____ _____. It can be just as dangerous as drunk driving. There are some tips you can use to _____ _____. If you start to feel sleepy, you should stop at a rest area to get out of the car and get some fresh air. You can also chew gum or sing a song loudly when you're _____.

16 대화를 듣고, 남자가 할 일로 가장 적절한 것을 고르시오.

① 아들 마중가기
② 캠핑 장소 알아보기
③ 캠핑 장비 준비하기
④ 아들에게 전화하기
⑤ 새 휴대전화 구입하기

M　Lisa, have you _____ _____ _____ from Mike?

W　Not yet. Why?

M　I think he's already arrived at the campsite. But why didn't he call us?

W　Don't worry. He'll surely call us soon.

M　But as you know, it's the first time our son has gone on a trip _____ _____ _____.

W　Right. If you're really worried about him, how about _____ _____ _____?

M　Yeah. I'll do that right away.

>> **WORDS**　**dangerous** 위험한　**drunk driving** 음주 운전　**rest area** 휴게소　**chew** 씹다　**campsite** 캠프장

17 대화를 듣고, 남자의 마지막 말에 대한 여자의 응답으로 가장 적절한 것을 고르시오.

① I'd better stay at home.
② That shirt looks good, too.
③ No, I can't pick you up there.
④ Yes. You are good at painting.
⑤ Sure. How about the green one?

M How do I look? Tonight is my first date with Kate.
W Let me see. Your shirt and pants look very nice.
M Thanks.
W Are you going to _____ _____ _____?
M Yes. I was trying to _____ _____ this one and that one.
W To be honest, I don't think either one would look good with _____ _____.
M Really? Choosing a tie is difficult. Can you pick one for me?

18 대화를 듣고, 여자의 마지막 말에 대한 남자의 응답으로 가장 적절한 것을 고르시오.

① I'll take the black one.
② The sooner, the better.
③ Sorry for keeping you waiting.
④ I just bought it five months ago.
⑤ It usually takes about three hours.

W May I help you?
M Yes. I bought this coffee machine about five months ago and I need to _____ _____ _____.
W Well, all repairs are free for the first year. What's the problem?
M It suddenly _____ _____ and I don't know why.
W Okay. Please leave it here and we'll _____ _____ what's wrong.
M Thanks.
W When do you _____ _____ _____?

19 대화를 듣고, 남자의 마지막 말에 대한 여자의 응답으로 가장 적절한 것을 고르시오.

① It's just three dollars.
② A paperback with 100 pages.
③ About two or three months ago.
④ It was written by a famous writer.
⑤ It's about the information revolution.

W I'd like to know if you have a book _____ *Revolution*.
M Well.... No, I don't think we do.
W Is there any way I can get the book?
M I could _____ _____ for you if you like.
W Oh, that would be great.
M Can you tell me the name of the _____ and the _____?
W I can't remember the author, but it's published by Star Press.
M Do you know when it was published, then?

20 다음 상황 설명을 듣고, Tony가 학생들에게 할 말로 가장 적절한 것을 고르시오.

① Do you want to help me?
② Is there anything else you want?
③ You should not listen to music in the library.
④ Did you do well on your test?
⑤ Would you mind being quiet?

M It was Sunday afternoon and Tony went to the library to study for his _____ _____. The library was quiet and he could concentrate well. However, about an hour later, two students came into the library and sat at the table _____ _____ him. They started _____ loudly. It was too _____ for him to study. He stared at them but they _____ _____. In this situation, what would Tony most likely say to them?

>> **WORDS**　**to be honest** 솔직히 말하면　**pick** 고르다　**author** 작가　**publish** 출판하다　**concentrate** 집중하다　**stare** 빤히 쳐다보다

01 대화를 듣고, 여자가 구입할 거울을 고르시오.

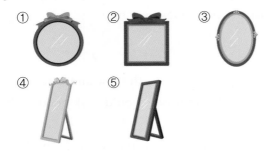

02 대화를 듣고, 여행에 가져갈 것으로 언급되지 <u>않은</u> 것을 고르시오.

① 수영복　　② 모자　　③선크림
④ 우산　　　⑤ 여권

03 대화를 듣고, 여자가 남자에게 전화한 목적으로 가장 적절한 것을 고르시오.

① 졸업을 축하하려고
② 자택 주소를 확인하려고
③ 졸업식 연설을 부탁하려고
④ 행사 장소 변경을 알리려고
⑤ 연설 시작 시간을 물어보려고

04 대화를 듣고, 두 사람이 만날 시각을 고르시오.

① 10 a.m.　② 11 a.m.　③ 1 p.m.
④ 2 p.m.　⑤ 3 p.m.

05 대화를 듣고, 두 사람이 대화하는 장소로 가장 적절한 곳을 고르시오.

① 가방 가게　　　② 버스
③ 버스 정류장　　④ 공항
⑤ 분실물 보관소

06 다음 그림의 상황에 가장 적절한 대화를 고르시오.

①　　②　　③　　④　　⑤

07 대화를 듣고, 남자가 여자에게 부탁한 일로 가장 적절한 것을 고르시오.

① 피아노 가르쳐주기
② 경시대회 참가하기
③ 여름 캠프 신청하기
④ 여름휴가 계획 세우기
⑤ 피아노 레슨 등록하기

08 다음을 듣고, Picasso Art Museum에 관해 언급되지 <u>않은</u> 것을 고르시오.

① 설립연도　　　　② 설립자
③ 보유 작품 수　　④ 연간 방문객 수
⑤ 문 닫는 시각

09 다음을 듣고, 무엇에 관한 설명인지 고르시오.

① 부채　　　② 양산　　　③ 우산
④ 선풍기　　⑤ 커튼

10 다음을 듣고, 두 사람의 대화가 <u>어색한</u> 것을 고르시오.

①　　②　　③　　④　　⑤

11 대화를 듣고, 여자가 이번 주 금요일 밤에 할 일로 가장 적절한 것을 고르시오.

① 공부하기　　　　② 운동하기
③ 병문안 가기　　④ 동생 돌보기
⑤ 콘서트 가기

12 다음 표를 보면서 대화를 듣고, 두 사람이 수강할 수업을 고르시오.

Swimming Class		
	Instructor	Time
①	Mr. Jackson	Mon. & Wed. 3-4 p.m.
②	Mr. Jackson	Tues. & Fri. 3-4 p.m.
③	Ms. Wilson	Mon. & Wed. 4-5 p.m.
④	Ms. Wilson	Tues. & Thur. 4-5 p.m.
⑤	Ms. Wilson	Wed. & Fri. 5-6 p.m.

13 대화를 듣고, 여자가 지불할 금액을 고르시오.

① $20　② $35　③ $40　④ $55　⑤ $60

14 대화를 듣고, 두 사람이 대화 직후에 할 일로 가장 적절한 것을 고르시오.

① 병원 가기　　　　② 도서관 가기
③ 보고서 제출하기　④ 식물에 물 주기
⑤ 과학 선생님 만나기

15 다음을 듣고, 여자가 하는 말의 목적으로 가장 적절한 것을 고르시오.

① 박물관을 홍보하려고
② 휴식 시간을 알려 주려고
③ 여행 일정을 안내하려고
④ 식사 메뉴를 추천하려고
⑤ 박물관 관람 주의사항을 전하려고

16 대화를 듣고, 남자가 지불할 금액을 고르시오.

① $10　② $12　③ $16　④ $18　⑤ $20

17 대화를 듣고, 여자의 마지막 말에 대한 남자의 응답으로 가장 적절한 것을 고르시오.

Man: _____

① I'm going to the dentist.
② I'll treat you to dinner tonight.
③ Yes. Brush your teeth well.
④ Yes. I want to be a dentist.
⑤ Yes. If you don't, the pain will get worse.

18 대화를 듣고, 남자의 마지막 말에 대한 여자의 응답으로 가장 적절한 것을 고르시오.

Woman: _____

① Sorry. I'm busy now.
② Great. I really appreciate it.
③ Go see the doctor right away.
④ Yes. I can help the children alone.
⑤ Sure. You just need to send in an application.

19 대화를 듣고, 여자의 마지막 말에 대한 남자의 응답으로 가장 적절한 것을 고르시오.

Man: _____

① I'm sorry but I can't play with you.
② I promise I'll go and cheer for you.
③ I wish I could have watched the match.
④ I'll teach you how to play tennis better.
⑤ I'm sorry to hear that you lost the match.

20 다음 상황 설명을 듣고, Emily가 Jack에게 할 말로 가장 적절한 것을 고르시오.

Emily: _____

① You haven't changed at all.
② You sure look healthier now.
③ Don't talk with your mouth full.
④ Fast food is really cheap and fast.
⑤ You should work out regularly.

01 대화를 듣고, 여자가 구입할 거울을 고르시오.

① ② ③
④ ⑤

W I'm looking for a mirror to put in my room.
M How about this round one _____ _____ _____?
W I don't need a ribbon. I'd like a _____ one.
M How about this simple _____ one?
W I like that one, but I want to buy a big mirror. It's important that it should be big enough so I can see my _____ _____.
M Then, this one is perfect for you. It's a simple full-length mirror.
W Oh, that's prefect. I'll take it.

02 대화를 듣고, 여행에 가져갈 것으로 언급되지 않은 것을 고르시오.

① 수영복 ② 모자 ③ 선크림
④ 우산 ⑤ 여권

M Honey, how long will it take to pack your things?
W About an hour.
M Don't forget your _____ _____. There is a beautiful beach just in front of the hotel.
W I already packed it with a hat and _____ lotion.
M Good. Did you bring your passport and airplane tickets?
W Oh, my! I totally forgot about them. If you hadn't reminded me, I _____ _____ _____ my plane.
M Where is your passport?
W It is in the top _____ of my desk. My tickets are inside the passport.
M Let me go get them.

03 대화를 듣고, 여자가 남자에게 전화한 목적으로 가장 적절한 것을 고르시오.

① 졸업을 축하하려고
② 자택 주소를 확인하려고
③ 졸업식 연설을 부탁하려고
④ 행사 장소 변경을 알리려고
⑤ 연설 시작 시간을 물어보려고

[Telephone rings.]
M Hello.
W Hello, Mr. Wilson. This is Alice Brown at Green Middle School.
M Hi, Ms. Brown. How have you been doing?
W I've been doing well. Mr. Wilson, could you _____ _____ _____ _____?
M Oh, what is it?
W Could you _____ _____ _____ at the graduation ceremony?
M Sure. When is the graduation ceremony _____ _____?
W Next Friday. It starts at 10:30. So, please come to the teachers' office by 10 o'clock.
M Okay. I will.

> **WORDS** **full-length** 전신이 다 보이는 **pack** 싸다, 꾸리다 **passport** 여권 **remind** 상기시키다 **graduation** 졸업, 졸업식

04 대화를 듣고, 두 사람이 만날 시각을 고르시오.

① 10 a.m.　　② 11 a.m.
③ 1 p.m.　　④ 2 p.m.
⑤ 3 p.m.

[Telephone rings.]

M Hi, Ms. James. This is Tom from *The Apple Times*.

W Hello, Tom. Are you calling for our _____?

M Yes. Are you free tomorrow at 11 a.m.?

W No. I'll be giving a two-hour _____ from 10 a.m. at the university.

M I see. When will you be free?

W Well, I have a book signing at a local bookstore at 1 p.m. That will _____ _____ _____, but then I'll be free.

M Good. I'll meet you at the bookstore _____ _____ the book signing.

W Okay.

05 대화를 듣고, 두 사람이 대화하는 장소로 가장 적절한 곳을 고르시오.

① 가방 가게　　② 버스
③ 버스 정류장　　④ 공항
⑤ 분실물 보관소

W Excuse me. I _____ _____ _____ in a bus.

M What was the number of the bus?

W 70.

M All right. We have _____ _____ _____ bags from no. 70 buses. What color is it?

W It's brown _____ _____ _____.

M I think we have. Just a moment, please. [Pause] Is this yours?

W Oh, yes. I didn't expect I would find it. Thank you so much.

M You're welcome. Have a nice day!

06 다음 그림의 상황에 가장 적절한 대화를 고르시오.

①　②　③　④　⑤

① M Hello. Can I buy these flowers?

　W Of course.

② M Excuse me. You are _____ _____ _____ pick the flowers here.

　W I'm sorry. I didn't know that. I won't do it again.

③ M Would you show me the way to the flower garden?

　W Sure. Walk _____ _____.

④ M Excuse me. Is there a trash can around here?

　W Yes, there is one near the flower garden.

⑤ M Do you come here often?

　W Yes, I come here _____ _____.

>> WORDS　**book signing** 책 사인회　**expect** 예상하다, 기대하다　**pick** (꽃을) 꺾다　**trash can** 쓰레기통

07 대화를 듣고, 남자가 여자에게 부탁한 일로 가장 적절한 것을 고르시오.

① 피아노 가르쳐주기
② 경시대회 참가하기
③ 여름 캠프 신청하기
④ 여름휴가 계획 세우기
⑤ 피아노 레슨 등록하기

M Lisa, where are you going?
W I'm going to _____ _____ _____ the summer camp.
M Summer camp? When does it start?
W It starts on July 25th. And it continues to July 28th.
M I'd love to _____ _____ _____ the camp, too.
W Really? Then, let's go to the camp together.
M Okay. Lisa, could you sign me up, too? I have _____ _____ _____ now.
W No problem. I'll do it for you.

08 다음을 듣고, Picasso Art Museum에 관해 언급되지 <u>않은</u> 것을 고르시오.

① 설립연도   ② 설립자
③ 보유 작품 수   ④ 연간 방문객 수
⑤ 문 닫는 시각

M Attention, please. We're _____ _____ the Picasso Art Museum soon. Before you enter the museum, I'll tell you about it briefly. The museum _____ _____ _____ 1988. It has more than 3,000 pieces of famous art works. More than 10,000 people _____ _____ _____ every year. The museum closes at 6 p.m. So you have to come back to this bus before then. Please enjoy your visit.

09 다음을 듣고, 무엇에 관한 설명인지 고르시오.

① 부채   ② 양산   ③ 우산
④ 선풍기   ⑤ 커튼

M This is a flat object having a wooden or _____ _____ with paper or cloth. In the old days before electric fans, people used it to make themselves _____ _____ _____. Sometimes, they used it as an accessory, too. In old movies, you may see some western noble ladies holding this. You can also see some noble people holding this in Korean old pictures. To make a _____ _____, you hold this in your hand and _____ _____ to make the air move.

10 다음을 듣고, 두 사람의 대화가 <u>어색한</u> 것을 고르시오.

①   ②   ③   ④   ⑤

① M What do you want to be when you _____ _____?
   W I love animals, so I want to run an animal hospital.
② M Have you heard of the lie detector?
   W Sure, but I've never been there before.
③ M Are you saying you've already finished your homework?
   W Dad, it was a _____ _____ _____.
④ M How much is the late fee?
   W It's two dollars in total.
⑤ M You're _____ _____ _____ a present for him.
   W Sorry, I was in such a _____ that I left it at home.

>> **WORDS** **continue** 계속되다 **briefly** 간단히 **flat** 평평한 **object** 물체 **electric** 전기의 **noble** 귀족의, 고귀한
lie detector 거짓말 탐지기 **late fee** 연체료

11 대화를 듣고, 여자가 이번 주 금요일 밤에 할 일로 가장 적절한 것을 고르시오.

① 공부하기　　② 운동하기
③ 병문안 가기　④ 동생 돌보기
⑤ 콘서트 가기

M　How was your week at school?

W　I'm so ＿＿＿＿＿ ＿＿＿＿＿ studying. I think I need a break.

M　I know what you mean. I'm going to a concert this Friday night. How about coming along?

W　Sorry, but I can't. I'm ＿＿＿＿＿ ＿＿＿＿＿ ＿＿＿＿＿ to the gym to exercise with my sister. She helps me exercise.

M　I thought you don't like exercise.

W　You're right. Actually I don't. The doctor said I needed ＿＿＿＿＿ ＿＿＿＿＿.

M　Well. Good luck. See you at school on Monday.

12 다음 표를 보면서 대화를 듣고, 두 사람이 수강할 수업을 고르시오.

Swimming Class		
	Instructor	Time
①	Mr. Jackson	Mon. & Wed. 3-4 p.m.
②	Mr. Jackson	Tues. & Fri. 3-4 p.m.
③	Ms. Wilson	Mon. & Wed. 4-5 p.m.
④	Ms. Wilson	Tues. & Thur. 4-5 p.m.
⑤	Ms. Wilson	Wed. & Fri. 5-6 p.m.

M　Yuna, you're ＿＿＿＿＿ ＿＿＿＿＿ the swimming classes at ABC Sports Center.

W　Yeah. I'm going to take one of the classes. Will you join me?

M　Sure.

W　Good. How about Mr. Jackson's class on Mondays and Wednesdays?

M　Sorry, I can't. I have guitar lessons ＿＿＿＿＿ ＿＿＿＿＿ and Wednesday.

W　Right. I can't take a Friday class, either.

M　Then let's take Ms. Wilson's class on Tuesdays and Thursdays.

W　Good. Let's ＿＿＿＿＿ ＿＿＿＿＿ for the class.

13 대화를 듣고, 여자가 지불할 금액을 고르시오.

① $20　② $35　③ $40
④ $55　⑤ $60

M　Hello. Can I help you?

W　Yes, please. ＿＿＿＿＿ ＿＿＿＿＿ is this shirt?

M　It's 20 dollars. But if you buy two, you can get them for 35 dollars.

W　Good. I'll take two of them. And I also need some socks.

M　How about these ones? We sell five pairs of socks for 20 dollars.

W　I'll ＿＿＿＿＿ ＿＿＿＿＿ ＿＿＿＿＿ then.

M　So let me check. 35 dollars for two shirts and 20 dollars for five pairs of socks. ＿＿＿＿＿ ＿＿＿＿＿?

W　No. That's all.

>> WORDS　**break** 휴식 시간　**gym** 체육관　**check** 확인하다, 점검하다

14 대화를 듣고, 두 사람이 대화 직후에 할 일로 가장 적절한 것을 고르시오.

① 병원 가기
② 도서관 가기
③ 보고서 제출하기
④ 식물에 물 주기
⑤ 과학 선생님 만나기

M Cathy, you don't look good.
W I have been in bed for three days because of a bad cold.
M That's too bad. Are you okay now?
W I'm okay except for a _____ _____. I heard our science teacher gave us homework.
M Right. Yesterday, we learned about life in the desert. We have to write a report about how _____ _____ _____.
W Do you have any ideas about that?
M No, actually I'm going to the library to _____ _____ _____. You can come with me.
W Okay, thank you.

15 다음을 듣고, 여자가 하는 말의 목적으로 가장 적절한 것을 고르시오.

① 박물관을 홍보하려고
② 휴식 시간을 알려 주려고
③ 여행 일정을 안내하려고
④ 식사 메뉴를 추천하려고
⑤ 박물관 관람 주의사항을 전하려고

W Good morning everyone. Did you sleep well? We're _____ _____ _____ the National Museum this morning. You can see lots of _____ _____ that local people used to use. We will then _____ _____ at the Chinese restaurant near the museum. After lunch, you'll have some _____ _____. We'll meet up again during the evening to have dinner at the hotel.

16 대화를 듣고, 남자가 지불할 금액을 고르시오.

① $10 ② $12 ③ $16
④ $18 ⑤ $20

W What can I do for you?
M I'd like to _____ _____ _____.
W How about this white one?
M Well, it's likely to get dirty too easily. How much is this blue one?
W It's 10 dollars. But if you _____ _____, we'll give them to you for 16 dollars.
M Good. I'll take two and _____ _____ to my brother then.

17 대화를 듣고, 여자의 마지막 말에 대한 남자의 응답으로 가장 적절한 것을 고르시오.

① I'm going to the dentist.
② I'll treat you to dinner tonight.
③ Yes. Brush your teeth well.
④ Yes. I want to be a dentist.
⑤ Yes. If you don't, the pain will get worse.

M Good morning. Please take a seat here.
W Thanks.
M What's your problem today?
W I have a _____ _____. I can't stand it any more.
M Let me _____ your teeth. Please open your mouth.
W All right. Ah.
M You have some cavities. The two upper ones look serious.
W Do you think I should get them _____ _____ _____?

>> **WORDS** except for …을 제외하고 desert 사막 stand 참다, 견디다 cavity 충치의 구멍 upper 위쪽의 serious 심각한

18 대화를 듣고, 남자의 마지막 말에 대한 여자의 응답으로 가장 적절한 것을 고르시오.

① Sorry. I'm busy now.
② Great. I really appreciate it.
③ Go see the doctor right away.
④ Yes. I can help the children alone.
⑤ Sure. You just need to send in an application.

M Jia, I heard you do volunteer work at the children's hospital every Saturday. Is that true?
W Yes. I have been doing volunteer work there since last year.
M Wow! What kind of work do you do there?
W I usually _____ _____ to the sick children.
M How nice you are! Actually, I'm _____ _____ _____ others, too.
W Really? Then _____ _____!
M Can I?

19 대화를 듣고, 여자의 마지막 말에 대한 남자의 응답으로 가장 적절한 것을 고르시오.

① I'm sorry but I can't play with you.
② I promise I'll go and cheer for you.
③ I wish I could have watched the match.
④ I'll teach you how to play tennis better.
⑤ I'm sorry to hear that you lost the match.

M Alice, I heard about your tennis match this Sunday.
W Did you? I really want to win the match, but I'm not sure I can.
M You're a very good player. I'm sure you'll _____ _____ _____.
W Thank you. But the player I'm going to play is really good.
M I'm sure you'll beat her if you try to be calm and _____ _____ _____.
W Okay, I'll keep that in mind. And I think I'll do better if you _____ _____ _____ the match.

20 다음 상황 설명을 듣고, Emily가 Jack에게 할 말로 가장 적절한 것을 고르시오.

① You haven't changed at all.
② You sure look healthier now.
③ Don't talk with your mouth full.
④ Fast food is really cheap and fast.
⑤ You should work out regularly.

W Jack used to eat a lot of fast food. But one day he decided to _____ _____ of it and eat more healthy foods. These days he's enjoying eating more vegetables and fruits. In addition, he has _____ _____ _____. He jogs every day. When his old friend Emily meets him, she sees that Jack is looking _____ _____. In this situation, what would Emily most likely say to Jack?

>> WORDS **volunteer work** 자원 봉사 **match** 경기, 시합 **beat** 이기다 **calm** 침착한 **decide** 결심하다, 결정하다

Memo

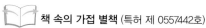

VISANG

중학 영어의 모든 것

All that

중학 영어 3-1

Answers

ABOVE IMAGINATION

우리는 남다른 상상과 혁신으로
교육 문화의 새로운 전형을 만들어
모든 이의 행복한 경험과 성장에 기여한다

실력 다지기

Lesson 01 to부정사

>> Grammar Practice   pp. 12~15

A1 (1) To play, 명사적 용법 (2) to talk, 형용사적 용법
(3) to win, 부사적 용법 (4) to move, 명사적 용법
(5) to be, 부사적 용법 (6) to eat, 형용사적 용법
(7) to hear, 부사적 용법

A2 (1) easy to finish (2) it stupid to try
(3) it important to get (4) advised me to be nice

B1 (1) for (2) of (3) of (4) for (5) of

B2 (1) easy for her (2) wise of Yuna (3) safe for you
(4) difficult for them

C1 (1) seems, is (2) seems, majored
(3) seemed, was (4) seemed, had been

C2 (1) to have dreamed (2) to have seen (3) to know

D1 (1) not to (2) never to (3) to (4) not to follow

D2 (1) visit her tomorrow (2) go

E1 (1) what to (2) how to (3) enough to (4) too, to
(5) so, that, can't

E2 (1) how, should (2) so, that, can't
(3) so, that, can (4) how to, fix

F1 (1) 이상한 말이지만, 그가 나를 좋아하는 것 같다.
(2) 말할 필요도 없이, 나는 축제에 갈 수 없다.
(3) 설상가상으로, 나는 감기에 심하게 걸렸다.
(4) 확실히, 그는 무례하다.
(5) 솔직히 말해서, 그는 정직하지 않다.

>> Grammar Test   pp. 16~17

01 ④ **02** ③ **03** ① **04** ⑤ **05** 솔직히 말해서, 그녀는 전혀 매력적이지 않다. **06** ④ **07** (1) to find (2) to give (3) to generate **08** be back by seven **09** (1) too, to stop (2) enough to support **10** ④ **11** for, of **12** ③ **13** ④ **14** (1) too, to (2) enough to

01 to부정사의 의미상 주어로 〈of+목적격〉을 쓰려면 빈칸에는 사람의 성격, 태도를 나타내는 형용사가 와야 하므로, difficult는 알맞지 않다.

02 목적어 역할을 하는 to부정사가 와야 한다.

03 to부정사의 부정은 to 바로 앞에 not이나 never를 쓴다.

04 ⑤ rock을 꾸미는 형용사적 용법으로 쓰인 to sit에서 동사 sit은 전치사가 필요하다. (→ to sit on)

05 To be frank with you는 독립부정사로 '솔직히 말해서'라는 의미이다.

06 ④는 결과를 나타내는 부사적 용법이며, 나머지는 명사적 용법이다. ① 목적어 ② 보어 ③ 주어 ⑤ 진주어

07 (1) 가목적어 it으로 보아 진목적어 to부정사가 알맞다. (2) ask는 to부정사를 목적격보어로 취하는 동사이다. (3) 가주어 it으로 보아 진주어 to부정사가 알맞다.

08 A가 B에게 7시까지 올 수 있냐고 하자 B는 (7시까지 돌아오는 것을) 노력해 보겠다고 말하고 있다. 앞에 나온 동사의 반복을 피하기 위해 대부정사 to가 쓰였으므로 빈칸에는 A에서 반복된 표현을 찾아 쓴다.

09 (1) 〈so+형용사(부사)+that+주어+can't ...〉 = 〈too+형용사(부사)+to부정사〉 (2) 〈so+형용사(부사)+that+주어+can ...〉 = 〈형용사(부사)+enough+to부정사〉

10 창문을 두드린 것을 들은 것은 어젯밤이고, 그렇게 생각하는 것은 현재이므로 완료부정사의 형태인 〈to have+과거분사〉로 나타낸다.

11 • to부정사의 의미상 주어는 일반적으로 〈for+목적격〉으로 나타낸다. / • 사람의 성격, 태도를 나타내는 형용사 nice가 있으므로 의미상 주어는 〈of+목적격〉으로 나타낸다.

12 ③ 〈의문사+to부정사〉는 〈의문사+주어+should+동사원형〉으로 바꿔 쓸 수 있다.

13 • 캠핑 여행에 무엇을 가져가야 하는지 묻고 있으므로 what이 알맞다. / • 체스를 하는 방법이 이해하기가 쉽지 않다는 내용이므로 how가 알맞다.

14 〈too+형용사(부사)+to부정사〉는 '너무 …해서 …할 수 없는'이라는 뜻이고, 〈형용사(부사)+enough+to부정사〉는 '…할 만큼 충분히 …한(하게)'라는 뜻이다.

>> Reading   pp. 18~19

1 made it possible for children to play music **2** ⑤
3 ③ **4** ①

[1~2]

정크 오케스트라

"세상이 우리에게 쓰레기를 보내면, 우리는 음악을 돌려준다." 이것은 내가 받은 음악회 입장권의 뒷면에 쓰여 있었다. '정크 오케스트라'는 완전히 쓰레기로만 만들어진 악기를 연주했다. 나는 그 음악에 너무나 감동해서 지휘자인 Favio Chávez를 만나 그에게 오케스트라에 대해 물었다.

당신은 왜 정크 오케스트라를 시작하셨나요?

Favio Chávez 제가 2005년에 파라과이에 있는 카테우라라고 불리는 작은 마을에 갔을 때, 저는 대부분이 쓰레기로 가득 차 있는 마을에 살고 있는 아이들을 봤습니다. 저는 그들의 삶에 긍정적인 뭔가를 더해 주고 싶어서 음악에 대한 저의 사랑을 그들과 나누기로 했습니다.

당신은 왜 악기를 만드는 데 쓰레기를 이용했나요?

Favio Chávez 한 사람의 쓰레기는 다른 사람의 보물입니다. 쓰레기 줍는 사람인 Nicolás Gómez가 저를 많이 도와주었습니다. 그는 쓰레기로 악기를 만들어 줌으로써 아이들이 음악을 연주하는 것을 가능하게 만들었습니다. 저는 사람들이 가치 없는 것도 영감을 주는 음악을 만들어 낼 수 있다는 것을 알게 되기를 원합니다.

1 〈make+가목적어(it)+목적격보어(possible)+의미상 주어+to부정사(진목적어)〉 구문이다.

2 ⑤ 쓰레기 줍는 사람인 Nicolás Gómez가 악기 만드는 것을 도와주었다고 했다.

3 　오늘날, 세계의 많은 대도시들은 환경오염과 범죄와 같은 비슷한 두 가지 문제에 직면한다. 도시 설계자들은 이러한 문제들을 해결하기 위해 무엇을 하고 있을까? 예를 들어, 인도의 한 도시인 Hyderabad는 나무를 심고 있다. 도시에 녹지를 조성하는 것은 많은 장점이 있다. 나무는 공기 중의 오염을 제거하여 공기를 더 깨끗하게 만든다. 몇 년 전 Hyderabad의 거리는 잿빛이고 보기 싫었다. 하지만 오늘날에는 나무와 꽃으로 가득하다. 녹지는 도시를 더 깨끗하고 다채롭게 만든다. 녹지는 또한 사람들이 휴식을 취할 수 있는 장소이다. 미국의 한 연구는 그 밖의 흥미로운 점을 보여주었다. 주변이 푸를수록, 범죄가 덜 발생한다는 것이다.

도시 문제를 해결하기 위해 나무를 심고 있는 인도의 도시 Hyderabad를 예로 들고 있으므로 ③이 알맞다.

4 　매년, 산불 때문에 수많은 사람들이 죽거나 집을 잃는다. 삼림 소방대원들은 이를 막는 것을 도와주고 있다. 삼림 소방대원들은 특수 소방대원들이다. 그들은 산속의 숲 한 가운데와 같이 자동차나 걸어서 가기 어려운 곳을 향해 비행기에서 뛰어내린다. 화재 현장에서, 삼림 소방대원들은 먼저 지대를 살피고 불을 끌 방법을 결정한다. 그들의 주된 목표는 불이 번지는 것을 막는 것이다. 삽이나 도끼와 같은 기본 장비들을 이용하여, 삼림 소방대원들은 풀과 그 밖의 마른 물질 같은 탈 수 있는 물질이 있는 땅을 정리한다. 그들은 또한 물을 가지고 다니는데, 단지 제한된 양이다.

삼림 소방대원들이 어떤 일을 하는지 소개하는 글이므로, ① '삼림 소방대원들이 하는 일'이 글의 주제로 알맞다.

1 should　**2** ③　**3** ③　**4** ④　**5** upset with　**6** ②

1 A가 자신이 어떻게 해야 할지 충고를 구하고 있으므로 B는 충고하는 말을 해야 한다.

2 잘못된 행동을 하고 있는 남자를 보고 화를 내는 표현이 알맞다.

3 화가 나 있는 상대방을 진정시킬 때 쓰는 표현으로 Calm down. / Take it easy. 등이 있다.

4 You'd better ....는 '...하는 게 좋겠다'라는 뜻으로 상대방에게 충고할 때 쓴다.

5 어떤 사람에게 화가 났음을 표현할 때 I'm upset with .... 등의 표현을 쓸 수 있다.

6 A: 나는 오후에 수학 시험이 있어. 너무 초조해. – (B) 걱정하지 마. 최선을 다하면 돼. – (A) 하지만 나는 너무 초조할 때 늘 실수를 해. 어떻게 해야 하지? – (C) 우선 쉬운 문제를 풀어. 그럼 기분이 나아질 거야.

1 (1) I'm upset about it. (2) Do you have any good ideas?　**2** (1) to enjoy water sports (2) to visit my grandmother　**3** (1) to ask (2) to visit (3) not to play　**4** (1) big that I couldn't eat it alone (2) easy that it can be solved (3) It is a wise thing　**5** (1) too smart → smart enough (2) talkative enough → too talkative

1 I'm upset about .... / I'm angry about .... 등으로 화냄을 표현할 수 있다. 충고를 구할 때는 Do you have any good ideas? / What should I do? 등으로 말할 수 있다.

2 to부정사의 부사적 용법 중 '...하기 위해서'라는 목적의 의미로 쓰였다.

3 (1), (2) want와 plan은 to부정사를 목적어로 취하는 동사이다. (3) tell은 목적격보어로 to부정사를 취하며, to부정사의 부정은 to앞에 not을 붙인다.

4 (1) 〈too+형용사(부사)+to부정사〉 = 〈so+형용사(부사)+that+주어+can't ...〉 (2) 〈형용사(부사)+enough+to부정사〉 = 〈so+형용사(부사)+that+주어+can ...〉 (3) to부정사가 주어 역할을 할 때 주어가 긴 경우, 주어를 문장 뒤로 보내고 그 대신 주어 자리에 가주어 it을 쓴다.

5 〈too+형용사(부사)+to부정사〉는 '너무 ...해서 ...할 수 없는'의 뜻이고, 〈형용사(부사)+enough+to부정사〉는 '...할 만큼 충분히 ...한(하게)'의 의미이다.

01 ⑤　02 ④　03 ⑤　04 I were you　05 ④　06 don't you go to the school nurse　07 (B) → (D) → (A) → (C)　08 ⑤　09 ⑤　10 To tell the truth　11 to not bark → not to bark　12 thinking → think　13 ④　14 ④　15 ①　16 ④　17 ③　18 as, order　19 (1) It, to persuade (2) I should put (3) that, can　20 ④　21 I told her not to call.　22 ③　23 ③　24 ⑤　25 ④　26 ⑤　27 ④　28 ④　29 ③　30 ⑤

01 '음악을 만들어 내는 데 쓰이는 물체'는 instrument(악기)에 해당하는 영영풀이이다.

02 conductor는 '지휘자'의 의미이므로 '음악가나 가수들 앞에 서서 연주나 노래를 지휘하는 사람'의 뜻이 되도록 빈칸에는 directs가 알맞다.

03 ⑤ '그에게 사과를 해야 한다고 생각하니?'라고 충고를 구하는 말에 '충고 고마워.'라고 대답하는 것은 어색하다.

04 상대방이 자신의 상황이라면 어떻게 할 것인지에 대한 충고를 구하므로 충고하는 표현인 If I were you ....가 오는 것이 알맞다.

05 B가 '무슨 일이야?'라고 하는 것으로 보아 친구에게 화가 났다는 표현인 ④가 알맞다.

06 그림은 양호 선생님께 진료를 받는 모습이고, B가 열이 난다고 했으므로 양호 선생님께 가 보라고 충고하는 내용이 알맞다.

07 (B) 이 과학 프로그램 못 보겠어요. 너무 지루해요. – (D) 정말이니? 난 네가 그것을 즐겨 본다고 생각했는데. – (A) 전혀요. 농구 경기를 보게 해주세요. – (C) 그래. 그럼.

08 ⑤는 상대방이 일찍 일어날 거라는 자신의 확신을 표현하는 문장이고, 나머지는 상대방에게 일찍 일어날 것을 충고하는 문장이다.

09 to부정사에 쓰인 동사에 전치사가 뒤따르는 경우에는 전치사를 잊지 않고 쓴다. 룸메이트는 '함께 살' 사람이므로 전치사 with가 필요하다.

10 To tell the truth는 '사실을 말하자면'의 의미를 나타낸다.

11 to부정사의 부정은 to 바로 앞에 not이나 never를 쓴다.

12 want는 목적격보어로 to부정사를 취하므로 to think가 되어야 한다.

13 to부정사의 의미상 주어는 대부분 〈for+목적격〉으로 쓰지만, 사람의 성격, 태도를 나타내는 형용사가 올 때에는 〈of+목적격〉으로 쓴다.

14 ④ To make matters worse는 '설상가상으로'의 뜻을 나타낸다.

15 ①은 forgot의 목적어로 쓰인 명사적 용법인 반면, 나머지는 목적을 나타내는 부사적 용법으로 쓰였다.

16 〈too+형용사(부사)+to부정사〉는 '너무 …해서 …할 수 없는'의 뜻으로 〈so+형용사(부사)+that+주어+can't ...〉로 바꿔 쓸 수 있다.

17 주어진 문장에서 주절의 동사(seems)는 현재이고 that절의 동사(knew)는 과거로, 본동사의 시제보다 이전에 일어난 일을 나타내는 완료부정사 〈to have+과거분사〉를 써야 한다.

18 so as to, in order to는 '…하기 위해서'라는 목적의 의미를 나타낸다.

19 (1) 문장의 주어가 To persuade him인 긴 to부정사구이므로, 이를 뒤로 보내고 주어 자리에 가주어 It을 쓴다. (2) 〈의문사+to부정사〉는 〈의문사+주어+should+동사원형〉으로 바꿔 쓸 수 있다. (3) 〈형용사(부사)+enough+to부정사〉는 '…할 만큼 충분히 …한(하게)'의 뜻으로 〈so+형용사(부사)+that+주어+can ...〉으로 바꿔 쓸 수 있다.

20 〈보기〉와 ④는 to부정사가 (대)명사를 꾸미는 형용사적 용법으로 쓰였다. ① 명사적 용법(진주어) ② 부사적 용법(감정의 원인) ③ 명사적 용법(보어) ⑤ 부사적 용법(목적)

21 to부정사의 부정은 to부정사 앞에 not을 써서 부정의 의미를 나타낸다.

22 to부정사의 의미상 주어는 앞에 나온 형용사가 성격이나 태도를 나타낼 때는 〈of +목적격〉으로 쓰므로 ①, ②, ③, ⑤에는 of가 들어가고, ④에는 for가 알맞다.

23 ③ to부정사가 꾸미는 (대)명사가 전치사의 목적어일 경우 to부정사 뒤에 전치사를 써야 한다. (play → play with)

24 ⑤ 동사 considered의 목적어 자리에 가목적어 it이 쓰였으므로, 진목적어로 to부정사를 써야 한다. (master → to master)

25

> 　어떤 동물의 눈은 시력을 쉽게 잃을 정도로 민감하다. 눈이 공격을 당하면, 눈이 멀게 되고 그 생명체의 목숨을 위험하게 할 수도 있다. 이러한 이유로, 어떤 동물들은 '가짜 눈'을 가지고 있다. 예를 들어, (과일을 먹고 사는) 큰박쥐는 싸우는 동안 눈을 보호하기 위해 귀 밑에 흰색 털을 가지고 있다. 공격자들은 그들의 진짜 눈 대신에 이것을 공격한다. 다른 동물들은 진한 무늬에 눈을 감추고 있다. 나비고기의 눈은 자신의 얼굴에 있는 진한 줄무늬에 숨겨져 있다.

큰박쥐는 진짜 눈을 보호하기 위해서 귀 밑에 눈처럼 보이는 흰색 털을 가지고 있다고 했으므로 ④ false(가짜의)가 알맞다.

26

> 　균형 잡힌 식사는 각 음식 군에서 적절한 양의 음식을 먹는 것을 포함한다. 균형 잡힌 식사를 하는 것은 당신의 몸이 건강을 유지하기 위해 필요로 하는 모든 영양소를 확실히 섭취하게 할 것이다. 그러므로 우리는 우리 몸이 필요로 하는 모든 영양소를 얻기 위해 다양한 음식을 먹는 것이 중요하다. 요컨대, 우리는 식사의 균형을 맞추려고 노력해야 한다.

우리 몸이 필요로 하는 영양소를 골고루 섭취하도록 균형 잡힌 식습관을 가지는 것이 중요하다고 했다.

[27~28]

> Herb Casey는 자신이 사는 도시의 시장이 되고 싶었다. 그래서 그는 홍보물을 붙이고, 집들을 방문하고, "저에게 투표해 주세요."라는 내용의 편지를 도시의 수천 명의 사람들에게 보냈다. 마침내, 선거일이 되었다. Herb는 훨씬 더 많은 홍보물을 붙였다. 그는 사람들에게 전화를 걸어 그들에게 "오늘은 선거일입니다. 저에게 투표해 주세요."라고 말했다. 8시에 Herb는 투표를 하러 갔고 8시 10분이 되어 기표소에 도착했다. 하지만 투표는 8시에 끝났기 때문에 그는 투표를 할 수 없었다. 다음 날, 개표를 했다. 그가 당선되었을까? 아니, 그렇지 않았다. 그는 한 표 차이로 선거에서 떨어졌다. 그는 인생 최대의 실수를 저질렀다.

27 시장으로 당선되기 위해 희망에 차서(hopeful) 선거 운동을 하다가 한 표 차이로 낙선하여 실망했다(disappointed).

28 (A) want는 to부정사를 목적어로 취한다. (B) put up, knocked on과 and로 병렬 연결된 구조이므로 과거형 sent가 알맞다. (C) allow는 to부정사를 목적격보어로 취한다.

[29~30]

> 운동을 하는 것은 여러분 신체의 건강을 유지하는 가장 중요한 방법들 중 하나이다. 운동을 할 때, 여러분은 뼈, 근육, 그리고 심장을 튼튼하게 한다. 여러분은 또한 과도한 지방을 연소시켜 균형을 향상하며 기분을 좋게 한다. 오늘날, 많은 사람들은 운동을 충분히 하지 않는다. 그들은 흔히 몇 시간 동안 텔레비전을 보거나, 비디오 게임을 하거나, 또는 인터넷을 한다. 이것이 여러분의 이야기처럼 들리는가? 만약 그렇다면, 이제 일어나서 움직일 시간이다! 축구를 하거나 춤을 추는 것은 모두 운동을 하는 훌륭한 방법이다. 건강을 유지하기 위해, 하루에 한 시간 정도의 운동을 하려고 노력하라. 그리고 한 번에 두 시간 이상 가만히 있지 않도록 노력하라.

29 건강을 유지하기 위해 운동을 하는 것이 중요하다는 내용이다.

30 ⓔ to부정사의 부정은 〈not＋to부정사〉 형태로 쓰므로, not to be inactive가 되어야 한다.

Part I 실력 다지기

Lesson 02 동명사

≫ Grammar Practice
pp. 32~35

A1 (1) ⓑ (2) ⓒ (3) ⓐ (4) ⓒ (5) ⓐ (6) ⓑ

A2 (1) not closing (2) winning
(3) Never making errors (4) Drinking

B1 (1) our(us) visiting (2) her succeeding
(3) my(me) sitting

C1 (1) shouting (2) getting (3) wearing (4) decorating
(5) arguing (6) playing (7) feeling (8) taking
(9) visiting (10) keeping

C2 (1) use trying (2) cry (3) On knowing
(4) like drinking

D1 (1) to lie (2) meeting (3) to go (4) to accept
(5) to undertake

D2 (1) to take → taking (2) coming → to come
(3) doing → to do

E1 (1) 동명사 (2) 동명사 (3) 동명사 (4) 현재분사

E2 (1) 저 날아가는 새를 봐.
(2) 엄마가 세탁기를 사셨다.
(3) 그녀는 울고 있는 아이를 돌보고 있다.

F1 (1) watching (2) getting (3) playing (4) walking
(5) buy

F2 swimming

≫ Grammar Test
pp. 36~37

01 (1) taking (2) cleaning (3) taking **02** ④ **03** for not arriving on time **04** ④ **05** reading **06** ⑤ **07** ③ **08** ④ **09** her winning **10** (1) finished studying math (2) wanted to go camping **11** ④ **12** ③ **13** ③ **14** ⑤

01 (1) feel like -ing: …하고 싶다 (2) spend＋시간＋(in) -ing: …하는 데 시간을 쓰다 (3) be worth -ing: …할 만한 가치가 있다

02 ④ want는 목적어로 to부정사를 취한다.

03 동명사의 부정은 동명사 앞에 not을 쓴다.

04 ④ put off는 목적어로 동명사를 취한다. (to meet → meeting)

05 enjoy는 동명사를 목적어로 취한다.

06 ⑤는 뒤에 있는 명사를 꾸미는 현재분사이고, 나머지는 동명사이다.

07 ③ look forward to -ing는 '…하는 것을 고대하다'라는 뜻이다.

08 give up은 동명사를, decide는 to부정사를 목적어로 취한다.

09 전치사 of 다음에는 동명사가 와야 하고, 동명사의 의미상 주어는 동명사 앞에 소유격이나 목적격으로 쓴다.

10 ⑴ finish는 동명사를 목적어로 취한다. ⑵ want는 to부정사를 목적어로 취한다.

11 ④ 전치사 at의 목적어인 동명사가 and로 연결된 병렬 구조이다. (write → writing)

12 ③ remember+동명사: …했던 것을 기억하다(과거) / remember+to부정사: …할 것을 기억하다(미래)

13 ③ try가 '…하려고 애쓰다'라는 의미로 쓰였으므로 to부정사가 알맞다. ① plant → planting(to plant) ② share → sharing ④ work → working ⑤ to see → seeing

14 〈보기〉의 complaining은 동사의 목적어로 쓰인 동명사이다. ⑤의 Discovering은 주어로 쓰인 동명사이고, 나머지는 명사를 꾸미는 현재분사이다.

>> Reading pp. 38~39

1 (A) buying (B) replacing   2 ⑤   3 ③   4 ⑤

[1~2]

우리가 사는 것을 구매하는 이유

여러분은 자신이 원하거나 필요로 하지도 않는 물건들을 왜 구매했는지 궁금해한 적이 있는가? 물건들을 구매하는 것에 관하여 무엇이 우리에게 영향을 주는지 생각해 보자.
나는 왜 코트를 구입한 후에 바지와 가방을 사는 걸까?
Lisa는 정말로 마음에 드는 코트를 산다. 즉시, 그녀는 자신의 바지가 새 코트와 어울리지 않는다는 것을 알아차린다. 그래서 그녀는 새 코트와 완벽하게 어울리는 새 바지를 산다. 하지만 그녀는 자신의 가방 중 어느 것도 새 옷과 어울리지

않는다는 것을 안다. 그래서 그녀는 새 가방을 산다. 그녀의 돈 대부분이 그녀의 새로운 모습을 완성하기 위한 새로운 물품을 사는 데 쓰인다.
무엇이 Lisa로 하여금 새 코트를 산 후 즉시 새로운 물품을 찾게 했을까? '디드로 효과'가 그것을 설명해 줄지도 모른다. 프랑스 작가인 Denis Diderot은 선물로 새 가운을 받았다. 그 선물을 받은 후에 곧 그는 자신의 모든 가구가 새 가운과 어울리지 않는다는 것을 알아차렸다. 그래서 그는 결국 대부분의 가구를 바꾸고 말았다. 그러므로 디드로 효과는 새로운 물품을 구입하는 것이 계획에 없던 더 많은 구매로 흔히 이어진다는 개념이다.

1 전치사 다음에는 동명사가 온다. end up -ing는 '결국 …하게 되다'라는 뜻이다.

2 ⑥ 문맥상 '디드로 효과'는 새로운 물품을 구매하는 것이 '계획에 없던' 구매로 이어진다는 개념이므로 planned를 unplanned로 써야 한다.

3

독일의 두 젊은이인 Jacob Grimm과 Wilhelm Grimm은 모험과 마술에 관한 전통 설화를 쓰는 것을 좋아했다. 그들의 이야기는 독일의 전통 생활양식과 믿음을 반영했다. 예를 들어, 중세 독일인들에게 숲은 위험한 장소였다. 그림 동화에서 마녀, 말하는 동물, 그리고 다른 마력을 지닌 존재들은 숲에 산다. 비록 그림 동화는 지금은 어린이들 이야기로 간주되지만, 그림 형제는 처음에는 주로 어른을 대상으로 이야기를 썼다. 많은 초기 이야기들은 어둡고 약간 무서웠다. 이후에 그림 형제는 많은 이야기들을 부드럽게 하고 그림도 추가했다. 이것이 이야기들을 어린이에게 보다 적절하도록 만들었다.

그림 형제의 이야기는 처음에는 어른을 대상으로 했지만, 나중에는 그림을 추가하고 이야기를 부드럽게 해서 어린이에게 적절한 이야기가 되었다는 내용이다.

4

옐로스톤공원을 운전해 지나간다고 상상해 보라. 당신은 길옆에서 곰 한 마리를 본다. 당신의 부모님은 (곰을) 더 가까이 보기 위해 자동차를 멈춘다. 당신이 눈을 깜빡하기도 전에, 곰은 자신의 코를 자동차 창문으로 넣는다. 곰은 당신의 소풍 도시락을 찾는 중이다. (C) 믿기 힘들겠지만, 인간과 곰 사이의 이러한 상호 작용은 흔했다. (B) 하지만 많은 곰들과 사람들이 이러한 근접성으로 인해 다치게 되자 상황은 바뀌었다. (A) 사람들과 곰들이 서로 너무 가까이 있는 것을 막기 위해, 사람들은 곰에게 먹이를 주는 것이 금지되었고 곰에게서 최소 91미터 떨어져 있어야 한다.

(C) 옐로스톤공원에서 인간과 곰 사이의 상호 작용은 흔했는데 (B) 이러한 근접성으로 인해 많은 곰들과 사람들이 다치면서 상황은 바뀌었고 (A) 곰과 사람이 서로 너무 가까이 있는 것을 막기 위해 여러 규칙이 생겼다는 흐름이 자연스럽다.

1 ⑤ **2** ② **3** ③ **4** ④ **5** ④ **6** ③

1 I'm looking forward to ....는 '나는 …을 몹시 기대하고 있다.'라는 뜻으로 기대를 나타내는 표현이다.

2 ②는 기쁨을 나타내는 표현이고, 나머지는 상대방이 잘되기를 기원할 때 쓰는 표현이다.

3 오랜만에 해변에 함께 가기로 했으므로 해변을 보는 것이 기대된다는 ③이 알맞다.

4 B가 A에게 행운을 빌어 주고 있으므로, A에는 중요한 일을 앞두고 있음을 표현하는 내용이 들어가야 한다.

5 I can't wait to ....는 기대를 표현하며, I'm looking forward to ....와 바꿔 쓸 수 있다.

6 (B) 너 걱정스러워 보인다. – (C) 응. 나는 내일 자전거 경주가 있어. – (A) 그냥 최선을 다해. 내가 너를 위해 행운을 빌게. – (D) 고마워.

1 can't wait to watch the movie **2** (1) Finding(To find)
(2) not forgetting (3) learning **3** Going(To go) fishing
4 (1) watching movies (2) walking(to walk) the dog
5 (1) to exercise (2) eating fast food (3) writing on
(4) to drink

1 기대를 표현할 때는 I can't wait to ....를 쓴다.

2 (1) 문장의 주어 자리이므로 동명사나 to부정사를 써야 한다. (2), (3) 전치사의 목적어로 동명사를 쓴다. 동명사의 부정은 동명사 앞에 not을 붙인다.

3 go fishing이 주어 자리에 올 경우 동명사 또는 to부정사로 쓴다.

4 (1) enjoy는 동명사를 목적어로 취한다. (2) like는 동명사와 to부정사 모두 목적어로 취한다.

5 (1) plan은 to부정사를 목적어로 취한다. (2) 〈stop+동명사〉: …하는 것을 멈추다 (3) 전치사 뒤에는 동명사가 목적어로 온다. (4) 〈try+to부정사〉: …하려고 애쓰다

01 ⑤ **02** (1) buy (2) match (3) realize **03** ④ **04** looking forward to **05** ⑤ **06** fingers crossed **07** hope to write a book **08** ③ **09** ⑤ **10** ⑤ **11** ⑤ **12** playing **13** grow → growing **14** having not → not having **15** ③ **16** ④ **17** (1) his coming (2) to give (3) answering **18** ① **19** ② **20** ⑤ **21** tried making cookies **22** ② **23** ⑤ **24** ④ **25** ⑤ **26** ④ **27** ③ **28** ④ **29** ⑤ **30** ③

01 ⑤ '다르게 되다'는 change(변하다)에 대한 설명이다. replace는 '교체하다, 바꾸다'라는 뜻이다.

02 (1) buy: 사다 (2) match: 어울리다 (3) realize: 깨닫다, 알아차리다

03 ④ 독도에 가 본 적이 있는지 묻는 질문에 독도에 가는 것이 기대된다고 답하는 것은 어색하다.

04 I'm looking forward to ....로 기대를 표현할 수 있다.

05 빈칸에는 희망을 표현하는 말이 알맞다.

06 누군가의 행운을 함께 기원하자고 할 때는 Let's keep our fingers crossed for ....를 쓸 수 있다.

07 I hope to ....로 희망이나 기대를 나타낼 수 있다.

08 중요한 시험이 있어서 걱정스러운 표정을 하고 있는 B에게 A가 최선을 다하라는 격려와 함께 할 말로는 행운을 기원하는 말이 알맞다.

09 동사가 주어로 쓰이려면 동명사 또는 to부정사의 형태로 바꿔야 하므로 Traveling이나 To travel을 써야 한다.

10 • consider는 동명사를 목적어로 취한다.
• keep ... from -ing: …가 …하지 못하게 하다

11 ⑤ coming은 전치사 to의 목적어로 쓰인 동명사이고, 나머지는 앞이나 뒤에 있는 명사를 꾸미는 현재분사이다.

12 의미상 '…하는 것을 멈추다'가 되어야 하므로 stop 다음에 동명사가 와야 한다.

13 전치사 in의 목적어로 동명사가 온다.

14 동명사의 부정은 동명사 앞에 not을 쓴다. 동명사가 주절보다 앞선 시제를 나타낼 때 완료동명사(having+과거분사)를 쓴다.

15 ③ want는 to부정사를 목적어로 취한다.

16 동명사의 의미상 주어는 소유격 또는 목적격으로 나타낸다.

17 (1) 전치사의 목적어 자리이므로 동명사 형태가 알맞고, 동명사의 의미상 주어는 소유격이나 목적격을 쓴다. (2) promise는 to부정사를 목적어로 취한다. (3) avoid는 동명사를 목적어로 취한다.

18 ① feel like -ing: …하고 싶다 (to have → having)

19 〈보기〉의 dancing은 앞에 있는 명사 girl을 꾸미는 현재분사이다. ②의 wearing도 앞에 있는 명사 man을 꾸미는 현

재분사이다. ① 동사의 목적어로 쓰인 동명사 ③ 전치사의 목적어로 쓰인 동명사 ④, ⑤ 주어로 쓰인 동명사

20 ⑤ feel like -ing는 '…하고 싶다'는 뜻으로 〈would like to＋동사원형〉으로 바꿔 쓸 수 있다.

21 '시험 삼아 해 보다'라는 의미를 나타낼 때는 try 다음에 동명사를 쓴다.

22 과거에 했던 일이 기억나지 않는다는 의미이므로 remember 다음에 동명사가 와야 한다.

23 ① '…하는 데 익숙하다'라는 의미가 되어야 하므로 be used to -ing 형태가 알맞다. (eat → eating) ② started의 목적어로 동명사나 to부정사가 와야 한다. (set → setting(to set)) ③ want는 to부정사를 목적어로 취한다. (having → to have) ④ cannot help -ing는 '…하지 않을 수 없다'의 의미이다. (to go → going)

24 ④ spend＋시간(돈)＋(in) -ing: …하는 데 시간(돈)을 쓰다 (collect → collecting)

25
> 동물들에게 지진에 대한 '육감'이 있을까? 어떤 과학자들은 동물들이 지진이 발생하기 전에 약한 진동을 느낄 것이라고 생각한다. 다른 과학자들은 동물들이 지하 암석들이 움직이면서 생기는 전기적 신호를 감지할 것이라고 생각한다. 사람들의 보고에 따르면, 중국의 2008년 5월 지진 전에 일부 동물들이 이상 행동을 보였다고 한다. 코끼리는 코를 거칠게 흔들었다. 공작은 꽥꽥 소리를 냈다. 몇몇 판다는 주변을 돌아다니기 시작했다.

동물들은 육감을 발휘하여 지진을 감지할 수 있다는 내용이다.

26
> 당신은 큰 시험 전에 조용히 앉아 있는 것이 두뇌를 압박감에 대비하게 한다고 생각할지도 모른다. 틀렸다! Beilock의 실험에서, 조용히 앉아 있는 것은 시험에 대한 걱정과 결과에 대한 의심으로 이어졌다. 이 스트레스는 비판적 사고를 더 어렵게 만들었다. 그녀의 해결책은 매 시험 전에 최소 10분을 당신의 생각이나 감정을 적는 데 쓰는 것이다. 스트레스가 심한 시험을 보기 전에 (자신의 감정을) 썼던 참가자들은 훨씬 더 쉬운 시험에서의 성적보다 평균 5퍼센트 더 높은 성적을 받게 되었다.

(A) 시험 전에 조용히 앉아 있는 것은 스트레스를 유발하고 이 스트레스는 비판적 사고를 '어렵게' 만들었다. (B) 시험 전에 자신의 감정을 '쓰는' 것이 좋은 성적을 받는 데 도움이 되었다.

[27~28]
> 최근의 한 연구에 따르면, 사람이 걸어 다니고 그 후에 곧 창의적인 사고가 증진된다고 한다. 연구는 실내와 실외에서 걷는 것이 비슷하게 창의적 영감을 끌어올린다는 것을 알아냈

다. 환경이 아닌 걷는 것 자체가 주된 요소였다. 걷는 사람들의 창의성 수준이 앉아 있는 사람들에 비해 현저히 높았다. 영국에서 학교들은 Daily Mile이라 불리는 새로운 운동의 일원이 되기 위해 가입을 하고 있다. 목표는 각 학교의 모든 학생들이 매일 수업 시작 전 최소 15분 동안 달리거나 걷게 하는 것이다. 이것은 학생들이 학문적, 사회적 성공을 이루는 데 도움이 될 것이다.

27 ⓒ 걷는 사람들의 창의성이 앉아 있는 사람들보다 더 높았다는 내용이 되어야 하므로 lower를 higher로 써야 한다.

28 위 글의 walking은 that절에서 주어 역할을 하는 동명사로 쓰였다. ③의 walking은 '걷고 있는'이라는 뜻으로 앞에 나온 A man을 꾸미는 현재분사로 쓰였고, 나머지는 모두 동명사로 쓰였다.

[29~30]
> 자금성은 황제들의 집으로서 역할을 했고, 종교적, 공식적 행사를 위한 장소로 쓰였다. 몇 세기 동안, 오직 황제의 가족과 관리들만 자금성에 들어갈 수 있었다. 1925년에 개방한 이후로, 수천 명의 방문객들이 자금성의 문을 드나들어 왔다. 그들은 자금성의 역사적 중요성뿐만 아니라 거대한 크기와 엄청난 건축물 때문에 그곳을 방문한다. 그곳은 또한 거의 5만 점의 그림, 32만 개의 도자기 등으로 이루어진 놀라운 황제의 보물들을 보유하고 있다.

29 ⓔ 뒤에 있는 imperial treasures를 꾸미는 현재분사 astonishing이 되어야 한다. 전체 문장의 동사는 houses이다.

30 ③ 1925년에 일반인들에게 개방되었다. 재건축에 관한 내용은 언급되지 않았다.

Lesson 03 시제

>> Grammar Practice
pp. 52~55

A1 (1) ⓑ (2) ⓒ (3) ⓓ (4) ⓐ (5) ⓑ (6) ⓒ

A2 (1) has gone (2) have lived

A3 (1) have you been → did you go
(2) experienced never → never experienced
(3) be → been (4) seeing → seen

B1 (1) been (2) have not (3) has been showing
(4) for (5) has been working (6) been writing
(7) have been studying

B2 (1) has been studying (2) have, been holding
(3) has not been taking

C1 (1) had (2) had behaved (3) had fixed
(4) had turned

C2 (1) had (2) had (3) lent

C3 (1) had broken (2) had studied (3) had, left

D1 (1) had (2) had (3) had (4) had been supporting

D2 (1) had been playing basketball
(2) that she had been crying
(3) had been learning German before

D3 (1) had been reading (2) had been writing
(3) had been living

>> Grammar Test
pp. 56~57

01 ③ **02** ③ **03** ⑤ **04** has been **05** (1) were
(2) have known **06** ④ **07** ④ **08** had eaten, arrived
09 ④ **10** ② **11** have → had **12** (1) have been to the
restaurant twice (2) How long have you known **13** ②
14 ③

01 현재완료는 last weekend처럼 명백한 과거를 나타내는 부사구와 함께 쓸 수 없다.

02 우리가 그곳에 도착한 것은 과거이고, 그가 떠난 것은 더 이전의 일이므로 과거완료를 써야 한다.

03 〈보기〉는 '나는 중학생 때부터 Brown 씨를 알아 왔다'라는 의미로 현재완료의 계속을 나타낸다. ①, ③ 경험 ② 완료 ④ 결과 ⑤ 계속

04 그녀가 지난달에 유럽에 갔다가 돌아왔고 지금은 한국에 있으므로, 현재완료의 경험 용법인 〈have(has) been to(…에 가 본 적이 있다)〉를 쓰는 것이 적절하다.

05 (1) '4학년 때 같은 반이었다'라는 내용이므로 과거시제로 써야 한다. (2) '그때 이후로 계속 그를 알아 왔다'라는 의미이므로 계속의 의미를 나타내는 현재완료가 알맞다.

06 Jake는 20분 전에 지하철을 기다리고 있었고 아직도 기다리고 있다는 의미이므로 빈칸에는 현재완료진행형이 알맞다.

07 ④는 결과를 나타내는 현재완료이고, 나머지는 경험을 나타낸다.

08 내가 집에 도착한 것은 과거시제로, 엄마가 저녁을 드신 것은 그 이전의 일이므로 과거완료로 쓴다.

09 친구를 기다린 것이 화가 난 것보다 더 이전의 일이므로 과거완료를 쓴다.

10 ② 의문사 when은 현재완료와 함께 쓸 수 없으므로 When did the girl leave Seoul?로 써야 한다.

11 교수님을 만난 것은 과거이고, 상대방이 그 교수님에 대해 이야기한 것은 더 이전의 일이므로 과거완료로 써야 한다.

12 (1) 현재완료는 〈have(has)+과거분사〉 형태로 쓴다. (2) 의문사가 있을 때 현재완료의 의문문은 〈의문사+have(has)+주어+과거분사 …?〉로 쓴다.

13 ② 그녀가 자고 있었던 것이 더 먼저 일어난 일이므로 과거완료진행형(had+been+-ing)으로 써야 한다. (has → had)

14 두 사람은 지난 일요일, 즉 특정한 과거 시점에 한 일에 대해서 대화를 나누고 있으므로, ③은 과거시제가 되어야 한다. (have studied → studied)

>> Reading
pp. 58~59

1 ① **2** ③ **3** ⑤ **4** ④

[1~2]

내 눈에 비친 세계
Lin Wang, 생태학자
Tsingy, 마다가스카르의 석림
나는 식물과 동물을 연구하기 위해서 20년 이상 동안 마다가스카르의 석림을 방문하고 있다. 이 지역의 뾰족한 돌들은 진정한 자연의 놀라움이다. 이 놀라운 모양은 비에 의해서 만들어져 왔다. 오랜 기간 동안 비가 돌을 침식해 돌을 날카롭고 뾰족하게 만들어 왔다. 그 환경은 동물들이 살기에 험난하지만, 그들은 생존할 방법들을 찾아냈다. 예를 들어, 마다가스카르에서만 사는 여우원숭이는 한 개의 돌탑에서 다른 돌탑으로 뛸 수 있도록 도와주는 개구리와 같은 다리를 가지고 있

다. 나에게 석림은 깜짝 장난감 상자와 같다. 그것은 늘 나를 놀라게 하고 정신을 바짝 차리게 한다!

1 ⓐ 과거에 시작해서 현재에도 계속하고 있는 일을 표현할 때는 현재완료진행형(have+been+-ing)을 쓴다. (visited → visiting)

2 ① Tsingy는 마다가스카르에 있는 석림이다. ② 비에 의해 돌이 침식되었다. ④ Tsingy는 동물들이 살기에 험난한 환경이다. ⑤ 여우원숭이는 마다가스카르에서만 산다.

3   열 살짜리 영국 여학생인 Tilly Smith는 태국의 해변에서 가족들과 휴식을 취하고 있었다. 갑자기, Tilly는 이상한 것을 느꼈다. 바다가 거품이 이는 것처럼 보였다. 또한, 물은 해변에서 반대쪽으로 흐르고 있었다. 많은 사람들이 물이 덮이지 않은 모래 위로 걸어가서 물고기와 조개를 모았다. 하지만 Tilly는 2주 전에 학교에서 배웠던 것을 기억했다. 그녀는 이상한 현상이 쓰나미의 징조라는 것을 알아차렸다. Tilly는 가족들에게 더 높은 지대로 달리라고 소리쳤다. 그녀와 그녀의 부모님은 다른 사람들에게 해변을 떠나라고 경고했다. 그 가족은 쓰나미가 들이닥칠 때, 호텔의 3층으로 달려갔다. 그들은 창문으로 지켜보았다. 재빠르게 기지를 발휘한 여학생이 약 백 명의 생명을 구했다.

가족뿐만 아니라 해변에 있던 사람들의 목숨을 구했다.

4   과학자들은 재생이 불가능한 화석 연료를 물, 바람, 그리고 태양 에너지와 같은 재생 가능한 자원들로 대체할 방법을 검토하고 있다. 이러한 자원들은 대체되거나 재사용될 수 있어서 고갈되지 않을 것이다. 수력 전기는 재생 가능한 자원의 한 예이다. 그것은 낙수 또는 유수의 에너지에서 생산되어 왔다. (우리의 태양 에너지 연구는 여전히 초기 단계이다.) 수력 전기는 직접적인 폐기물을 생산하지 않으며, 화석 연료에 의해 가동되는 에너지 발전소보다 온실 가스를 덜 발생시킨다.

대체에너지의 예로 수력 전기에 대해 이야기하고 있는데, ⓓ는 태양 에너지에 대한 내용이다.

1 ⑤   2 ④   3 ③   4 makes, sad   5 ④   6 ②

1 A가 수학 시험을 통과했다고 했으므로 빈칸에는 기쁨을 나타내는 표현이 알맞다.

2 ④는 망각을 표현하는 문장이고, 나머지는 알고 있음을 표현하는 문장이다.

3 B의 대답으로 보아 Have you heard about ...?으로 알고 있는지 묻는 표현이 알맞다.

4 That makes me sad.로 슬픔을 표현할 수 있다.

5 I've heard that ....은 알고 있음을 표현하는 말로, I've been told that ....으로 바꿔 쓸 수 있다.

6 (B) 무슨 일 있어, Michael? – (A) 나 드디어 학교 야구팀에 들어갔어! – (C) 와, 잘됐다! 그 말을 들으니 정말 기뻐! – (D) 고마워.

1 I have heard that the shooting stars will peak around 10 p.m.   **2** (1) had already explained (2) found (3) had risen   **3** (1) has been sick since (2) has been writing a novel for (3) has been working for a bank since   **4** has rained   **5** (1) have just ordered (2) have already decorated the classroom (3) have not(haven't) written the thank you card yet (4) have you cleaned

1 누군가에게 듣거나 정보를 읽어 알고 있음을 표현할 때는 I have heard that ....을 써서 나타낸다.

2 (1), (3) 과거의 어느 시점보다 더 앞서 일어난 일이 그 시점까지 영향을 미칠 때 과거완료(had+과거분사)를 쓴다. (2) 특정 과거 시점을 나타내는 yesterday와 같은 부사는 과거시제와 함께 쓴다.

3 현재완료는 〈have(has)+과거분사〉, 현재완료진행형은 〈have(has)+been+-ing〉 형태로 나타낸다. since는 과거의 특정 시점을 나타내는 말과, for는 일정 기간과 함께 쓰인다.

4 3일 동안 비가 계속 오고 있으므로, 계속의 의미를 나타내는 현재완료로 쓰는 것이 알맞다.

5 현재완료는 〈have(has)+과거분사〉의 형태로, 과거에 일어난 일이 현재까지 영향을 미치고 있을 때 쓴다. 현재완료의 부정문은 〈have(has)+not+과거분사〉, 의문문은 〈Have(Has)+주어+과거분사 …?〉로 쓴다.

01 ③ **02** ⑤ **03** ③ **04** glad(happy) to hear **05** ④
06 ④ **07** (D) → (A) → (B) → (C) **08** ④ **09** ④
10 has learned → learned **11** ④ **12** ⑤ **13** ②
14 had broken **15** for, since **16** ④ **17** ⑤ **18** hasn't
(has not) booked **19** ② **20** has been talking **21** ④
22 ⑤ **23** (1) ⓒ (2) ⓑ (3) ⓐ **24** ① **25** ⑤ **26** ④
27 ② **28** ② **29** Vertical farms **30** ⓐ been ⓑ been

01 ③은 동사 – 명사 관계이고, 나머지는 명사 – 형용사 관계이다.

02 '시작과 끝이 있는 특정한 기간'은 period(기간)의 영영풀이이다.

03 알고 있는지 묻고 답하는 대화이므로 빈칸에는 know가 알맞다.

04 기쁨을 표현할 때는 I'm glad(happy) to hear that. 등을 쓴다.

05 알고 있음을 표현할 때는 I've heard of ....로 할 수 있다.

06 A가 1등상을 받았다고 했으므로, 잘했다고 하며 기쁨을 표현하는 것이 알맞다.

07 (D) 나 때문에 축구 시합에서 졌어. – (A) 기분 풀어. 누구나 질 수 있잖아. – (B) 하지만 내가 큰 실수를 했어. 그게 나를 슬프게 해. – (C) 기운 내. 내일은 나아질 거야.

08 과거(열 살 때)부터 현재까지 계속 영어를 배우고 있다는 의미이므로 현재완료를 써야 한다.

09 Tony가 책을 사준 것은 내가 그것을 잃어버린 것보다 먼저 일어난 일이므로 과거완료가 알맞다.

10 명백한 과거를 나타내는 부사(yesterday)는 현재완료와 함께 쓸 수 없고, 과거시제와 함께 쓰인다.

11 10년 전에 캘리포니아로 이사하여 계속 그곳에 살고 있는 중이라는 의미이므로 현재완료진행형을 써야 한다.

12 ⟨have(has) gone to⟩는 '…에 가고 없다'라는 결과의 의미를 나타내고, '…에 가 본 적이 있다'라는 경험의 의미를 나타낼 때는 ⟨have(has) been to⟩로 쓴다.

13 ②는 경험을 나타내고, 나머지는 계속을 나타내는 현재완료로 쓰였다.

14 팔이 부러진 것이 목욕을 할 수 없었던 것보다 먼저 일어난 일이므로 과거완료로 써야 한다.

15 현재완료의 계속 용법으로 for(…동안)는 기간과 함께 쓰이고, since(…이후로)는 과거의 특정 시점을 나타내는 말과 함께 쓰인다.

16 기차가 떠난 것이 먼저 일어난 일이므로 과거완료를 쓴다.

17 전화벨이 울렸던 과거 시점보다 앞서 Jason이 자기 시작해서 그때까지 자고 있었던 동작을 나타내므로 ⟨had+been+-ing⟩ 형태의 과거완료진행형이 알맞다.

18 현재 시점을 기준으로 아직 호텔을 예약하지 못한 것이므로, ⟨have(has)+과거분사⟩ 형태의 현재완료시제로 써야 한다. 현재완료의 부정은 ⟨have(has)+not+과거분사⟩로 나타낸다.

19 ⟨보기⟩와 ②는 계속을 나타낸다. ①, ④ 완료 ③, ⑤ 경험

20 한 시간 전부터 지금까지 통화를 하고 있으므로 현재완료진행형으로 써야 한다.

21 열 살이 되었을 때인 과거 시점이 기준이고 그때까지 바다를 본 경험이 없었음을 나타내므로 과거완료로 써야 한다.

22 ·과거를 나타내는 부사구 last night으로 보아 과거시제가 알맞다. / ·'2시 이후로 계속 체스를 두고 있다'는 의미이므로 현재완료진행형이 알맞다.

23 (1) '일주일 동안 계속 아팠다'는 계속의 의미이다. (2) '어렸을 때 한 번 가 본 적이 있다'는 경험의 의미이다. (3) '기차가 이미 떠났다'는 완료의 의미이다.

24 ① 인형을 잃어버린 것은 그 사실을 알았던 것보다 먼저 일어난 일이므로 과거완료를 쓴다. (has → had)

25
> 사람들은 수 세기 동안 토핑을 올려 구운 빵인 피자와 같은 음식을 먹고 있다. 하지만 토마토소스, 모차렐라치즈, 그리고 바질을 얹은 오늘날 우리가 아주 흔히 보는 피자에는 알려진 이야기가 하나 있다. 1899년에, 이탈리아의 움베르토 왕과 마르게리타 여왕은 나폴리에 있는 한 식당에 방문해서 세 가지 특별한 피자를 먹었다. 여왕은 빨간색, 흰색, 그리고 녹색이 있는 피자가 가장 마음에 든다고 말했는데, 그것이 그녀에게 이탈리아 국기를 떠올리게 했기 때문이었다. 이것이 마르게리타피자가 탄생하게 된 과정이다.

마르게리타피자가 어떻게 탄생하게 되었는지에 대한 내용이다.

26
> 매년 3만 명이 넘는 사람들이 교통사고로 죽고, 더 많은 사람들이 부상으로 고통을 받는다. 좋은 소식은 1990년 이후로, 자동차 사고 사망자의 수가 20퍼센트 이상 떨어지고 있다는 것이다. 이것은 부분적으로는 유아용 안전 의자, 에어백, 안전벨트 법규, 그리고 운전 중 휴대전화 금지법 덕분이다. 그리고 새로운 전자 장비의 혁신이 자동차를 더 안전하게 만들 것이다. 어떤 자동차 디자이너들은 심지어 충돌 없는 자동차에 대해 논의하고 있다.

다양한 기술의 발전이 자동차를 안전하게 만들었고, 자동차 사고율을 떨어지게 했다는 내용이다.

[27~28]

> 올림픽 경기 역사를 통틀어서 유명한 챔피언들이 많이 있어 왔다. 하지만 가장 유명하고 성공한 올림픽 선수들 중 한 명은 Milo라는 힘이 센 이탈리아 사람이었다. Milo는 레슬링 경기에서 다섯 번 우승했다. 이는 그가 20년 이상 챔피언이

었음을 의미한다! Milo의 힘은 유명했다. 때때로 그는 한 손을 뻗어 누군가에게 자신의 손가락을 움직일 것을 요구했다. 아무도 그의 가장 작은 손가락조차 움직이지 못했다. 어느 전설에서, 그는 건물이 무너지고 있을 때 지붕을 받쳐 들어서 친구들을 지켰다. 그는 모든 친구들이 안전하게 빠져나올 때까지 (지붕을) 붙잡고 있었다.

27 역사상 가장 유명한 올림픽 챔피언들 중 한 명이자 힘이 아주 셌던 Milo에 대한 이야기이다.

28 (A) '유명한 챔피언들이 많이 있어 왔다'라는 뜻으로 현재완료(have+과거분사) 형태가 알맞다. (B) 조동사 would 다음에 hold out과 병렬로 연결된 형태로 challenge가 알맞다. (C) 친구들이 빠져나온 것이 더 먼저 일어난 일이므로 과거완료를 쓴다.

[29~30]

대도시에서 지역 농장으로부터 나온 신선한 음식을 얻기란 어려울 수 있다. 가능한 해결책은 있다. 농사를 위로 짓는 것이다. 몇몇 건축가들과 과학자들은 사람들이 고층 건물에 수직 농장을 짓도록 독려하고 있다. '하늘 농장'은 도시에 이상적인데, 그것이 전통 농장의 땅의 일부분을 이용하기 때문이다. 이러한 농장은 실내에 있기 때문에 허리케인, 가뭄, 홍수에 의해 피해를 입지 않는다. 몇몇 수직 농장은 한국, 미국, 네덜란드와 같은 곳에서 이미 실행 중에 있다. 컬럼비아 대학의 교수인 Dickson Despommier는 "높은 건물에서의 농업은 우리가 도시에서 먹고 사는 방식을 곧 혁신적으로 바꿀 것"이라고 말한다.

29 Sky farms는 문맥상 Vertical farms(수직 농장)와 바꿔 쓸 수 있다.

30 ⓐ와 ⓑ는 각각 현재완료진행형(have+been+-ing)과 현재완료(have+과거분사)가 쓰인 형태이다.

Lesson 04   관계사

▶▶ Grammar Practice
pp. 72~75

A1 (1) who (2) which (3) what (4) that (5) that (6) whose
A2 (1) who(that) (2) whose (3) which(that)
B1 (1) 그녀는 아들이 있는데, 그는 영국에서 공부한다.
(2) 그녀는 영국에서 공부하는 아들이 있다.
B2 (1) and he (2) but he (3) for it
C1 (1) which (2) which was (3) which was (4) whom
(5) who is
C2 (1) ○ (2) × (3) ×
D1 (1) where (2) why (3) when (4) where (5) why
D2 (1) where (2) why (3) when
D3 (1) the way(how) / the way in which
(2) where(in which)
E1 (1) whenever (2) Wherever (3) Whenever
(4) whatever (5) however
E2 (1) Whatever (2) Whoever (3) Wherever
(4) However

▶▶ Grammar Test
pp. 76~77

01 (1) who (2) when (3) whose **02** ② **03** ④ **04** whose
05 ③ **06** ④ **07** ④ **08** ③ **09** ① **10** ③ **11** whom
Jia likes the most is my uncle **12** (1) No matter how
cold (2) whoever brings me **13** ② **14** ②

01 (1) 선행사가 사람이고 주격이 와야 하므로 who가 알맞다.
(2) 때를 나타내는 관계부사 when이 알맞다. (3) 바로 뒤에 top(정상)이라는 명사가 이어지므로 소유격 관계대명사인 whose가 알맞다.
02 선행사가 사람(a singer)이고 빈칸은 관계대명사절의 목적어 자리이므로 목적격 whom이 알맞다.
03 선행사에 all이 포함된 경우 관계대명사 that을 주로 쓴다.
04 소유를 표현할 때는 관계대명사 whose를 쓴다.
05 목적격 관계대명사 which는 생략할 수 있다.
06 선행사가 동물이고 계속적 용법이므로 관계대명사 which가 알맞다. 관계대명사 that은 계속적 용법으로 쓸 수 없다.
07 ④ '…하는 것은 무엇이든지'의 뜻으로 명사절을 이끄는 Whatever가 알맞다.
08 • 선행사를 포함하는 관계대명사 what이 알맞다.
• 선행사 the reason에는 이유의 관계부사 why 또는 for which가 알맞다.

09 ① 목적격 관계대명사가 생략된 형태이다. try on은 '…을 입어 보다'라는 뜻이다.

10 〈보기〉와 ③의 what은 선행사를 포함하는 관계대명사로 명사절을 이끌며 '…하는 것'이라는 뜻이고, 나머지는 모두 '무엇'으로 해석하는 의문사로 쓰였다.

11 whom이 이끄는 목적격 관계대명사절이 주어인 The guitarist를 꾸미는 구조이다.

12 (1) 양보의 부사절을 이끄는 However는 No matter how와 바꿔 쓸 수 있다. (2) anyone who는 명사절을 이끄는 whoever와 바꿔 쓸 수 있다.

13 ① the way와 how는 같이 쓸 수 없고 둘 중 하나만 써야 한다. (the way how → the way(how) / the way in which) ③ 선행사가 the house이므로 관계부사 where 또는 in which가 와야 한다. (which → where(in which)) ④ 선행사가 the reason일 때는 관계부사 why 또는 for which가 와야 한다. (in which → why(for which)) ⑤ 선행사 the drawer가 장소를 나타내므로 관계부사 where 또는 in which가 와야 한다. (when → where(in which))

14 ② that은 주격 관계대명사이므로 생략할 수 없다. ①, ③ 목적격 관계대명사로 생략할 수 있다. ④, ⑤ 분사 앞의 〈주격 관계대명사+be동사〉이므로 생략할 수 있다.

>> Reading
pp. 78~79

1 ③ **2** ④ **3** ② **4** ②

[1~2]

> 당신의 마음을 효과적으로 말하라!
> 오늘 우리는 자신을 효과적으로 표현하기 위해 적절한 의사소통 기술을 쓰는 것에 대해 이야기할 것입니다.
> Brian에 대한 동영상으로 시작해 봅시다. Brian이 남동생과 이야기하려고 할 때, 그는 항상 남동생과 말다툼을 하게 됩니다. 그에게 이런 문제가 있는 이유를 알아봅시다.
> "너 또 내 이어폰 잃어버렸지. 너는 왜 그렇게 조심성이 없니?"
> Brian은 자신의 감정을 표현하기 위해 '너'로 문장을 시작하고 있습니다. <u>대신에</u>, 그는 '나 메시지'를 써야 합니다. '나'로 시작하는 것은 그가 남동생을 비난하기보다는 자신이 느끼거나 생각하는 것에 집중하도록 도울 수 있습니다. 우리 자신을 표현하는 방식에서의 작은 변화는 의사소통 문제를 해결하거나 심지어 막을 수도 있습니다.
> "내가 가장 좋아하는 이어폰이 없어져서 난 정말 속상해."

1 (A) 이유를 나타내는 선행사 the reason으로 보아 관계부사 why가 알맞다. (B) 선행사를 포함하는 관계대명사 what이 알맞다.

2 자신의 감정을 표현할 때 '너'로 문장을 시작하는 것 대신에 '나 메시지'를 써야 한다는 내용이다. Instead는 '대신에'라는 뜻이다.

3
> 화산은 막대한 힘을 지니고 있다. 화산은 엄청난 파괴와 죽음을 야기할 수 있다. 하지만 화산이 많은 측면에서 유용할 수 있다. 화산재는 식물이 자라는 데 도움이 되는 무기질을 많이 함유하고 있다. 재는 토양과 섞여 식물에게 비옥한 땅을 만든다. 또한 화산 아래에 지구의 열기는 지하수가 끓도록 만든다. 뜨거운 물과 증기는 지표면까지 올라온다. 이것이 온천을 만들어낸다. 뜨거운 물과 증기는 또한 집을 데우고 전기를 생산하는 데 쓰일 수 있다. 땅속에서 올라오는 증기는 거대한 터빈을 돌리는 데 쓰인다. 이것은 오염을 거의 일으키지 않으며 세계 전기의 소량을 생산하지만 그 비율이 점차 늘고 있다.

화산이 주는 이점에 대한 내용이다.

4
> 우리는 눈꺼풀에 대해 많은 관심을 기울이지 않지만, 눈꺼풀은 많은 기능을 한다. 눈꺼풀은 우리 눈을 촉촉하게 유지하고 먼지와 티끌을 내보낸다. 물고기와 뱀과 같은 동물들은 눈꺼풀이 아예 없다. 그것은 눈이 항상 젖어 있는 물고기에게는 괜찮다. 하지만 뱀은 눈꺼풀 없이 어떻게 잠을 잘까? 뱀은 눈을 뜬 채 잠을 잔다. 뱀의 뇌는 잠들기 위해 기능을 멈출 수 있다. 반면에, 낙타는 완전히 운이 좋다. 한쪽 눈에 눈꺼풀이 세 개 있다. 그 중 하나는 투명해서 낙타는 사막 모래바람이 부는 동안 그것을 통해 볼 수 있다. 하지만 눈싸움에서는 뱀과 물고기가 이길 것이다.

눈싸움을 한다면, 물고기와 뱀은 눈꺼풀이 없어서 눈을 감을 필요가 없으므로 눈꺼풀이 세 개나 되는 낙타를 이길 것이다.

>> Expression Test
pp. 80~81

1 ④ **2** ② **3** ④ **4** ④ **5** ④ **6** ⑤

1 ④는 '너는 그것을 기억하니?'라는 뜻으로 기억 여부를 묻는 표현이고, 나머지는 '이해하겠니?'의 뜻으로 이해를 점검하는 표현이다.

2 B가 긍정의 답을 하고 나서, 그림 그리는 것을 좋아한다고 말하는 것으로 보아, A의 말이 '너는 그림 그리는 것을 정말 좋아하는 것 같아.'의 의미가 되도록 It seems (to me) that .... 표현이 알맞다.

3 Do you know what I mean?은 자신이 말한 것을 상대방이 이해했는지를 점검하는 표현이다. ④ Do you see that?은 '너는 그게 보이니?'라는 의미이다.

4 In my opinion, ...은 자신의 의견을 말할 때 쓰는 표현이다.

5 A가 Peter의 파티에 대해 비밀로 하자고 했는데, B가 잘못 알아들은 상황이다. 오해를 지적해 줄 때 That's not what I meant.를 쓸 수 있다.

6 (C) 너 영화 〈어린왕자〉 봤니? – (B) 물론이지. 나는 지난주에 그것을 봤어. – (A) 너는 그 영화를 어떻게 생각했니? – (D) 음, 나에게는 약간 지루했어.

▶▶ 서술형 평가
p. 82

1 That's not what I meant. **2** (1) who(that) is sitting on the bench (2) which(that) is beautiful (3) which(that) her teacher recommended **3** (1) where (2) how (3) when **4** (1) whenever you want to talk to me (2) wherever you are (3) choose whoever practices hard **5** (1) who (whom/that) you met at the party (2) a friend whose uncle was a famous singer (3) the cartoon character which(that) I like best

1 오해를 지적해 줄 때는 That's not what I meant.라고 말한다.

2 (1) 선행사가 사람이고 주격이 필요하므로 who(that)를 이용한다. (2) 선행사가 사물이고 주격이 필요하므로 which(that)를 이용한다. (3) 선행사가 사물이고 목적격이 필요하므로 which(that)를 이용한다.

3 (1) 선행사가 장소이므로 관계부사 where (2) 방법에 관한 것이므로 관계부사 how (3) 선행사가 시간이므로 관계부사 when

4 (1) whenever는 '…할 때는 언제나'라는 의미로 시간의 부사절을 이끈다. (2) wherever는 '…하는 곳은 어디든지'라는 의미로 장소의 부사절을 이끈다. (3) whoever는 '…하는 사람은 누구든지'라는 의미로 명사절을 이끈다.

5 (1) 선행사가 사람이고 목적격이 필요하므로 who(whom/that)를 이용한다. (2) 소유를 표현할 때는 whose를 쓴다. (3) 선행사가 사물이고 목적격이 필요하므로 which(that)를 이용한다.

▶ Final Test
pp. 83~87

01 ⑤ **02** (1) effectively (2) prevent (3) communication **03** ③ **04** mean **05** do you think about that yellow backpack **06** ③ **07** ④ **08** ① **09** ③ **10** ②, ④ **11** where **12** ④ **13** where **14** However **15** ③ **16** ② **17** ⑤ **18** ④ **19** ② **20** ① **21** which **22** ② **23** ③ **24** ④ **25** ④ **26** ③ **27** ④ **28** ④ **29** ③ **30** ⑤

01 '말, 표정, 또는 행동으로 당신이 느끼거나 생각하는 것을 말하거나 보여주다'는 express(표현하다)의 영영풀이이다. ① 환영하다 ② 언쟁을 하다 ③ 초대하다 ④ 집중하다

02 (1) effectively는 '효과적으로' (2) prevent는 '막다, 예방하다' (3) communication은 '의사소통'이라는 뜻이다.

03 (D) 너 어제 왜 내 생일 파티에 오지 않았니? – (B) 미안해. 난 어제 정말 열심히 공부해야 했어. – (A) 왜 네 책을 쳤니? – (C) 오 아니, 내 말은 그런 뜻이 아니야. 오늘 아침에 시험이 있어서 난 어제 공부해야 했어.

04 대화 도중에 상대방이 이해했는지 점검하는 표현으로 Do you know what I mean?을 쓸 수 있다.

05 의견을 물을 때 What do you think about(of) ...?을 쓸 수 있다.

06 I think ....는 '나는 …라고 생각한다'라는 뜻으로, 의견을 표현할 때 쓴다. ③은 '나는 …라고 들었다'라는 뜻이다.

07 B가 미안하지만, 한 번 더 보여줄 수 있는지 묻고 있으므로, A에는 이해를 점검하는 표현이 알맞다.

08 선행사 the man은 사람이고 조동사 can의 주어가 필요하므로 주격 관계대명사 who가 와야 한다.

09 선행사가 없는 것으로 보아 선행사를 포함하는 관계대명사 what이 알맞다.

10 선행사가 사람(the man)이고 목적격 관계대명사 자리이므로 who나 whom, that이 올 수 있다.

11 〈전치사+관계대명사〉는 관계부사로 바꿔 쓸 수 있으며 선행사가 장소이므로 where가 알맞다.

12 의미상 각각 양보의 부사절을 이끄는 wherever(어디서 … 할지라도)와 whatever (무엇을 …할지라도)가 알맞다.

13 두 문장의 공통 요소인 the shop을 선행사로 취하는 관계부사 where를 이용하여 한 문장으로 쓸 수 있다.

14 양보의 부사절(아무리 …할지라도)을 이끌면서 뒤에 있는 형용사 rich를 꾸밀 수 있는 것은 However이다.

15 ⓐ 계속적 용법의 주격 관계대명사가 와야 한다. (whom → who) ⓒ 사람과 동물이 모두 선행사로 올 경우에는 주로 관계대명사 that을 쓴다. (who → that)

16 ② 목적격 관계대명사로 생략할 수 있다. ① 관계대명사 what은 목적격으로 쓰여도 생략할 수 없다. ③, ⑤ 주격 관

계대명사는 생략할 수 없다. ④ 선행사가 이미 생략되어 있으므로 관계부사 when은 생략할 수 없다.

17 • 선행사가 사람(the children)이고 주격이 필요하므로 who(that)가 알맞다.
• 선행사에 -thing이 포함된 경우에는 주로 관계대명사 that을 쓴다.

18 • for which는 이유를 나타내는 관계부사 why와 바꿔 쓸 수 있다.
• in which는 장소를 나타내는 관계부사 where과 바꿔 쓸 수 있다.

19 ② 선행사가 없으므로 선행사를 포함하는 관계대명사 what을 써야 한다.

20 ① 의문사로 '무엇'이라는 뜻이고, 나머지는 관계대명사 what이다.

21 〈접속사+대명사〉는 계속적 용법의 관계대명사 〈콤마(,)+관계대명사〉로 바꿔 쓸 수 있다.

22 • 선행사가 all을 포함하고 있으므로 관계대명사 that이 알맞다.
• 선행사가 the season(계절)이므로 관계부사 when이 알맞다.

23 ③은 Semi will stay in the room.에서 in the room을 대신할 수 있는 관계부사 where가 들어가야 한다.

24 ④ 관계대명사 that은 계속적 용법으로 쓸 수 없다. (that → which)

25
> 지진이 자주 일어나는 도시에서, 일부 건물들은 지진에 대한 안전성을 염두에 두고 지어진다. 그 건물들은 진동을 흡수하도록 설계된다. 이제 공학자들은 '스마트 빌딩'도 개발하고 있다. 이 건물들에는 지진이 일어나는 동안 특별한 시스템을 자동으로 활성화하는 센서가 있다. 시스템들 중 하나는 자동차에 있는 것과 비슷한 일종의 충격 흡수기를 이용한다. 공학자들은 피해를 줄일 더 많은 시스템을 개발하고 있다.

주어진 문장은 스마트 빌딩에 있는 특별한 시스템 중 하나에 대한 내용이므로 ④에 들어가는 것이 알맞다.

26
> 허수아비는 건초로 채워진 격자무늬 셔츠를 입고 있는 우스꽝스러운 막대기 형상이다. 그것은 단지 장식용으로 들판에 서 있는 것이 아니다. 까마귀가 농작물을 먹기 때문에 농부들은 겁을 주어 까마귀를 쫓아내려고 허수아비를 세워 둔다. 하지만 허수아비는 사람처럼 보여서가 아니라 사람처럼 냄새가 나서 새들을 겁먹게 한다. 우리의 옷을 입음으로써, 허수아비는 우리처럼 냄새가 나고, 새들은 분명히 우리의 냄새가 좋다고 여기지 않는다. 그것이 우리가 흘린 케첩이거나 사과 주스일까? 그것은 상관없다. 어떤 것이든 허수아비는 새들로부터 농작물을 보호한다.

새들이 허수아비의 옷에서 나는 냄새 때문에 도망을 간다는 내용이다.

[27~28]
> 고기와 생선은 대부분의 사람들의 식단에서 중요한 부분이다. 그것들은 단백질을 함유하고 있는데, 그것은 우리 몸이 필요로 하는 것이다. 우리의 근육과 기관들은 주로 단백질로 이루어져 있다. 단백질은 몸이 자라고 스스로 회복하도록 도와준다. 어떤 단백질원은 다른 것들보다 우리 몸에 더 좋다. 흰색 고기와 생선은 붉은색 고기보다 지방 함유량이 훨씬 적다. 이것 때문에, 붉은색 고기를 먹는 것보다 흰색 고기를 먹는 것이 더 낫다. 모든 음식들처럼, 우리가 고기를 요리하는 방식은 그것이 얼마나 건강한지에 영향을 미칠 수 있다. 튀긴 음식은 구운 음식만큼 우리에게 좋지는 않다.

27 ④ 흰색 고기는 지방 함유량이 적어서 붉은색 고기보다 몸에 더 좋다고 했다.

28 ④ 관계부사 how와 선행사 the way는 함께 쓸 수 없고, 둘 중 하나만 써야 한다.

[29~30]
> 사막은 동물들이 살기에 만만한 곳은 아니다. 그들은 극도의 온도를 견뎌야 한다. 사막에 사는 많은 동물들은 그저 햇빛에서 벗어나 있다. 그들은 많은 시간을 땅속에서 보낼 것이고, 음식을 찾아 밤에만 나온다. 어떤 동물들은 열기와 싸우는 데 도움이 되는 적응력을 지니고 있다. 낙타는 모래의 열기로부터 몸을 멀리 있게 해주는 긴 다리를 가지고 있다. 사막여우와 산토끼는 열기를 빼 주는 큰 귀를 가지고 있다. 사막에 사는 많은 동물들은 다른 기후에 사는 친족들보다 더 연한 털이나 피부를 가지고 있다. 연한 색은 진한 색보다 열을 덜 흡수한다.

29 사막에 사는 동물들이 어떻게 자신의 몸을 시원하게 유지하는지에 대한 내용이다.

30 밑줄 친 that은 주격 관계대명사이다. ① 접속사 that(so ... that ...: 너무 …해서 …하다) ② 관계부사 when을 대신하는 that ③ '그렇게'라는 의미의 부사 ④ 대명사 ⑤ 주격 관계대명사

Lesson 05 수동태

>> Grammar Practice
pp. 92~95

A1 (1) was written (2) was (3) was trusted (4) was (5) written (6) is located

A2 (1) him (2) made (3) signed (4) made (5) drunk (6) caught (7) built

B1 (1) 그 식당은 건축 중이었다.
(2) 그 도둑은 그 경찰관에 의해 처벌될 것이다.
(3) 그는 내일 선생님께 칭찬받을 것이다.

B2 (1) The work will be finished by her.
(2) A new hospital was being built here (by us).
(3) The problem had been solved by me.
(4) The house on the corner has been sold (by them).
(5) Our lives have been changed by technology.

C1 (1) will be changed (2) may be elected (3) must be cut

C2 (1) bake → be baked (2) reading → read (3) is → be

D1 (1) to (2) for (3) of

D2 (1) was given, was given to her (2) are bought for me (3) was told to me

E1 (1) walk → to walk (2) calling → called (3) coming → to come

E2 (1) made happy (2) was elected President (3) seen to relax

F1 (1) to (2) with (3) at (4) in

F2 (1) was run over by (2) is spoken well of by (3) is said that

>> Grammar Test
pp. 96~97

01 ③ 02 was written 03 ④ 04 ② 05 ③ 06 torn
07 (1) been washed (2) scolded 08 ② 09 were bought for the poor children 10 ⑤ 11 protect → be protected 12 It was, that 13 ① 14 ①

01 도둑이 어제 체포된 것이므로 과거시제 수동태 〈was+과거분사〉가 알맞다.

02 수동태는 〈주어+be동사+과거분사+by+목적격(행위자)〉의 형태이다.

03 사역동사가 있는 문장의 수동태는 목적격보어인 동사원형을 to부정사로 바꾼다.

04 의미상 '아이들이 Jane에 의해 돌봐질 것'이므로 미래시제 수동태인 〈will be+과거분사〉형태로 써야 한다. (② → will be cared for)

05 be filled with: …로 가득 차다 / be satisfied with: …에 만족하다

06 진행시제 수동태는 〈be동사+being+과거분사〉형태로 나타내며, tear는 '찢다'라는 뜻의 동사로 빈칸에는 과거분사형인 torn이 알맞다.

07 (1) 현재완료 수동태이므로 〈has been+과거분사〉로 써야 한다. (2) 의문문 수동태로 빈칸에는 scolded가 알맞다.

08 ① be married to: …와 결혼하다 ② be surprised at: …에 놀라다 ③ be satisfied with: …에 만족하다 ④ 4형식 동사 show의 수동태로 간접목적어 앞에 전치사 to를 써야 한다. ⑤ be covered with: …으로 덮이다

09 buy는 직접목적어만을 주어로 해서 수동태를 만들며, 간접목적어 앞에 전치사 for를 쓴다.

10 의문사가 있는 의문문의 수동태는 〈의문사+be동사+주어+과거분사+by+목적격 …?〉의 형태이다.

11 이 지역은 사람들에 의해 보호를 받아야 하는 대상이므로 조동사가 있는 수동태인 〈조동사+be+과거분사〉형태가 되어야 한다.

12 목적어가 that절인 문장의 수동태는 주어 자리에 가주어 It을 쓰고, that절(진주어)은 문장의 뒤로 보낸다.

13 ② → should be protected ③ → was bought for her ④ → were sent ⑤ → was surprised at

14 ① 현재시제 수동태인 The trees are cut ....이나, 진행시제 수동태인 The trees are being cut .... 혹은 완료시제 수동태인 The trees have been cut ....으로 써야 알맞다.

>> Reading
pp. 98~99

1 ③ 2 The people at *The Daily News* were harshly criticized by the public. 3 ⑤ 4 ②

[1~2]

당신은 가짜 뉴스를 알아챌 수 있는가?

한 뉴스 기사 뒤에 숨겨진 동기를 생각하면서 기사를 살펴보자.

슬라브인이 전쟁 중에 친구에게 총을 쏘다

컬럼비아 광산 소속의 슬라브인 노동자인 Mejk Swenekafew가 목요일 저녁에 채굴 야영지 근처에서 John Pecitello에 의해 총상을 입고 다쳤다. 그 두 사람은 언쟁을 벌였다. 언쟁이 싸움으로 이어졌고, Pecitello는 Swenekafew를 가슴과 다리에 두 번 쐈다. 그는 지금 입원 중이다. Pecitello는 총격 이후에 도주했다. 경찰이 그를 찾고 있다.

이 기사에 뭔가 이상한 점이 있는가? 그 슬라브인의 이름을 거꾸로 읽어 보아라. 그것의 철자는 "우리는 뉴스를 조작한다."가 된다. 〈데일리 텔레그램〉 사는 그들의 경쟁사인 〈데일리 뉴스〉 사가 그들의 기사를 훔치는지를 증명하기 위해서 이 거짓 기사를 발행했다. 〈데일리 뉴스〉 사는 'Swenekafew'에 대한 동일한 기사를 발행해서 훔친 것이 발각되었다. 대중들은 〈데일리 뉴스〉 사의 사람들을 혹독하게 비난했다.

1 〈데일리 텔레그램〉 사는 경쟁사인 〈데일리 뉴스〉 사가 기사를 훔치는지 증명하기 위해 '거짓' 기사를 발행했다.

2 수동태는 〈be동사+과거분사+by+목적격(행위자)〉의 형태로 나타낸다.

3
1989년, 프랑스 정부는 Tarn 계곡의 교통 문제를 해결할 방법을 찾고 있었다. 공무원들은 자동차들이 계곡 안에서 갇히는 것을 막기 위해 새로운 다리를 짓고 싶어 했다. 하지만 그들은 경관을 해치거나 계곡에 사는 사람들을 속상하게 만들 수 있는 것을 건설하는 것에 대해 염려했다. 2004년 12월에, 미요 대교가 개통되었다. 그 다리는 너무 아름다워서 거의 계곡의 자연스러운 일부인 것처럼 보인다. 다리의 어떤 부분은 에펠탑보다 높아서, 다리 위를 운전하는 관광객들은 계곡 위를 날아다니는 것처럼 느낄 것이다. 다리 아래에 계곡에 사는 사람들은 차와 오염이 적은 생활을 즐기고 있다.

⑤ 계곡에 살고 있는 사람들은 차와 오염이 적은 생활을 즐기고 있다고 했다.

4
수년간, 공룡은 크고 멍청한 냉혈 동물이라고 여겨졌다. 하지만 많은 공룡들은 오늘날의 새나 개 정도의 크기였다. 물론, 인간만큼 똑똑한 공룡은 없었지만, 2미터짜리 트로오돈과 같은 더 작은 공룡들은 꽤 큰 두뇌를 가지고 있었다. 티라노사우루스 렉스는 강력한 포식자로 알려져 있다. 영화에서 티라노사우루스 렉스는 흔히 빠르고 거대한 존재이지만, 사실 이 공룡은 아주 빨리 달릴 수 없었다. 신체적으로 그것은 너무 컸다. 실제로 티라노사우루스 렉스는 아마도 코끼리 정도로 빨리 움직였을 것이다. 또한, 티라노사우루스 렉스는 매우 작은 팔을 지니고 있었다. 강한 팔 없이, 이 공룡은 아마도 강력한 사냥꾼은 아니었을 것이다.

② 일부 공룡들은 인간만큼 똑똑하지는 않지만, 꽤 큰 두뇌를 지니고 있었다고 했다.

1 (m)ind   2 ①   3 ③   4 ①   5 ④   6 what

1 No로 답했는데 빌려줄 수 있다고 말하는 것으로 보아 A는 Do you mind ...?로 허락을 요청했음을 알 수 있다.

2 Can you tell me about ...?은 상대방에게 설명을 요청하는 표현으로 Can you explain ...?과 바꿔 쓸 수 있다.

3 ③은 '너는 너의 컴퓨터를 사용할 수 있니?'라는 뜻이고, 나머지는 '내가 너의 컴퓨터를 사용해도 될까?'라고 허락을 요청하는 표현이다.

4 ① I don't mind at all.로 보아 Of course not.으로 답해야 자연스럽다.

5 빈칸 뒤에 Go ahead.가 있으므로, 승낙하는 표현이 와야 한다. ④ Of course not.은 승낙하지 않는 표현이다.

6 상대방이 한 말을 잘 이해하지 못했을 때 반복을 요청하는 표현으로 I don't know what you mean.이 있다.

1 Is it okay if I   2 are surrounded by   3 (1) The secret must be kept by the members. (2) All the patients have been treated by the doctor.   4 (1) are satisfied with (2) was taken (3) is covered with   5 (1) be put (2) be taken out (3) be returned

1 허락을 요청할 때는 Is it okay if I ...?로 묻는다.

2 탑이 나무들에 의해 둘러싸인 것이므로 수동태로 써야 한다. 수동태는 〈be동사+과거분사+by+행위자(목적격)〉의 형태로 쓴다.

3 수동태는 〈be동사+과거분사+by+행위자(목적격)〉의 형태로 쓴다.

4 (1) be satisfied with: …에 만족하다 (2) 사진이 찍힌 것이므로 수동태로 써야 한다. (3) be covered with: …으로 덮이다

5 조동사가 있는 수동태는 〈조동사+be+과거분사〉로 쓴다.

01 ④ **02** (1) fake (2) spell (3) backwards **03** ①
04 explain **05** ④ **06** ⑤ **07** (C) → (D) → (B) → (A)
08 ⑤ **09** ④ **10** ② **11** (1) was asked (2) built (3) be
kept **12** (1) will be published (2) has been stolen
13 ④ **14** ② **15** to **16** was made for her **17** ②
18 (1) The man is looked up to by everyone. (2) I was
elected president of my class. **19** ③ **20** ② **21** ④
22 seen to enter **23** It, that, said to be getting **24** ②
25 ② **26** ③ **27** ③ **28** was made **29** ④ **30** ③

01 '누군가가 어떤 것을 하게 만드는 이유인데, 특히 그것이 숨겨져 있을 때'는 motive(동기)의 영영풀이이다.

02 (1) fake: 거짓된, 가짜의 (2) spell: 철자를 쓰다
(3) backwards: 거꾸로

03 Do you mind if ...?는 '…해도 될까요?'라는 뜻으로 허락을 요청하는 표현이다.

04 설명을 요청하는 표현으로 Can you explain ...?이 있다.

05 '내가 네 펜을 써도 될까?'라는 뜻으로 허락을 요청하는 표현인데, ④는 '너는 네 펜을 쓸 수 있다.'라는 뜻이다.

06 B가 A가 한 말을 이해하지 못한 상황이므로 반복을 요청하는 표현인 ⑤가 알맞다.

07 (C) 너 어떻게 퍼즐을 풀었니? – (D) 그것은 식은 죽 먹기였어. – (B) 식은 죽 먹기? 그게 무슨 말이니? – (A) 그건 어떤 일이 하기 쉽다는 뜻이야.

08 현재완료 수동태의 부정문인 〈has not been+과거분사〉의 형태가 알맞다.

09 be pleased with: …에 즐거워하다 / be known to: …에게 알려져 있다

10 의문사가 있는 의문문의 수동태는 〈의문사+be동사+주어+과거분사 …?〉의 형태이다.

11 (1) 내가 질문을 받은 것이므로 수동태가 알맞다. (2) 왕이 성을 지은 것이므로 능동태가 알맞다. (3) 약은 보관되는 것이므로 수동태로 써야 하고, 조동사가 있는 수동태는 〈조동사+be+과거분사〉 형태이다.

12 (1) 잡지가 발행되는 것이므로 수동태로 써야 한다. (2) 지갑이 도난을 당한 것이므로 수동태로 써야 한다. 현재완료시제의 수동태는 〈have(has)+been+과거분사〉로 쓴다.

13 우리가 수학을 가르침 받는다는 수동의 의미가 필요하고, 미래시제로 물었으므로 〈will be+과거분사〉로 대답해야 한다.

14 현재진행시제 수동태는 〈is(am, are) being+과거분사〉 형태이며, 수동태의 주어가 단수이므로 be동사는 단수형인 is를 써야 한다.

15 teach, send는 직접목적어를 주어로 하여 수동태로 쓸 때

간접목적어 앞에 전치사 to를 쓴다.

16 4형식 동사 make의 수동태는 간접목적어 앞에 전치사 for를 쓴다.

17 ② 차는 세차되는 대상이므로 동사는 수동형이 되어야 한다. (washed → was washed)

18 (1) look up to는 '…을 존경하다'라는 뜻의 동사구이므로 수동태가 될 때 하나의 덩어리로 움직여야 한다. (2) 〈elect+목적어+목적격보어〉의 5형식 문장이 수동태가 된 형태이다.

19 ③ 진행시제 수동태는 〈be동사+being+과거분사〉로 쓴다. (was been built → was being built)

20 행위자가 일반인이거나 밝힐 필요가 없을 때는 〈by+목적격〉을 생략할 수 있다.

21 ④ 사역동사의 수동태이므로 wash는 to부정사의 형태가 되어야 한다. (wash → to wash)

22 지각동사의 목적격보어인 동사원형은 수동태로 전환할 때 to부정사로 쓴다.

23 목적어가 절인 문장의 수동태는 주어 자리에 가주어 It을 쓰고 본래의 절은 문장의 맨 뒤로 보낸다. that절의 주어를 수동태의 주어로 하여 나타낼 때는 〈that절의 주어+be동사+과거분사+to부정사〉로 쓴다.

24 ① 사역동사가 있는 문장의 수동태는 목적격보어인 동사원형을 to부정사로 바꿔야 하므로 to go가 되어야 한다. ③ resemble은 수동태로 쓸 수 없는 동사이다. ④ by 다음에는 목적격 them이 와야 한다. ⑤ 조동사 다음에는 동사원형이 와야 한다.

25
> 때때로 사람들은 너무 바빠서 실제로 앉아서 지루해질 시간이 좀 필요하다. 2014년도 영국의 한 연구에서, 80명의 참가자들은 사전의 내용을 읽고 베껴 쓰는 것과 같은 지루한 과업을 부여받았다. 그들이 플라스틱 컵을 이용하는 창의적인 방법을 떠올려 보도록 요구받았을 때, 그들은 지루한 과업을 부여받지 않았던 사람들보다 더 창의적인 방법을 고안해 내는 경향이 있었다.

때로 지루한 시간을 보내는 것이 창의적인 사고를 하는 데 필요하다는 내용이다.

26
> 거의 450년 동안, 잉카 제국의 도시인 마추픽추는 세상에서 숨겨져 있었다. 그 도시는 페루의 산 높은 곳에 위치해 있었다. 마추픽추는 잉카인들에 의해 지어졌고, 종교적 중심지였다. 그 잉카 제국의 도시에 살던 사람들은 사라진 듯 보였다. 왜일까? 그것은 미스터리로 남아있다. 한 이론은 질병으로 마추픽추 사람들이 죽었다는 것이다. 오늘날, 마추픽추는 가장 중요한 관광지들 중 하나인데, 그 잃어버린 도시가 매우 놀랍고 아름답기 때문이다.

마추픽추에서 재배되었던 농작물은 언급되지 않았다.

> 1974년에, 중국 산시성 지역의 농부들은 엄청난 발견을 했는데, 묻혀 있던 거대한 군대를 발견했다. 실제 크기의 조각상인 병사들은 자신들의 지도자의 무덤을 조용히 보호하며, 2,200년 이상 숨겨져 있었다. 발굴되었을 때, 조각상들은 실제 군대와 똑같은 위치로 서 있었다. 전문가들은 이 위치로부터 고대 중국의 전술에 대해 많은 것을 알아냈다. 오늘날 이 용감한 군대는 또한 세계적으로 유명한 경이로운 예술이다. 각 조각상들은 손으로 만들어졌고, 독특한 얼굴을 지니고 있다. 57제곱킬로미터에 달하는 전체 구조는 아직도 발굴 중이다.

27 주어진 문장의 this position이 가리키는 내용이 ③ 바로 앞에 나와 있으므로 ③에 들어가는 것이 알맞다.

28 조각상은 만들어지는 대상이므로 수동태로 써야 한다.

[29~30]

> 2006년 8월 24일에, 세계의 천문학자들은 명왕성이 더 이상 행성이 아니라고 결정했다. 이제 우리의 태양계에는 9개가 아닌 오직 8개의 행성이 있다. 과학자들은 명왕성이 정말로 행성인지 아닌지에 대해 논쟁을 했다. 명왕성에 대한 의문은 태양에서 아주 멀리 떨어져 있는 얼음체인 에리스의 발견으로 증가되었다. 마침내, 과학자들은 어떤 물체가 행성으로 분류되기 위해서는 3가지 기준을 충족해야 한다고 결정했다. (1) 그것은 태양 주변을 돌아야 한다. (2) 그것은 크고 둥글어야 한다. (3) 그것의 궤도에 다른 물체가 없어야 한다.
>
> 명왕성과 에리스 둘 다 태양 주변을 돌고 둥근 모양이다. 하지만 그것들의 궤도는 이상하고, 궤도에 다른 물체가 있다. 이와 같은 이유로, 그것들은 행성으로 불릴 수 없다. 대신에, 그것들은 이제 '왜행성'이라고 불린다.

29 명왕성과 에리스는 태양을 돌고 둥글지만, 궤도가 이상하고 다른 물체와 궤도를 공유하고 있어서 행성이 될 수 없다고 했다.

30 ⓒ to부정사의 의미상 주어(for an object)에서 물체는 분류되는 대상이므로 to be classified 형태의 수동태로 써야 한다.

PART II 듣기 실전 모의고사

▶▶ 01회 듣기 실전 모의고사   pp. 112~119

01 ④ 02 ④ 03 ⑤ 04 ③ 05 ④ 06 ③ 07 ① 08 ④
09 ① 10 ⑤ 11 ① 12 ③ 13 ③ 14 ⑤ 15 ⑤ 16 ③
17 ④ 18 ⑤ 19 ⑤ 20 ⑤

Dictation Test

01 collection of mugs, small dots, inside the circle **02** How much, per kilo, anything else **03** got burned, treat my burn, Rinse off **04** only a week, make it, ends earlier **05** my photos printed, your files, about two hours **06** another one, cats and dogs, share my umbrella **07** dust to float, clean the fan, turn on the light **08** swimming technique, main goal, are rescued, relax your body **09** on your finger, belong to, on the thickness **10** on the cupboard, spell, each, doing the assignment **11** about to, every other day, forgot about **12** consume rice, would be enough, cheaper, domestic products **13** empty bottle, be recycled, quite costly, creative way **14** sleep well, not until, your eyes closed, avoid using **15** don't feed, greatly increased, a lot of inconvenience **16** was exhausted, help him, remove the weeds **17** feel chilly, have a fever, immune system, cinnamon powder **18** be delayed, studying hard, study together **19** my report yet, some feedback, for improvement **20** lost her wallet, the last time, gets angry, clear up

01 ④

M Rachel, you have a nice collection of mugs.

W All of these are my creation. You may have one if you wish.

M Wow, really? Can I have that white mug with the black circle?

W You mean the one with small dots around the circle?

M That one's nice too but I meant the one with the word "MUG" inside the circle.

W I got it. There you go.

M I owe you one. Thanks a lot.

남 Rachel, 너 멋진 머그컵 모음을 가지고 있구나.
여 전부 내가 만든 거야. 원하면 하나 가져도 돼.
남 와, 정말? 검은색 원이 있는 저 흰색 머그컵 가져도 되니?
여 원 주변에 작은 점들이 있는 것 말이니?
남 그것도 멋진데, 나는 원 안에 'MUG'라는 단어가 있는 걸 말했어.
여 알겠어. 여기 있어.
남 내가 한 번 빚졌네. 정말 고마워.

02 ④

M Good morning, ma'am.
W Good morning. How much are the strawberries?
M They are 6 dollars per kilo. But the strawberries are on sale this week. They are 25 dollars for 5 kilograms.
W That is good. I would like 10 kilograms of strawberries.
M Here you are. Do you need anything else?
W No, it's okay.

남 안녕하세요. 손님?
여 안녕하세요. 딸기가 얼마예요?
남 킬로그램 당 6달러입니다. 하지만 이번 주에 딸기가 할인 중입니다. 5킬로그램에 25달러입니다.
여 좋군요. 딸기 10킬로그램 주세요.
남 여기 있습니다. 더 필요하신 것 있습니까?
여 아니요. 없습니다.

03 ⑤

[Telephone rings.]
M Rose Clinic, how may I help you?
W I'm calling because I just got burned from boiling water.
M So would you like to come to the clinic?
W No, I don't think it is that serious.
M Then, what do you need?
W I just want to know how to treat my burn.
M Okay. Rinse off the burned area with cool running water until the pain goes away.
W Thanks a lot.

[전화벨 소리가 울린다.]
남 Rose 병원입니다. 무엇을 도와 드릴까요?
여 제가 방금 끓는 물에 데어서 전화했어요.
남 그럼 병원에 오시겠어요?
여 아뇨, 그렇게 심각하지는 않은 것 같아요.
남 그럼, 무엇이 필요하신가요?
여 전 그저 화상 입은 걸 치료하는 방법을 알고 싶습니다.
남 네. 통증이 사라질 때까지 시원한 흐르는 물에 화상 부위를 씻어 내십시오.
여 정말 감사합니다.

04 ③

M Jiwon, can we finish writing the script for the English presentation tomorrow after school?
W I'm sorry I can't. I have to go to the piano lesson.
M It's September 10th already and we have only a week from now, you know.
W Why don't we make it on Friday?
M You mean the 14th? It's only three days before the presentation and I don't think it's a good idea.
W How about the 12th then? School ends earlier that day.
M Okay. I have an appointment with the dentist, but I think I can reschedule it.

남 지원아, 내일 방과 후에 영어 발표를 위한 대본 쓰는 걸 끝낼 수 있을까?
여 미안하지만 안 돼. 나 피아노 수업을 가야 해.
남 벌써 9월 10일이고, 너도 알다시피 이제 일주일밖에 안 남았어.
여 금요일에 만나면 어때?
남 14일 말이니? 발표하기 겨우 3일 전이라 좋은 생각이 아닌 것 같은데.
여 그러면 12일은 어떠니? 그날 학교 일찍 마치잖아.
남 좋아. 치과 예약이 있는데, 조정할 수 있을 것 같아.

05 ④

W Hello, can I have my photos printed today?
M Yes, we can. Did you bring the memory card?
W Here it is. How long does it take?
M Let me see your files. Oh, it's more than 100 photos!

W I took many photos during the holidays.

M It will take about two hours.

W I see. I'll stop by a bank and come back after two hours.

여 안녕하세요, 오늘 제 사진들을 인화할 수 있을까요?

남 네, 가능합니다. 메모리 카드를 가져오셨습니까?

여 여기요. 시간이 얼마나 걸릴까요?

남 파일 좀 보겠습니다. 오, 100장이 넘는군요!

여 휴가 중에 사진을 많이 찍었어요.

남 2시간 정도 걸릴 거예요.

여 알겠습니다. 은행에 들렀다가, 2시간 후에 올게요.

---

06 ③

① W Can I borrow your umbrella?

　 M Yeah, I have another one in my car.

② W It's raining cats and dogs.

　 M You had better wear a raincoat and boots.

③ W Wasn't it supposed to rain all day long today?

　 M I thought so too.

④ W Did you buy a new raincoat?

　 M Yes, I bought it yesterday.

⑤ W I didn't know that it was going to rain.

　 M Maybe you can share my umbrella.

---

① 여 우산 좀 빌려도 될까요?

　 남 네, 제 차에 하나 더 있어요.

② 여 비가 정말 심하게 오네.

　 남 우비와 장화를 착용하는 게 좋겠어.

③ 여 오늘 하루 종일 비가 오기로 되어 있지 않니?

　 남 나도 그렇게 생각했어.

④ 여 우비를 새로 샀니?

　 남 응, 어제 샀어.

⑤ 여 비가 올 줄 몰랐어.

　 남 내 우산 같이 쓰자.

---

07 ①

M It's gotten really hot recently. Can we turn on the fan?

W We have to clean it first unless you want dust to float everywhere.

M Okay. I'll clean the fan.

W It's so nice of you. Do you need a screwdriver?

M No, I don't. Just turn on the light for me, please? It's getting dark.

W Okay. Do you need anything else?

M Not really. Thanks.

남 최근에 날씨가 너무 더워졌네요. 선풍기를 켤까요?

여 먼지가 사방에 떠다니기를 원치 않는다면, 먼저 그걸 청소해야 해요.

남 알겠어요. 내가 선풍기를 청소할게요.

여 정말 고마워요. 나사돌리개가 필요한가요?

남 아뇨, 필요 없어요. 그저 불 좀 켜줄래요? 어두워지네요.

여 좋아요. 또 필요한 게 있나요?

남 없어요. 고마워요.

---

08 ④

M Let me tell you about survival swimming. It is a swimming technique you can apply when you fall into water by accident. The main goal of survival swimming is to float on the surface of the water until you are rescued. To swim for survival, float on the water as if you're lying down on your bed. Remember, you should relax your body so that it doesn't sink and try not to move a lot to save your energy.

남 생존 수영에 대해 말씀드리겠습니다. 그것은 여러분이 사고로 물에 빠졌을 때 적용할 수 있는 영법입니다. 생존 수영의 주된 목표는 구조될 때까지 물의 표면에 떠 있는 것입니다. 생존을 위해 수영하려면, 침대에 누워 있는 것처럼 물에 떠 있으십시오. 가라앉지 않기 위해 몸에 힘을 빼고, 에너지를 비축하기 위해 많이 움직이지 않아야 한다는 점을 기억하세요.

---

09 ①

W This is something you wear on your finger. Some people wear this to make their hands more beautiful or to look nice, and other people exchange this when they get married or engaged. Still others wear this to show that they belong to a certain group. It can be designed in all kinds of shapes and its size may vary depending on the thickness of your finger.

여 이것은 손가락에 착용하는 것입니다. 어떤 사람들은 이것을

손이 더 아름답게 보이거나 멋지게 보이기 위해 착용하고, 또 어떤 사람들은 결혼하거나 약혼할 때 이것을 교환합니다. 어떤 그룹에 소속되어 있다는 것을 표시하기 위해 이것을 착용하는 사람들도 있습니다. 이것은 갖가지 모양으로 디자인될 수 있고, 손가락의 굵기에 따라 크기도 다양할 수 있습니다.

10 ⑤

① W Have you seen the movie, *Parasite*?
　 M Yes, it was really great.
② W Can I get some water?
　 M Of course. You can use the cup on the cupboard.
③ W How do you spell your last name, sir?
　 M It's D-A-R-S-Y.
④ W How much are these carrots?
　 M They are 1,000 won each.
⑤ W Did you finish doing the assignment?
　 M Yeah. I'm going to write about the global warming.

---

① 여 영화 〈기생충〉 본 적 있니?
　 남 응, 매우 좋았어.
② 여 물 좀 마셔도 될까요?
　 남 물론이죠. 찬장에 있는 컵을 쓰세요.
③ 여 당신의 성의 철자가 어떻게 되십니까?
　 남 D-A-R-S-Y입니다.
④ 여 이 당근들 얼마인가요?
　 남 각각 1,000원입니다.
⑤ 여 숙제 다 했니?
　 남 응. 난 지구 온난화에 대해 쓰려고.

11 ①

[Telephone rings.]

W Hi, Mark. Did you get up already?
M Sure, I'm about to go to school now. How was your trip to France, Mom?
W It was such a beautiful place. By the way, have you been watering the plants every other day?
M Oops, I totally forgot about it.
W I knew it. Make sure you water them before you leave for school.
M Yes, Mom.

[전화벨 소리가 울린다.]

여 여보세요, Mark. 벌써 일어났니?
남 그럼요, 이제 학교 가려던 참이에요. 프랑스 여행은 어떠셨어요, 엄마?
여 정말 아름다운 곳이었어. 그나저나, 이틀에 한 번 식물에 물을 주고 있니?
남 이런, 저 그걸 완전히 까먹었어요.
여 그럴 줄 알았다. 학교로 출발하기 전에 꼭 식물에 물을 주렴.
남 네, 엄마.

12 ③

W Oh, no. There's no more rice at home. Let's order it online.
M Okay. I think we'd better buy a large sack since we consume rice a lot. There's a 10-kilogram sack and it's 30,000 won.
W We don't need that much. A 5-kilogram sack would be enough.
M Okay. Rice from China is cheaper than domestic rice.
W I do prefer domestic products.
M Good. Then, let's buy this one.

여 이런. 집에 쌀이 떨어졌어요. 인터넷으로 쌀을 주문해요.
남 알겠어요. 우리는 쌀을 많이 먹으니까 큰 포대를 사는 게 좋을 것 같아요. 10킬로그램짜리 포대가 있는데 30,000원이네요.
여 그렇게 많이는 필요 없어요. 5킬로그램짜리 포대면 충분할 것 같아요.
남 그래요. 중국 쌀이 국내 쌀보다 더 싸네요.
여 저는 국산을 선호해요.
남 좋아요. 그럼, 이걸 사요.

13 ③

W You just drank a bottle of coke. What do you do with the empty bottle? Well, you can recycle it, but not a lot of used materials can actually be recycled. Besides, recycling can sometimes be quite costly. So some innovators have come up with reusing those old materials in a creative way. This is what upcycling is.

여 여러분이 방금 콜라 한 병을 마셨습니다. 그 빈 병을 가지고 무엇을 하나요? 음, 그것을 재활용할 수 있지만, 많은 중고 물품들이 실제로 재활용될 수는 없습니다. 게다가, 재활용하는 것은 때때로 꽤 비용이 들 수 있습니다. 그래서 몇몇 혁신

자들은 그러한 오래된 물품들을 창의적인 방법으로 재사용하는 방법을 생각해 냈습니다. 이것이 바로 업사이클링입니다.

14 ⑤

M You look tired. What's wrong?

W I can't sleep well at night.

M What time do you usually go to bed?

W I go to bed at around 10 but it's not until 12 that I actually fall asleep.

M So do you just lie on your bed with your eyes closed for two hours?

W No, I surf on the Internet until I get drowsy.

M I think that's the problem. You should avoid using electronic devices one hour before you sleep.

W Okay, I'll try that.

남 너 피곤해 보인다. 무슨 일 있니?

여 나 밤에 잠을 잘 못 자.

남 주로 몇 시에 자러 가는데?

여 10시쯤 자러 가는데 실제로는 12시나 되어서야 잠이 들어.

남 그래서 두 시간 동안 눈을 감은 채로 침대에 그저 누워 있는 거야?

여 아니, 졸릴 때까지 인터넷 검색을 하지.

남 그게 문제인 것 같다. 잠자기 한 시간 전에는 전자 기기 이용하는 것을 피해야 해.

여 알겠어, 그렇게 해 볼게.

15 ⑤

W Good afternoon. I have an announcement for visitors of our park. Please don't feed the pigeons. The number of pigeons has greatly increased because of the food that have been continually given by visitors. This causes a lot of inconvenience to the other visitors. So please don't give food to the pigeons. We hope you enjoy your visit.

여 안녕하십니까. 저희 공원을 방문하신 분들께 안내 말씀드리겠습니다. 비둘기들에게 먹이를 주지 마십시오. 방문객들에 의해 지속적으로 제공된 음식물로 인해 비둘기의 수가 엄청나게 늘었습니다. 이것은 다른 방문객들에게 많은 불편을 초래합니다. 그러므로 비둘기에게 먹이를 주지 마세요. 즐거운 시간 보내시기 바랍니다.

16 ③

W Paul, how can you sleep at school all day?

M Well, I was exhausted from working all weekend long.

W You said that you were going to visit your uncle during the weekend, right?

M Yeah. My uncle runs a farm so my Dad and I went to help him pull out all the weeds.

W Couldn't he just use some chemicals to remove the weeds?

M It's an organic farm and he never uses weed killers.

W So you went there as a human weed killer.

M That's right. I was so tired that I couldn't help but get sleepy in class.

여 Paul, 어쩜 학교에서 하루 종일 잘 수가 있니?

남 음, 주말 내내 일을 해서 지쳤어.

여 주말에 삼촌 뵈러 간다고 했잖아?

남 맞아. 삼촌이 농장을 운영하셔서 아버지와 내가 잡초를 전부 뽑는 걸 도와드리러 갔었어.

여 삼촌께서 잡초를 없애는 화학 약품 같은 걸 그냥 쓰시면 안 되었던 거니?

남 유기농 농장이어서 삼촌께서는 제초제를 절대 안 쓰셔.

여 그래서 네가 인간 제초제로 거기 간 거구나.

남 그렇지. 난 너무 피곤해서 수업 때 졸리지 않을 수 없었어.

17 ④

W Could you turn off the air conditioner? I feel chilly.

M Are you sure? The current room temperature is 26 degrees Celsius.

W Oh, yeah? I didn't know that.

M Are you feeling okay? Maybe you have a fever.

W I guess you're right. I've also had a sore throat since this morning.

M Try some honey cinnamon tea before you go to bed tonight. It helps improve your immune system.

W I don't know how to make it.

M Do you have cinnamon powder and some honey at home?

W Yes, I do. What do I do with them?

여 에어컨을 좀 꺼 주실래요? 춥네요.

남 정말요? 지금 실내 온도가 26도인데요.

여 아 그래요? 몰랐네요.

남 괜찮으세요? 열이 있는 것 같기도 하네요.

여 그런 것 같아요. 아침부터 목도 따끔거렸어요.

남 오늘 밤 자기 전에 벌꿀계피차를 좀 마셔 보세요. 면역력을 향상하는 데 도움이 되거든요.

여 그걸 어떻게 만드는지 몰라요.

남 집에 계핏가루와 꿀이 좀 있나요?

여 네, 있어요. 그걸로 뭐 하면 되죠?

---

18 ⑤

M I hope there's an earthquake or blizzard this week.

W What do you mean?

M I was hoping our final exams would be delayed if there was a disaster.

W Haha! I never thought of it that way.

M Forget it. I'm just being silly. So are you studying hard for the exams?

W Well, I've been studying harder for it than for the midterms but I'm not sure if I'm doing it right.

M Me too. Do you want to go to the library and study together?

남 이번 주에 지진이나 눈보라가 발생하면 좋겠다.

여 그게 무슨 소리니?

남 자연 재해가 발생하면 기말고사가 늦춰질 수도 있잖아.

여 하하! 그렇게 생각해 본 적이 없네.

남 잊어버려. 그냥 잠시 바보처럼 굴어 봤어. 시험공부 열심히 하고 있니?

여 음, 중간고사 때보다 열심히 공부하고 있는데, 잘하고 있는지 모르겠어.

남 나도 그래. 도서관에 가서 함께 공부할래?

---

19 ⑤

W Fred, did you go over my report yet?

M Yes, I did.

W Please give me some feedback.

M Overall, I think you wrote it very well.

W Could you be more specific?

M It's informative and well-organized with good examples.

W Is there any room for improvement?

여 Fred, 내 보고서 읽어 봤니?

남 응, 읽어 봤어.

여 피드백을 좀 부탁해.

남 전반적으로, 아주 잘 썼다고 생각해.

여 좀 더 구체적으로 말해줄 수 있겠니?

남 유익하고 좋은 예들로 잘 구성된 것 같아.

여 개선해야 하는 부분이 있니?

---

20 ⑤

M Rebecca has lost her wallet earlier today. She remembers that Isaac was with her the last time she took money from her wallet. So Rebecca asks if Isaac has seen her wallet. However, Isaac gets angry because he thinks that Rebecca is suspecting him of stealing the wallet. She wants to clear up the misunderstanding. In this situation, what would Rebecca most likely say to Isaac?

남 Rebecca는 오늘 일찍 지갑을 잃어버렸다. 그녀는 자신이 마지막으로 지갑에서 돈을 꺼냈을 때 Isaac이 함께 있었다는 것을 기억한다. 그래서 Rebecca는 Isaac에게 자신의 지갑을 봤는지 묻는다. 그러나 Isaac은 Rebecca가 자신이 지갑을 훔쳤다고 의심하고 있다고 생각하여 화를 낸다. 그녀는 오해를 풀고 싶어 한다. 이 상황에서, Rebecca가 Isaac에게 뭐라고 말할까?

01 ③	02 ③	03 ⑤	04 ②	05 ④	06 ②	07 ①	08 ④
09 ②	10 ④	11 ③	12 ②	13 ③	14 ②	15 ②	16 ③
17 ④	18 ①	19 ⑤	20 ⑤				

── Dictation Test ──

01 quite modern, square shape, with flower patterns, any patterns **02** right across, take orders, work every day **03** have a question, how to do it, log on **04** should have left, ahead than, actually **05** reduce the waist, measure, be dry-cleaned **06** out of order, something hot, swim here **07** eat out, tired of, order **08** terms to you, means milk, stained **09** purchase goods, means of payment, used to **10** most beautiful smile, can't stand, feel stupid **11** an important decision, instead, removing harmful chemicals, whether to try **12** mosquitos hate, spend more than, look like **13** five days later, the weekend before, going camping **14** kept shouting, played soccer, got tanned **15** have found, is wearing, take him **16** busy, visit my grandparents, a week later **17** was due, hand it in, let me submit **18** reading books, used to read, passed away **19** missed classes, allergic to, made of **20** read an article, suits them best, didn't think

01 ③

W Now let's choose a clock for our bedroom.

M Since the interior of our bedroom is quite modern, let's pick a clock that isn't round.

W I agree. How about a clock with a square shape?

M Well, it definitely looks better than the round one.

W Yeah. It's decorated with flower patterns. Do you like this design better?

M I don't know. What do you think?

W I prefer a clock without any patterns.

M Okay, let's buy that one then.

─────────────────

여 이제 침실에 걸 시계를 골라요.

남 우리 침실의 인테리어가 꽤 현대적이니 둥글지 않은 시계를 골라요.

여 동의해요. 사각형 시계는 어때요?

남 음, 둥근 것보다는 확실히 좋아 보이네요.

여 네. 꽃무늬로 장식이 되어 있네요. 이 디자인이 더 좋은가요?

남 모르겠어요. 어떻게 생각해요?

여 전 아무 무늬가 없는 것을 선호해요.

남 좋아요, 그럼 저걸 사죠.

02 ③

W How have you been doing these days, Jacob?

M I've started a part-time job at a coffee shop and I've been quite busy lately.

W Which coffee shop do you work at?

M I work at Roast Coffee. It's right across our apartment complex.

W Oh yeah. I've been there once and it was really nice. What do you do there?

M I mostly take orders from the customers and clean up the desks after the customers leave.

W I see. Do you work every day?

M No, I just work on Wednesdays and Fridays.

W I see.

─────────────────

여 Jacob, 요새 어떻게 지내니?

남 카페에서 아르바이트를 시작해서 최근에 꽤 바빴어.

여 어느 카페에서 일하니?

남 난 Roast Coffee에서 일해. 우리 아파트 단지 바로 건너편에 있어.

여 아 그래. 한 번 가 봤는데 정말 좋더라. 거기서 무슨 일을 하는데?

남 주로 고객들의 주문을 받고 고객들이 떠난 후에 탁자 청소를 해.

여 그렇구나. 매일 일하니?

남 아니, 수요일과 금요일에만 일해.

여 그렇구나.

03 ⑤

[Telephone rings.]

W ABC Radio Station. How can I help you?

M Hello, I'm a listener of ABC Radio and I have a question.

W Okay, please go on.

M I want to send my story and song request to the radio program, *With You* and I don't know how to do it.

W You can either log on to the webpage of the program or download ABC Radio application.

M I see. Thank you for your help.

W You're welcome.

─────────────────

[전화벨 소리가 울린다.]

여 ABC 라디오 방송국입니다. 무엇을 도와 드릴까요?

남 안녕하세요, 저는 ABC 라디오 청취자인데요, 질문이 있어서요.

여 네, 말씀하세요.

남 제 사연과 신청곡을 〈당신과 함께〉 라디오 프로그램에 보내고 싶은데요, 방법을 모르겠어요.

여 그 프로그램의 웹사이트에 접속하시거나 아니면 ABC 라디오 애플리케이션을 다운받으실 수 있습니다.

남 알겠습니다. 도와주셔서 감사해요.

여 천만에요.

---

04 ②

W Oh, my God. I'm late for my swimming class.

M When does class start?

W Class starts at 5 p.m. I should have left at 4:45 at the latest.

M You can go now, then.

W But the clock says it's already 4:55.

M Oh, I've adjusted the clock 10 minutes ahead than the actual time.

W Why would anybody do that?

M I do it so that I won't be late. Since it's 4:45 actually, you won't be late for your class if you get going now.

여 오, 이런. 수영 수업에 늦었다.

남 수업이 몇 시에 시작하는데?

여 수업은 5시 시작해. 늦어도 4시 45분에는 출발했어야 해.

남 그러면 지금 출발하면 되겠네.

여 하지만 시계는 벌써 4시 55분이라고 가리키고 있는데.

남 아, 내가 시계를 실제 시각보다 10분 빠르게 맞춰 놨어.

여 대체 왜 그렇게 하는 거야?

남 늦지 않으려고 그렇게 해. 실제로는 4시 45분이니까 지금 출발하면 수업에 안 늦을 거야.

---

05 ④

M Hello, how may I help you?

W I've lost some weight recently and so I want to reduce the waist of this skirt.

M Okay. How much would you like to reduce the size?

W I'm not so sure. Could you please measure my waist?

M Sure. Let me see.... I guess a half an inch would be enough.

W Okay. I also want these coats to be dry-cleaned.

M All right. They will be ready by Thursday.

W Great.

남 안녕하세요, 무엇을 도와 드릴까요?

여 최근에 살이 좀 빠져서 이 치마 허리를 좀 줄이고 싶어요.

남 좋습니다. 사이즈를 얼마나 줄여드릴까요?

여 확실히 모르겠어요. 제 허리를 좀 재어 주시겠어요?

남 물론이죠. 어디 보자. 반 인치면 충분할 것 같아요.

여 네. 이 코트들도 드라이클리닝 부탁드려요.

남 알겠습니다. 목요일까지는 준비될 거예요.

여 좋습니다.

---

06 ②

① **M** Stay away from there.

   W All right. The oven looks very hot.

② **M** This vending machine ate my coins again.

   W Really? It must be out of order.

③ **M** How about drinking something hot?

   W Good idea. I'd love to have warm milk.

④ **M** It's so cold and windy today.

   W Yeah. We'd better not go out today.

⑤ **M** It's really nice to swim here.

   W Yes. This is the perfect place in this hot weather.

---

① **남** 거기서 떨어져 있어.

   여 알겠어. 오븐이 무척 뜨거워 보이네.

② **남** 이 자판기가 또 내 동전을 먹어버렸어.

   여 정말? 그것은 고장 난 게 틀림없어.

③ **남** 뜨거운 것을 마시는 게 어떨까?

   여 좋은 생각이야. 나는 따뜻한 우유를 먹고 싶어.

④ **남** 오늘 정말 춥고 바람이 분다.

   여 그래. 오늘은 밖에 나가지 않는 게 좋겠어.

⑤ **남** 여기서 수영하니까 정말 좋아.

   여 그래. 이곳은 이런 더운 날씨에는 완벽한 곳이야.

---

07 ①

W What do you want to have for dinner, Jason?

M What do we have in the fridge, Mom?

W We've got some beef stew and some side dishes.

M Can we please eat out today?

W No way. I've already prepared the rice for cooking.

M But I'm tired of eating the beef stew for three days in a row.

W I've got an idea. Why don't you order some *jokbal*? We can have it with cooked rice.

M Yay, I'll order it right away.

여 Jason, 저녁 뭐 먹고 싶니?

남 냉장고에 뭐 있는데요, 엄마?

여 소고깃국이랑 반찬이 좀 있지.

남 오늘 외식하면 안 돼요?

여 안 돼. 벌써 쌀을 안쳐 놨단다.

남 하지만 3일 연속으로 소고깃국 먹는 데 질렸어요.

여 좋은 생각이 났다. 족발을 좀 주문하면 어떨까? 밥이랑 먹으면 되잖아.

남 오예, 지금 바로 주문할게요.

---

08 ④

W Let me explain some coffee-related terms to you. The first term is *café latte*. In French, *café* means coffee, and *latte* means milk. So *café latte* means coffee with milk. The second term is caramel *macchiato*. *Macchiato* is an Italian word which means "stained or marked." So caramel *macchiato* refers to coffee stained with caramel syrup.

여 커피와 관련된 용어를 몇 가지 설명해 드리겠습니다. 첫 번째 용어는 '카페라테'입니다. 프랑스어로 '카페'는 커피를 의미하고, '라테'는 우유를 뜻합니다. 따라서 '카페라테'는 우유를 곁들인 커피를 의미하죠. 두 번째 용어는 '캐러멜마키아토'입니다. '마키아토'는 '얼룩진 혹은 표시된'이라는 의미의 이탈리아어입니다. 그래서 '캐러멜마키아토'는 캐러멜 시럽으로 얼룩진 커피를 가리킵니다.

---

09 ②

M It is something you need when you purchase goods. It has two main kinds: coins and paper. Every country has its own design. These days, credit cards and other means of payment have been replacing it. As a result, people don't bring it in their wallets as often as they used to.

남 그것은 여러분이 물건을 구입할 때 필요한 것입니다. 그것에는 두 가지 주된 종류가 있는데, 동전과 지폐입니다. 각 국가에는 자신만의 디자인이 있습니다. 오늘날에는 신용카드와

다른 지불 수단들이 그것을 대체하고 있습니다. 결과적으로, 사람들은 전보다 그것을 지갑에 들고 다니지 않습니다.

---

10 ④

① **W** I feel so small these days.

　M I sometimes feel that way too. Cheer up.

② **W** I'm afraid I won't be able to do well on final exams.

　M You've been studying really hard. I'm sure you'll do great.

③ **W** I think I look ugly.

　M Come on. You have the most beautiful smile in the world.

④ **W** Nobody cares for me. In fact, everybody hates me.

　M I can't stand people like her.

⑤ **W** I feel stupid when people ask me about my dream.

　M Don't worry. You've got plenty of time to think about it.

---

① **여** 나 요즘 너무 초라한 느낌이야.

　남 나도 때때로 그렇게 느껴. 힘내.

② **여** 나 기말고사를 잘 보지 못할 것 같아서 두려워.

　남 너 정말 열심히 공부해 왔잖아. 난 네가 잘할 거라고 확신해.

③ **여** 나 너무 못생긴 것 같아.

　남 왜 그래. 넌 세상에서 가장 아름다운 미소를 지녔잖아.

④ **여** 아무도 날 좋아하지 않아. 실제로, 모두가 날 싫어해.

　남 난 그녀와 같은 사람들을 참을 수가 없어.

⑤ **여** 사람들이 내 꿈에 대해 물을 때 난 바보가 된 느낌이야.

　남 걱정 마. 그것에 대해 생각할 시간이 많이 있어.

---

11 ②

M I saw a documentary about water pollution yesterday and I made an important decision.

W Oh, yeah? What is it?

M I decided not to use hair conditioner from now on.

W Won't your hair be too stiff if you don't use it?

M The documentary suggested that we use vinegar instead.

W Vinegar? I wouldn't want to use vinegar for my hair.

M   Not only is it good for the environment, it is good for your health too. It's really effective at removing harmful chemicals of shampoo.

W   Hmm, let me watch the documentary before I decide whether to try it or not.

남   나 어제 수질 오염에 대한 다큐멘터리를 보고 중대한 결심을 했어.

여   그래? 뭔데?

남   난 이제부터 헤어 컨디셔너를 안 쓰기로 했어.

여   그걸 안 쓰면 머리가 너무 뻣뻣하지 않겠니?

남   다큐멘터리에서 대신 식초를 쓰라고 제안했어.

여   식초? 나는 식초를 내 머리에 쓸 의향이 없어.

남   그건 환경에 좋을 뿐만 아니라 건강에도 좋아. 그건 샴푸의 해로운 화학 물질을 제거하는 데 매우 효과적이야.

여   흠, 시도해 볼지 말지를 결정하기 전에 내가 그 다큐멘터리를 볼게.

---

12 ②

M   Honey, this is the list of the plants I selected. I think you can choose one for our living room from the list.

W   Awesome. Oh, does the Rose geranium keep away mosquitos?

M   Yes, it has a smell that mosquitos hate.

W   That's interesting but I prefer the ones that purify the air.

M   That leaves us three options.

W   The Areca palm seems gorgeous but I'm not willing to spend more than 30,000 won on plants.

M   How about the Coral wood then? It has shiny red fruits which look like coral.

W   That's nice. Let's buy it.

남   여보, 이게 내가 고른 식물들의 목록이에요. 이 목록에서 우리 거실에 놓을 것 하나를 고르면 될 것 같아요.

여   굉장하네요. 오, 로즈제라늄은 모기를 쫓아요?

남   네, 그것은 모기가 싫어하는 냄새를 지녔어요.

여   흥미롭지만 전 공기를 정화하는 식물을 선호해요.

남   그러면 선택할 수 있는 게 세 개 남네요.

여   아레카야자가 멋져 보이긴 하는데 전 식물에 3만원 이상 쓰고 싶지 않아요.

남   그러면 산호수는 어때요? 그것은 산호처럼 보이는 빛나는 빨간색의 열매가 나요.

여   좋네요. 그걸로 사요.

---

13 ③

M   Judy, what's the date today?

W   It's June 13th.

M   Isn't your birthday five days later?

W   Right. My birthday is June 18th. Why?

M   I want to throw a party for you on that day.

W   Thank you. But it's a Wednesday. I think the weekend before my birthday will be better for having a party.

M   Right. Then how about June 14th?

W   It's Saturday, right? I'm going camping with my family on that day.

M   I see. Then let's have the party on the next day, the 15th.

W   Okay. How sweet you are!

남   Judy, 오늘이 며칠이야?

여   6월 13일이야.

남   5일 후가 네 생일 아니니?

여   맞아. 내 생일은 6월 18일이지. 왜?

남   그날 널 위해 파티를 열어주고 싶어서.

여   고마워. 하지만 그날은 수요일이야. 내 생일 전의 주말이 파티를 열기에는 더 나을 것 같아.

남   맞아. 그럼 6월 14일은 어때?

여   토요일 맞지? 그날은 가족과 함께 캠핑을 갈 거야.

남   알았어. 그러면 그 다음 날인 15일에 파티를 하자.

여   좋아. 넌 정말 친절하구나!

---

14 ②

W   Hi, David.

M   Hey, Becky. What happened to your voice? Did you catch a cold?

W   No, I went to the K-pop concert yesterday. I kept shouting throughout the concert. It was a fantastic night.

M   I can imagine.

W   How was your weekend?

M   I played soccer with my friends all day yesterday.

W   So that's why you got tanned. I thought you've been to the beach or something.

M   You don't have to go to the beach to get a sun burn.

여   안녕, David.

남   이봐, Becky. 네 목소리가 왜 그러니? 감기 걸렸니?

여 아니, 어제 케이팝 콘서트에 갔어. 콘서트 내내 계속 소리를 질렀지. 황홀한 밤이었어.

남 상상이 간다.

여 넌 주말 어떻게 보냈니?

남 어제 하루 종일 친구들과 축구했어.

여 그래서 탔구나. 해변 같은 곳에 다녀온 줄 알았지.

남 해변에 가야만 타는 건 아니니까.

15 ②

W Hello, here's a quick announcement from the management booth. We have found a 4-year-old boy. He is wearing a black jumper, blue jeans and white sneakers. He was found crying alone near the water fountain. If you are his parent or guardian, please come to the management booth and take him. Thank you.

여 안녕하십니까, 관리 사무소에서 잠시 안내 말씀드리겠습니다. 네 살짜리 소년을 발견했습니다. 그 아이는 검정색 점퍼와 청바지, 그리고 흰색 운동화를 착용하고 있습니다. 그 아이는 음수대 근처에서 혼자 울고 있는 모습이 발견되었습니다. 부모님이나 보호자께서는 관리 사무소로 오셔서 아이를 데려가시기 바랍니다. 감사합니다.

16 ③

M Jane, let's go hiking this Saturday.

W This Saturday is April 10th, right?

M Right. Are you busy on that day?

W Well, I'll have to visit my grandparents in the country. That day is my grandfather's birthday.

M Then how about making it a week later?

W You mean on the 17th?

M Yes.

W I don't have any plans on that day. Let's go hiking on that day.

남 Jane, 이번 토요일에 하이킹 가자.

여 이번 토요일은 4월 10일이지, 맞지?

남 맞아. 그날 바쁘니?

여 음, 시골에 계신 조부모님을 찾아뵈어야 해서. 그날이 할아버지 생신이거든.

남 그러면 한 주 후에 만나면 어떨까?

여 17일에 말이니?

남 그래.

여 그날에는 계획이 없어. 그날 하이킹 가자.

17 ④

M Oh, no.

W What's the matter?

M The application for the musical audition was due on Monday. I totally forgot to submit it and it's already Wednesday.

W Oh... why don't you call the office and ask if you can hand it in late?

M I don't think they will let me submit it late.

W If I were you, I would try it. You know, trying wouldn't hurt.

M Do you really think so?

남 오, 이런.

여 무슨 일이야?

남 뮤지컬 오디션 지원서가 월요일에 마감이었어. 제출하는 것을 완전히 까먹었는데 벌써 수요일이야.

여 아… 사무실에 전화해서 늦게 제출할 수 있는지 문의해 보는 게 어때?

남 늦게 제출할 수 없을 것 같아.

여 내가 만일 너라면, 나는 시도해 볼 거야. 너도 알다시피, 밑져야 본전이잖아.

남 정말 그렇게 생각해?

18 ①

W Mark, why are you always reading books?

M Well, I love reading books. I think it is because of my Grandma.

W What did she do to you? Did she force you to read books?

M Not at all. She used to read books to me before I went to bed when I was little.

W I see.

M They are my favorite memories when I was little.

W I wish I had such great memories with my own Grandma too. However, both of my grandmothers passed away before I was born.

여 Mark, 넌 어째서 항상 책을 읽니?

남 음, 난 책 읽는 걸 좋아해. 우리 할머니 때문인 것 같아.

여 할머니께서 어떻게 하셨는데? 책 읽으라고 강요하셨니?

남 전혀. 할머니께서는 내가 어릴 때 자기 전에 책을 읽어주곤 하셨어.

여 그렇구나.

남 그 시간들이 내 어린 시절의 가장 좋은 기억이야.

여 나도 할머니와의 그런 좋은 기억이 있으면 좋겠다. 하지만 할머니 두 분 모두 내가 태어나기 전에 돌아가셨어.

남 Esther와 Tim은 영어 교과서에서 퍼스널 컬러에 대한 글을 막 읽었다. 글에 따르면, 모든 사람에게는 자신에게 가장 잘 어울리는 개인적인 색깔이 있다고 했다. Esther는 Tim에게 자신이 입고 있는 셔츠의 색깔이 자신에게 어울리는지 물어보았는데, Tim은 그 색깔이 그녀의 퍼스널 컬러라고 생각하지 않았다. 이 상황에서, Tim은 Esther에게 뭐라고 말할까?

19 ⑤

W Paul, can I borrow your notes for the Chinese class?

M Here you go. But why do you need it?

W I missed classes yesterday, and I didn't want to miss anything important.

M Oh, right. I was about to ask you why you didn't come to class.

W You know how I'm allergic to shrimps, right?

M Yeah, of course.

W I didn't know that the fries we ate for lunch yesterday were made of shrimp. So I just ate them.

M Oh, no. Did you have to go to the hospital?

여 Paul, 네 중국어 수업 공책 좀 빌릴 수 있을까?

남 여기 있어. 그런데 왜 그게 필요하니?

여 어제 수업을 빠졌는데, 중요한 것들을 놓치고 싶지 않아서.

남 아, 맞다. 네가 왜 수업에 오지 않았는지 물어보려던 참이었어.

여 내가 새우 알레르기 있는 거 알고 있지?

남 응, 물론이지.

여 어제 점심으로 먹은 튀김이 새우로 만들어진 줄을 몰랐어. 그래서 그냥 먹었거든.

남 오, 안 돼. 그래서 병원에 가야 했니?

20 ⑤

M Esther and Tim just read an article about personal color on their English textbook. The article said that everyone has a personal color that suits them best. Esther asked Tim if the color of her shirt suited her but Tim didn't think the color was her personal color. In this situation, what would Tim most likely say to Esther?

>> 03회 듣기 실전 모의고사   pp. 128~135

01 ⑤	02 ⑤	03 ⑤	04 ③	05 ①	06 ①	07 ④	08 ⑤
09 ①	10 ③	11 ⑤	12 ③	13 ⑤	14 ④	15 ③	16 ①
17 ⑤	18 ⑤	19 ⑤	20 ④				

Dictation Test

01 a nice blanket, something cute, smaller rabbits
02 something wrong, sick in bed, appreciate it
03 ask for, pick them up, come after   **04** beloved artists, started her career, continued painting   **05** go for, at least, while waiting   **06** bring, Stay calm, temporary password   **07** all over them, wash away, recommend using   **08** smoky flavor, is cooked, directly on   **09** brush your teeth, thread, might bleed
10 nobody got hurt, offend you, homeroom teacher
11 neck pain, go away, from the side, fix my posture
12 that begins, third period, Korean class together
13 my pronunciation, repeat after, try your method
14 buy two, two packs, large-sized one   **15** dying from, preparing for, help starving children   **16** once a month, having dinner, pay the fee   **17** to go, sprinkle pepper, anything else   **18** perfect match, just like raindrops, entire piece   **19** behind it, got a haircut, laughed at   **20** one week left, be worried, waits until

01 ⑤

M Is there anything you want for Christmas?

W I would like to have a nice blanket.

M What kind of blanket do you want?

W I usually prefer something simple without any patterns but I'd like to have something cute this time.

M Like what?

W I don't have anything specific in mind.

M I once saw Cindy using a blanket that had an image of a big rabbit on it. Everybody thought it was cute. How about that?

W That'll be nice but please buy me one that has smaller rabbits on it if you can find one.

남 크리스마스 선물로 받고 싶은 것 있니?

여 좋은 담요 하나 가지고 싶어.

남 어떤 종류의 담요를 원하는데?

여 나는 보통 아무 무늬도 없는 단순한 것을 선호하는데, 이번에는 귀여운 것을 가지고 싶어.

남 이를테면 어떤 것?

여 특별히 생각한 것은 없어.

남 Cindy가 커다란 토끼가 그려진 담요를 쓰는 것을 본 적이 있는데. 모두 그게 귀엽다고 생각했어. 그건 어때?

여 그거 좋겠는데. 혹시 찾을 수 있다면 나는 더 작은 토끼들이 있는 것을 사 줘.

02 ⑤

M Did you finish your math assignment?

W I've only solved two problems and I still have eight left.

M You had the whole weekend to finish it. Was there something wrong?

W Well, I've been sick in bed. So I've slept for almost 30 hours during the weekend.

M Wow. Are you feeling any better?

W Yeah, but I think I should go to the hospital after school.

M Yes, you should. By the way, do you want me to help you with the math assignment?

W I appreciate it but I would like to do it myself.

남 수학 숙제 다 했니?

여 두 문제만 풀고 아직도 여덟 문제가 남았어.

남 숙제를 마치려고 주말을 다 보냈잖아. 무슨 일 있었어?

여 음, 아파서 누워 있었어. 그래서 주말 동안 거의 30시간은 잤다니까.

남 와. 좀 나아졌니?

여 응, 하지만 방과 후에 병원에 가야 할 것 같아.

남 응, 그래야겠다. 그나저나, 수학 숙제 좀 도와줄까?

여 고맙지만 내가 스스로 할게.

03 ⑤

[Telephone rings.]

M Grace Pediatrics. How may I be of assistance?

W Hello, I visited the hospital an hour ago and I just realized that I had forgotten to ask for a doctor's note. I have to submit it to my school.

M Your name and birthday, please.

W It's Sophia Hong and I was born in November 17, 2005.

M Okay. We'll have the documents ready for you. When would you like to pick them up?

W I'll be right there in 30 minutes.

M It's lunch time soon and if you can't come in 10 minutes, I suggest that you come after 1 o'clock.

W I see.

남 은혜 소아과입니다. 무엇을 도와 드릴까요?

여 안녕하세요, 제가 한 시간 전에 병원을 방문했는데요, 진단서 요청하는 것을 깜빡했다는 것을 방금 알았어요. 그것을 학교에 제출해야 해서요.

남 이름과 생일을 말씀해주세요.

여 Sophia Hong이고요, 생일은 2005년 11월 17일입니다.

남 네. 서류를 준비해 놓겠습니다. 언제 가지러 오시겠어요?

여 30분 안에 갈게요.

남 곧 점심시간이어서 10분 안에 오실 수 있는 게 아니면 1시 이후에 오실 것을 권장합니다.

여 알겠습니다.

04 ③

W What are you reading, David?

M I'm reading a book called "My Life's History" written by Grandma Moses.

W Who's Grandma Moses?

M She is one of the most beloved artists in America.

W And why is she called Grandma Moses?

M She got her nickname from the fact that she started her career as a painter when she was 76.

W That's unbelievable.

M Indeed. Grandma Moses continued painting for 26 years until she died at the age of 102. She published this book when she was 92.

여 David, 뭐 읽고 있니?

남 Grandma Moses가 쓴 〈My Life's History〉라는 책을 읽고 있어.

여 Grandma Moses가 누군데?

남 그녀는 미국에서 가장 사랑받는 예술가들 중 한 명이야.

여 그런데 왜 Grandma Moses라고 불리는 거야?

남 그녀가 76세 때 화가로서 경력을 시작한 사실로 인해 붙여진 별명이야.

여 도저히 믿기 어렵다.

남 정말 그래. Grandma Moses는 102세의 나이로 별세하기 전까지 26년 동안 그림을 계속해서 그렸어. 그녀는 이 책을 92세 때 출판했어.

05 ①

W Which ride do you want to go for next?

M Why don't we try the roller coaster one more time?

W No way. It was scary. How about bumper cars?

M That'll be fun too. Where is it?

W Right over there. Oh, my. Look at the line.

M I'm sure we'll have to wait for at least two hours.

W Let's grab a bite before we get on the line.

M Or we can buy some burgers and fries and eat while waiting for our turn.

W Great idea.

여 다음엔 어떤 놀이기구 타고 싶니?

남 롤러코스터 한 번 더 타면 어때?

여 안 돼. 무서웠어. 범퍼카 타는 건 어때?

남 그것도 재미있겠다. 어디에 있지?

여 바로 저기에. 오, 이런. 줄 좀 봐.

남 분명 최소 두 시간은 기다려야 할 거야.

여 줄 서기 전에 뭐 좀 먹자.

남 아니면 햄버거랑 감자튀김을 좀 사서 우리 차례를 기다리면서 먹어도 되겠다.

여 좋은 생각이야.

06 ①

① W Make sure you bring your passport.
  M No worries. I already put it in my backpack.

② W I don't remember where I put my passport.
  M Stay calm and try to search for it again.

③ W May I see your passport?
  M Can I show you another ID card instead?

④ W I forgot my password for the website.
  M Just tap the blue button and try to set a temporary password.

⑤ W What do I need to bring to reissue my passport?
  M You need two pictures and your ID card.

---

① 여 여권 가져가는 거 잊지 마.
  남 걱정 마. 이미 배낭에 넣었어.

② 여 여권을 어디에 뒀는지 기억이 안 나요.
  남 침착하게 다시 한 번 찾아보세요.

③ 여 여권 좀 보여주시겠어요?
  남 대신 다른 신분증을 보여드려도 되나요?

④ 여 웹사이트 비밀번호를 잊어버렸어요.
  남 파란 버튼을 클릭해서 임시 비밀번호를 설정해 보세요.

⑤ 여 여권을 재발급 받으려면 무엇을 가져가야 해?
  남 사진 두 장과 신분증이 필요해.

07 ④

W Tim, what happened to your sneakers? There are stains all over them.

M I accidentally spilt coffee on them in the morning.

W Oh, no. Were you burned?

M Fortunately, it was iced coffee.

W That's a relief.

M Yeah. Anyway, is there a way I can wash away all of the stains?

W I recommend using baking soda when you brush sneakers.

M Can you give me some if you have it at home?

W Of course. I can give it to you tomorrow.

여 Tim, 네 운동화에 무슨 일이 생긴 거야? 온통 얼룩이네.

남 아침에 실수로 그 위에 커피를 쏟았어.

여 오, 이런. 데었니?

남 다행히도, 아이스 커피였어.

여 다행이다.

남 응. 그나저나, 얼룩을 다 지울 수 있는 방법이 있을까?

여 운동화를 닦을 때 베이킹 소다를 쓸 것을 권해.

남 베이킹 소다가 집에 있으면 좀 줄 수 있니?

여 물론이지. 내일 가져다줄게.

08 ⑤

W Here's how you can add a smoky flavor to your *bulgogi*. First, add oil to a hot pan and fry some scallions which are called "pa" in Korean. Then put the *bulgogi* into the pan and cook them until the meat is cooked. Now, here's the most important part. Don't pour soy sauce directly on the *bulgogi* but around it. This way, you'll have a tasty *bulgogi* dish that has a mouth-watering smoky flavor.

여 불고기에 훈제한 맛을 더하는 방법을 설명해 드릴게요. 먼저, 달궈진 팬에 기름을 두르고, 한국어로는 '파'라고 불리는 것을 좀 볶으세요. 그런 다음에 팬에 불고기를 넣고 고기가 익을 때까지 볶으세요. 자, 여기가 가장 중요한 부분입니다. 간장을 불고기 위가 아닌 주변에 부으세요. 이렇게 하면, 군침이 도는 훈제한 맛이 나는 맛있는 불고기 요리를 하실 수 있어요.

09 ①

M It is something that you can use before or after you brush your teeth. It is basically a piece of thread that you can use to remove any remaining food between your teeth. You should be careful when using it because your gums might bleed if you push it in too hard. Dentists recommend using it two to three times a week.

남 이것은 이를 닦기 전이나 후에 이용할 수 있는 것입니다. 이것은 기본적으로 치아 사이에 남아있는 음식물을 제거하기 위해 쓰는 실 조각입니다. 실을 너무 힘차게 밀어 넣으면 잇몸에서 피가 날 수 있으므로 이것을 이용할 때 조심해야 합니다. 치과 의사들은 이것을 일주일에 두세 번 쓰기를 권장합니다.

10 ③

① W Can you go get me some coffee?

　 M Sure. What kind of coffee would you like?

② W Look, there must have been a traffic accident.

　 M That's why there's a traffic jam. I hope nobody got hurt.

③ W What time can you pick me up?

　 M Sorry, I didn't mean to offend you.

④ W Where have you been during lunch time?

　 M I talked with my homeroom teacher.

⑤ W Why don't we have chicken soup for dinner?

　 M Sorry but we don't have the ingredients in the fridge.

① 여 가서 커피 좀 사다 줄래요?

　 남 물론이죠. 어떤 커피를 원하나요?

② 여 봐, 차 사고가 났네.

　 남 그래서 차가 막혔구나. 아무도 안 다쳤으면 좋겠다.

③ 여 몇 시에 날 데리러 올 수 있나요?

　 남 미안해요, 기분 나쁘게 할 생각은 없었어요.

④ 여 점심시간에 어디에 갔었니?

　 남 담임 선생님과 이야기를 나눴어.

⑤ 여 저녁에 닭죽을 먹는 게 어때요?

　 남 미안하지만 냉장고에 닭죽 재료가 없어요.

11 ⑤

W I've been suffering from severe neck pain.

M Come here. Let me massage your neck a little bit.

W Thanks. Ouch, it really hurts.

M Why don't you do some neck exercises from time to time?

W Well, I do it all the time but the pain won't go away.

M Then I think you need to fix your posture.

W Do you think so?

M Yeah. Let me take a picture of you from the side and show you. Here, look.

W Wow, seriously, I look like a turtle. I guess I should try really hard to fix my posture.

여 나 심각한 목 통증에 시달리고 있어요.

남 이리 와 봐요. 내가 목을 좀 마사지해 줄게요.

여 고마워요. 아야, 정말 아프네요.

남 때때로 목 운동을 좀 하지 그래요?

여 음, 매일 하는데 통증이 사라지지 않네요.

남 그러면 자세를 고쳐야 할 것 같군요.

여　그렇게 생각해요?

남　네. 옆에서 당신의 사진을 찍어서 보여줄게요. 자, 봐요.

여　와, 정말, 제가 거북이처럼 보이네요. 자세를 고치기 위해 정말 열심히 노력해야겠어요.

12 ③

W　Brian, did you decide on which classes to take during the summer?

M　Not yet. Shall we take the English class that begins at 8 o'clock together?

W　Hey, I can't wake up that early during vacation. Why not take the 11:20 English class with me?

M　I want to take the math class in the third period.

W　How about this then? You take English and math on the first and the third period, and we take the Korean class together in the second period.

M　That schedule looks exhausting to me. I want to enjoy my summer vacation.

W　Come on, buddy.

M　All right.

여　Brian, 여름에 어떤 수업 들을지 결정했니?

남　아직. 8시에 시작하는 영어 수업 같이 들을래?

여　야, 난 방학 때 그렇게 일찍 일어날 수는 없어. 11시 20분 영어 수업을 나랑 같이 들으면 어때?

남　나 3교시에는 수학 수업을 듣고 싶어.

여　그럼 이렇게 할까? 네가 1교시와 3교시에 영어와 수학 수업을 듣고, 2교시에 우리가 같이 국어 수업을 듣는 거지.

남　그 일정은 내게 힘들 것 같아. 나 여름 방학을 즐기고 싶어.

여　제발, 친구야.

남　알았어.

13 ⑤

M　Olivia, I think your English pronunciation is really good.

W　Thanks. I've been practicing my pronunciation while watching American television shows.

M　Do you repeat after the actors?

W　Yeah. When there's a line I want to memorize, I pause and repeat after the line is said.

M　How many times do you repeat each line?

W　I go over again and again until I am satisfied.

M　I want to try your method. Can you recommend any television shows to me?

W　Since you like thrillers, how about "Grimm?"

M　Awesome. I'm going to download the show right now.

남　Olivia, 너 영어 발음 정말 좋은 것 같아.

여　고마워. 미국 텔레비전 쇼 보면서 발음을 연습하고 있어.

남　배우들을 따라 말하는 거야?

여　응. 내가 암기하고 싶은 문장이 나올 때, 일시 정지하고 대사를 따라해.

남　각 대사를 몇 번이나 반복하니?

여　내가 만족스러울 때까지 계속 반복해.

남　네 방법을 시도해 보고 싶다. 내게 텔레비전 쇼 추천해줄래?

여　넌 스릴러를 좋아하니까 〈Grimm〉 어떠니?

남　좋다. 지금 바로 그 쇼를 다운받아야겠다.

14 ④

W　May I help you?

M　Yes. I want some cookies. How much is this pack?

W　It's 6 dollars. But if you buy two, we'll sell them to you for 10 dollars.

M　Sounds good. I'll take two packs of them. And I need an orange juice.

W　A large-sized one is 3 dollars and a medium-sized one is 2 dollars.

M　One medium-sized orange juice, please.

W　Anything else?

M　That's all.

여　도와 드릴까요?

남　네. 저는 쿠키를 좀 원해요. 이 묶음은 얼마죠?

여　6달러입니다. 하지만 두 개를 사시면, 10달러에 드릴게요.

남　좋네요. 두 묶음 살게요. 그리고 오렌지 주스도 필요해요.

여　큰 사이즈는 3달러이고 중간 사이즈는 2달러입니다.

남　중간 사이즈 오렌지 주스로 주세요.

여　다른 것은요?

남　그게 전부입니다.

15 ③

W　Isn't it sad to think that children are dying from hunger in some parts of the world when people have been throwing so much food away? In response to this situation, the world-famous rock band, BYS, has been preparing for a fundraising concert. The tickets will be sold from Monday 7 p.m. and all profit will be used to help starving children.

여 사람들이 너무나 많은 음식물 쓰레기를 버리고 있을 때 세계의 어느 부분에서는 아이들이 굶주림으로 죽어가고 있다는 사실을 생각하면 너무 슬프지 않으신가요? 이에, 세계적으로 유명한 록 밴드인 BYS가 기금 마련 콘서트를 준비했습니다. 티켓은 월요일 7시부터 판매될 예정이며, 모든 수익금은 굶주림에 허덕이고 있는 아이들을 돕는 데 쓰일 것입니다.

16 ①

M Hello, students. Today, I'm going to introduce our Friday Evening Movie Club to you. We gather once a month at school and watch a movie. Then we discuss the movie while having dinner together. You have to pay 10 dollars for every meeting. But if you join us, you don't need to pay the fee for the first month.

남 안녕하세요, 학생 여러분. 오늘 저는 우리의 Friday Evening 영화 동아리를 여러분께 소개해 드리겠습니다. 우리는 한 달에 한 번 학교에서 모여서 영화를 봅니다. 그런 다음 함께 저녁 식사를 하면서 그 영화에 대해 토론합니다. 여러분은 매번 모임마다 10달러를 내야 합니다. 하지만 가입하시면, 첫 달에는 회비를 내실 필요가 없습니다.

17 ⑤

W Hi, Mr. Williams. What would you like to have for today?

M I'd like to have a hot americano and a ham cheese bagel.

W Great. Is it for here or to go?

M I want to have it for here. By the way, could you not sprinkle pepper on the bagel?

W Really? It would probably taste better with it.

M Yeah, but I personally don't like the smell of pepper.

W No problem. Is there anything else you need?

여 안녕하세요, Williams 씨. 오늘은 어떤 것을 드시겠어요?
남 뜨거운 아메리카노와 햄치즈베이글을 먹을게요.

여 좋습니다. 여기에서 드시나요, 아니면 포장해 드릴까요?
남 여기에서 먹는 걸로 할게요. 그런데, 베이글에 후추를 뿌리지 말아 주시겠어요?
여 정말요? 그게 있는 편이 더 맛있을 텐데요.
남 네, 하지만 개인적으로 후추의 향을 안 좋아해서요.
여 문제없습니다. 다른 필요하신 게 더 있으신가요?

18 ⑤

M What is the title of this piano piece on the computer?

W It's "Raindrop" by Chopin.

M Oh, yeah? I thought it was a perfect match for today's rainy weather.

W You can say that again. This part sounds just like raindrops.

M Indeed. Sometimes it's softer, and other times it's louder.

W Yeah, this part sounds just like pouring rain.

M It's so beautiful. Can we listen to the entire piece one more time?

남 컴퓨터에서 나오는 피아노곡의 제목이 뭐야?
여 쇼팽의 〈빗방울 전주곡〉이야.
남 아, 그래? 오늘의 비 오는 날씨와 정말 잘 어울린다고 생각했거든.
여 동감이야. 이 부분은 마치 빗방울 소리처럼 들린다.
남 정말 그래. 때로는 더 부드럽고, 때로는 더 크게 들리네.
여 응, 이 부분은 꼭 비가 퍼붓는 것처럼 들리지.
남 너무 아름답다. 우리 전체 곡을 한 번 더 들을 수 있을까?

19 ⑤

W Chris, I like your new hair style.

M I'm glad you like it but there's a long story behind it.

W I'd like to hear about it.

M Well, I heard the girl I like talking to a friend. She said that she liked boys with short hair. So, I got a haircut and showed it to her.

W What happened then?

M It was a disaster. She laughed at my hair. She said that it made me look like a chestnut.

W Oh, no. So that's why you permed your hair.

여	Chris, 새로운 머리 스타일 마음에 든다.
남	마음에 든다니 기쁜데 그 뒤에는 긴 이야기가 있지.
여	그것에 대해 듣고 싶다.
남	음, 내가 좋아하는 여자아이가 친구와 이야기하는 걸 들었어. 그녀는 머리가 짧은 남자아이를 좋아한다고 하더라고. 그래서 난 머리를 자르고 그걸 그녀에게 보여줬지.
여	그 다음엔 어떻게 됐어?
남	완전히 망쳤어. 그녀는 내 머리를 비웃었어. 머리 때문에 내가 밤처럼 보인다고 했어.
여	오, 저런. 그래서 파마를 한 거구나.

20 ④

M: Ruth is very upset because she has only one week left until her science report is due. Meanwhile, Paul, who hasn't even started doing it, seems very relaxed. Ruth asks why he doesn't seem to be worried at all. Paul wants to explain that he sometimes waits until the last moment on purpose and thinks it is not bad. In this situation, what would Paul most likely say to Ruth?

남: Ruth는 과학 보고서 제출 기한까지 겨우 한 주가 남았기 때문에 너무 속상하다. 한편, Paul은 심지어 그것을 시작도 안 했는데, 매우 여유로워 보인다. Ruth는 그가 어째서 전혀 걱정하지 않는 것처럼 보이는지 묻는다. Paul은 자신이 때때로 일부러 마지막 순간까지 기다리며, 이것이 나쁘지 않다고 생각한다는 것을 설명하려 한다. 이 상황에서, Paul은 Ruth에게 뭐라고 말할까?

01 ③	02 ③	03 ③	04 ③	05 ⑤	06 ⑤	07 ②	08 ④
09 ④	10 ③	11 ③	12 ①	13 ⑤	14 ④	15 ②	16 ④
17 ⑤	18 ②	19 ③	20 ⑤				

Dictation Test

01 buy something, new arrivals, stripes, dots **02** get to school, comes every, half price **03** bought a jacket, left my camera, must have lost, let me know **04** taking place, meeting earlier, while watching, ten to eight **05** inviting, broadcasting, film dramas, not to touch **06** recommend, turn on, looking for, turn off **07** get up early, a wake-up call, sleep through **08** brush, turn, off, save the resources, plastic bags **09** mark, wedding anniversary, made with **10** first prize, look like, turning, was taken **11** sign up for, should buy, in total **12** booked tickets, except, gold medal **13** make an appointment, closed, either, or, make it **14** went to, museums, tried various, penguins **15** driving habit, become sleepy, stay awake, sleepy **16** received a call, apart from us, calling him yourself **17** wear a tie, decide between, your outfit **18** get it repaired, stopped working, find out, need it back **19** titled, order it, author, publisher **20** final exam, next to, chatting, noisy, kept talking

01 ③

M: May I help you?

W: Yes, I'm looking to buy something for my father.

M: How about a tie? These are our new arrivals.

W: Wow! They all look very great.

M: What about the one with a lot of stripes? It sells very well.

W: Umm.... My father doesn't like stripes.

M: Then how about the one with a lot of big and small dots?

W: Oh, I like that one. I'll take it.

남: 도와 드릴까요?

여: 네, 아빠를 위해 살 것을 찾고 있어요.

남: 넥타이는 어떠세요? 이것들은 새로 들어온 것들입니다.

여: 와! 모두 정말 멋져 보이네요.

남: 줄무늬가 많은 것을 어떠세요? 매우 잘 팔리는 것입니다.

여: 음…. 아빠가 줄무늬를 안 좋아하세요.

남   그럼 크고 작은 점들이 많은 것은 어떠세요?
여   오, 그게 마음에 들어요. 그것으로 할게요.

02 ③

M   Mom, I'm always late to school because it takes over forty minutes to get to school by bus.

W   Oh, that's too bad. But I heard that the new subway line stops near your school.

M   I didn't know that. That's good news. But is it fast enough?

W   Sure. From here it will take only about fifteen minutes. The subway train comes every ten minutes. There is also a special discount for students.

M   Really? How much is the discount rate?

W   Students can take the train at half price.

M   That's good.

남   엄마, 저 학교에 가는 데 버스로 40분 이상 걸려서 학교에 항상 지각해요.

여   오, 그거 안됐구나. 그런데 새 지하철 노선이 너희 학교 근처에 정차한다고 들었어.

남   몰랐어요. 좋은 소식이네요. 하지만 충분히 빠른가요?

여   물론이지. 여기서부터 15분 정도밖에 안 걸릴 거야. 열차는 10분마다 운행되고, 학생들에게는 특별 할인도 있다는데.

남   정말요? 할인율은 얼마예요?

여   학생들은 반값에 열차를 탈 수 있어.

남   좋네요.

03 ③

[Telephone rings.]

W   Hello. Phil's clothing. What can I do for you?

M   I bought a jacket at your store about an hour ago.

W   Oh, is there any problem with your jacket?

M   No. I think I left my camera at your store. Have you seen it?

W   I'm sorry but I haven't. You must have lost it just before I started work.

M   Oh, really? Then what should I do?

W   If you let me know your phone number, I'll ask the manager and then I'll call you.

M   Oh, I see. My phone number is 234-5678. Thanks.

[전화벨 소리가 울린다.]

여   여보세요. Phil의 옷가게입니다. 무엇을 도와 드릴까요?

남   한 시간쯤 전에 그 가게에서 재킷 한 벌을 샀어요.

여   오, 재킷에 문제라도 있나요?

남   아니요. 제 생각에는 그 가게에 제 카메라를 놓고 온 것 같아서요. 그것을 보셨나요?

여   죄송합니다만 보지 못했어요. 제가 일을 시작하기 방금 전에 그것을 잃어버리신 게 틀림없습니다.

남   오, 정말요? 그러면 어떻게 해야 하나요?

여   고객님의 전화번호를 알려 주시면, 점장님께 여쭤 보고 그러고 나서 전화를 드리겠습니다.

남   오, 알겠습니다. 제 전화번호는 234-5678입니다. 감사합니다.

04 ③

M   The film festival is taking place at Central Park. They are showing *New Moon* tonight. Can you watch it with me?

W   I'd love to. What time does the movie start?

M   Eight, but how about meeting earlier and having dinner together?

W   I don't think I have time for dinner because I have piano lesson until seven in the evening.

M   Then I will bring some sandwiches and we can eat them while watching the movie.

W   That's a good idea. We can meet at the main gate of the park at ten to eight.

M   Okay.

남   영화 축제가 센트럴 파크에서 열리고 있어. 오늘밤에 〈New Moon〉을 상영하는데, 같이 보러 갈래?

여   그러고 싶어. 영화는 몇 시에 시작하지?

남   8시, 하지만 좀 더 일찍 만나서 같이 저녁 먹는 게 어때?

여   저녁 7시까지 피아노 레슨이 있어서 저녁 먹을 시간이 없을 것 같아.

남   그럼 내가 샌드위치를 좀 가져갈게. 영화를 보면서 그것을 먹을 수 있어.

여   좋은 생각이야. 공원 정문에서 8시 10분 전에 만나자.

남   알았어.

05 ⑤

M   Hi, Lisa. Come in.

W   Oh, Tom! Thank you for inviting me here! Wow! I can't believe you work here.

M Yes, it's a great job. I've always been interested in broadcasting.

W So, is this where they film dramas?

M Some of them. I can show you where they film *Sweet Princess*, if you'd like.

W That would be great! That's one of my favorite dramas.

M Follow me then. It's right down this hall. Please try not to touch anything while you are here. The cameras they use are very expensive.

남 안녕, Lisa. 들어와.

여 오, Tom! 날 여기에 초대해 줘서 고마워! 와! 네가 여기서 일 하다니 믿을 수가 없어.

남 그래, 정말 좋은 일이야. 나는 항상 방송에 관심이 있었어.

여 그럼, 여기가 드라마를 찍는 곳이야?

남 그 중 몇 곳이야. 네가 원한다면, 〈Sweet Princess〉 찍는 곳을 보여줄 수 있어.

여 그거 좋겠다! 그건 내가 가장 좋아하는 드라마들 중 하나야.

남 그럼 날 따라와. 이 복도 바로 아래에 있어. 여기 있는 동안에 는 아무것도 만지지 않도록 해. 여기서 쓰는 카메라는 매우 비싸거든.

06 ⑤

① W What can I do for you?
   M Can you recommend a nice TV?

② W Do you mind if I turn on the TV now?
   M Sorry, but I don't want to watch the TV now.

③ W Do you know where the remote control is?
   M No. I was looking for it to turn on the TV, too.

④ W How about buying a new TV?
   M I don't think we need a new one now.

⑤ W You'd better turn off the TV while you're studying.
   M Mom, I'll turn it off after watching this show.

---

① 여 무엇을 도와 드릴까요?
   남 괜찮은 텔레비전 한 대 추천해 주시겠어요?

② 여 지금 텔레비전을 켜도 될까?
   남 미안하지만, 지금은 텔레비전을 보고 싶지 않아요.

③ 여 리모컨이 어디에 있는지 아니?
   남 아니요. 저도 텔레비전을 켜려고 그것을 찾고 있었어요.

④ 여 새 텔레비전을 사는 게 어때?
   남 지금은 새 텔레비전이 필요하지 않은 것 같아요.

⑤ 여 공부를 하고 있는 동안에는 텔레비전을 끄는 것이 좋겠다.
   남 엄마, 이 쇼를 보고 나서 끌게요.

07 ②

W David, do you still get up early in the morning?

M Yes, I usually get up about 5:30.

W Wow! Amazing! Then, can you give me a wake-up call tomorrow morning? I'm supposed to catch the first train at 6:30.

M Sure. No problem. But why don't you set your alarm clock?

W Of course, I will do that. But sometimes it doesn't help me at all. I sleep through it.

M I see. Then, what time do you want me to call?

W 5:30 will be fine.

여 David, 너 여전히 아침 일찍 일어나니?

남 응, 보통 5시 30분쯤 일어나.

여 와! 놀랍다! 그러면 내일 아침에 전화로 나를 좀 깨워줄 수 있 겠니? 6시 30분에 첫 기차를 타기로 되어 있거든.

남 물론이야. 문제없어. 하지만 자명종을 맞춰 놓지 그러니?

여 물론 그렇게 할 거야. 하지만 가끔은 전혀 소용이 없어. 나는 깨지 않고 자.

남 알았어. 그러면 몇 시에 전화해줄까?

여 5시 30분이 좋겠어.

08 ④

W "Going green" is not difficult. Here are some simple ways to help the environment. First, use a cup when you brush your teeth. Second, turn your computers off at night before you go to bed. It can help save 40 watt-hours a day. Third, buy things from a second-hand store to save the resources to make them. Lastly, try to use less plastic bags each day. It is an easy way to protect the environment.

여 '친환경적이 되는 것'은 어렵지 않습니다. 여기 환경을 돕는 몇 가지 간단한 방법이 있습니다. 먼저, 양치질을 할 때는 컵 을 이용하세요. 둘째, 잠자리에 들기 전에 밤에는 컴퓨터를 끄세요. 그것은 하루에 40와트시를 절약하는 데 도움을 줄 수 있습니다. 셋째, 중고 상점에서 물건을 구입해서 그것을 만들 자원을 절약하세요. 마지막으로, 매일 비닐봉지를 적게 쓰도록 노력하세요. 그것은 환경을 보호하는 쉬운 방법입 니다.

09 ④

M This helps you remember special days. You mark things like your friend's birthday and your parents' wedding anniversary on it. This also tells you what day of the week it is today. In the old days, it was mostly made with paper. By the way, these days even your smartphone has it.

남 이것은 당신이 특별한 날들을 기억하도록 도와줍니다. 당신은 친구의 생일과 부모님의 결혼기념일과 같은 것들을 그 위에 표시합니다. 이것은 또한 당신에게 오늘이 일주일 중 무슨 요일인지를 알려 줍니다. 옛날에 그것은 주로 종이로 만들어졌습니다. 하지만 요즘은 당신의 스마트폰조차도 그것을 가지고 있습니다.

10 ③

① **M** I think health is the most important.

  W You can say that again.

② **M** I won the first prize in the marathon.

  W I can't believe that!

③ **M** What does it look like?

  W It's used for playing games.

④ **M** Do you mind turning down the volume? It's too loud.

  W Not at all. I'm sorry.

⑤ **M** Where was the picture taken?

  W I think it was taken in Paris.

---

① **남** 건강이 가장 중요하다고 생각해.

  여 동의해.

② **남** 나 마라톤 경기에서 1등상을 받았어.

  여 믿을 수가 없다!

③ **남** 그것은 어떻게 생겼니?

  여 그것은 게임을 하는 데 쓰여.

④ **남** 볼륨을 낮춰 주시겠어요? 소리가 너무 커서요.

  여 그럼요. 죄송합니다.

⑤ **남** 그 사진은 어디에서 찍은 거니?

  여 그것은 파리에서 찍은 것 같아.

11 ③

W May I help you?

M Yes, please. I'd like to sign up for this art class here. How much is it?

W It's 80 dollars a month.

M I'll take the class.

W All right. And do you have your brushes, paints, pencils and erasers?

M No. I should buy them. Oh, do you sell them here?

W Yes. They cost 50 dollars in total.

M Okay. I'll take them.

여 도와 드릴까요?

남 네, 부탁드려요. 여기 미술 수업에 등록하고 싶은데요. 얼마죠?

여 한 달에 80달러입니다.

남 그 수업을 수강하겠습니다.

여 알겠습니다. 그리고 붓, 물감, 연필, 지우개가 있으세요?

남 아뇨. 사야 합니다. 오, 여기서 파나요?

여 네. 전부해서 50달러입니다.

남 좋아요. 그것들을 사겠습니다.

12 ①

W Have you booked tickets for the ice show?

M I was just about to. Look at this schedule and tell me when is good for you.

W Any day is fine with me except Sunday.

M Sunday is the 24th, right? Then we won't be able to see Amy Gray's performance.

W The performers on the 23rd are also great.

M Sorry, but I already have plans for that day.

W Then, let's see the one with Brian Gwen. He beat Steven Foster and won the gold medal at the Winter Olympics.

M Okay. I'll make a reservation online.

여 아이스 쇼 입장권은 예약했니?

남 막 하려던 참이었어. 이 일정표를 보고 언제가 좋은지 말해 줘.

여 일요일만 빼고 아무 날이나 괜찮아.

남 일요일은 24일이지? 그러면 우리는 Amy Gray의 공연을 볼 수가 없네.

여 23일 공연자들도 대단해.

남 미안하지만, 난 이미 그날은 계획이 잡혀 있어.

여 그럼 Brian Gwen이 있는 공연을 보자. 그는 Steven Foster를 이기고 동계 올림픽에서 금메달을 땄어.

남 알았어. 인터넷으로 예약할게.

13 ⑤

[Telephone rings.]

W Dr. Kim's Dental Clinic. May I help you?

M Can I make an appointment? I have a toothache.

W Oh, I see. How about Friday at 11 o'clock?

M Sorry, but I'm quite busy on that day. Are you open on Saturday morning?

W I'm afraid we are closed on Saturdays.

M Then, can I visit on Monday?

W You can come at either 9:30 a.m. or 1:30 p.m. next Monday, sir.

M 9:30 is too early for me. Please make it at 1:30 in the afternoon next Monday. My name is Kevin Peterson.

W All right, Mr. Peterson. We'll see you then.

[전화벨 소리가 울린다.]

여 김 박사 치과입니다. 무엇을 도와 드릴까요?

남 예약을 할 수 있을까요? 이가 아파서요.

여 아, 알겠습니다. 금요일 11시 어떠세요?

남 죄송하지만, 그날은 꽤 바빠요. 토요일 아침에 여나요?

여 유감이지만 토요일마다 문을 닫습니다.

남 그럼, 월요일에 방문할 수 있을까요?

여 다음 주 월요일 오전 9시 30분이나 오후 1시 30분에 오실 수 있습니다.

남 9시 30분은 너무 일러요. 다음 주 월요일 오후 1시 30분으로 해 주세요. 제 이름은 Kevin Peterson입니다.

여 알겠습니다, Peterson 씨. 그때 뵙겠습니다.

---

14 ④

M Hi, Cathy. Long time no see. How was your summer vacation?

W I went to Australia.

M Australia? What did you do there?

W I enjoyed an opera at the Sydney Opera House and visited lots of museums and parks in Sydney. I also tried various Australian food.

M Fantastic! What else did you do?

W I went to see the penguins on Philip Island near Melbourne. They were so cute.

M That sounds fun.

남 안녕, Cathy. 오랜만이야. 여름 방학은 어땠니?

여 난 호주에 갔었어.

남 호주? 거기서 뭐 했어?

여 시드니 오페라 하우스에서 오페라를 즐기고, 시드니의 많은 박물관과 공원을 방문했어. 다양한 호주 음식도 먹어 보고.

남 환상적이다! 또 뭐 했어?

여 나는 멜버른 근처에 있는 필립 섬에 펭귄들을 보러 갔어. 그들은 너무 귀여웠어.

남 재미있겠다.

---

15 ②

W I'd like to talk about a dangerous driving habit. If you drive for many hours, it is very easy to become sleepy. It can be just as dangerous as drunk driving. There are some tips you can use to stay awake. If you start to feel sleepy, you should stop at a rest area to get out of the car and get some fresh air. You can also chew gum or sing a song loudly when you're sleepy.

여 저는 위험한 운전 습관 한 가지에 대해 말씀을 드리고자 합니다. 오랜 시간 동안 운전을 하게 되면 졸음이 오기 매우 쉽습니다. 그것은 음주 운전만큼이나 위험합니다. 당신이 맑은 정신을 유지하기 위해 이용할 수 있는 몇 가지 팁이 있습니다. 졸리기 시작할 때 당신은 휴게소에 내려서 차에서 나와 신선한 공기를 마셔야 합니다. 또한 졸릴 때 당신은 껌을 씹거나 노래를 크게 부를 수도 있습니다.

---

16 ④

M Lisa, have you received a call from Mike?

W Not yet. Why?

M I think he's already arrived at the campsite. But why didn't he call us?

W Don't worry. He'll surely call us soon.

M But as you know, it's the first time our son has gone on a trip apart from us.

W Right. If you're really worried about him, how about calling him yourself?

M Yeah. I'll do that right away.

남 Lisa, Mike에게 전화 받았어요?

여 아직 못 받았어요. 왜요?

남 그 애가 벌써 캠핑장에 도착한 것 같아요. 그런데 왜 우리에게 전화를 하지 않았을까요?

여 걱정하지 말아요. 틀림없이 곧 전화를 할 거예요.

남 하지만 당신도 알다시피, 우리 아들이 처음으로 우리와 떨어져 여행을 간 거잖아요.

여 맞아요. 당신이 정말로 그 애가 걱정된다면, 직접 전화를 하는 게 어때요?

남 그래요. 당장 그렇게 해야겠어요.

---

17 ⑤

M How do I look? Tonight is my first date with Kate.

W Let me see. Your shirt and pants look very nice.

M Thanks.

W Are you going to wear a tie?

M Yes. I was trying to decide between this one and that one.

W To be honest, I don't think either one would look good with your outfit.

M Really? Choosing a tie is difficult. Can you pick one for me?

남 나 어때? 오늘밤에 Kate와 첫 데이트를 해.

여 어디 보자. 네 셔츠와 바지가 아주 멋져 보여.

남 고마워.

여 넥타이를 매려고?

남 응. 이것과 저것 중에서 하나를 결정하려고 하고 있었어.

여 솔직히 말해서, 어느 쪽도 네 옷과 잘 어울릴 것 같지 않아.

남 정말? 넥타이 고르는 건 어려워. 하나 골라 줄래?

---

18 ②

W May I help you?

M Yes. I bought this coffee machine about five months ago and I need to get it repaired.

W Well, all repairs are free for the first year. What's the problem?

M It suddenly stopped working and I don't know why.

W Okay. Please leave it here and we'll find out what's wrong.

M Thanks.

W When do you need it back?

여 제가 도와 드릴까요?

남 네. 제가 약 5개월 전에 이 커피 머신을 샀는데, 수리를 받아야 해요.

여 음, 첫해에는 모든 수리가 무료입니다. 문제가 뭐가요?

남 갑자기 작동이 멈췄는데 왜 그런지 모르겠어요.

여 알겠습니다. 여기 두시면 뭐가 문제인지 알아보겠습니다.

남 고맙습니다.

여 언제 다시 필요하신가요?

---

19 ③

W I'd like to know if you have a book titled *Revolution*.

M Well.... No, I don't think we do.

W Is there any way I can get the book?

M I could order it for you if you like.

W Oh, that would be great.

M Can you tell me the name of the author and the publisher?

W I can't remember the author, but it's published by Star Press.

M Do you know when it was published, then?

여 〈혁명〉이라는 책이 있는지 알고 싶어요.

남 글쎄요…. 아뇨, 저희는 없는 것 같습니다.

여 그 책을 구할 수 있는 방법이 있을까요?

남 원하신다면 제가 주문해 드릴 수 있습니다.

여 오, 좋네요.

남 작가의 이름과 출판사를 말씀해 주시겠어요?

여 작가는 기억나지 않지만, Star 출판사에서 출판한 거예요.

남 그럼 언제 출판됐는지 아시나요?

---

20 ⑤

M It was Sunday afternoon and Tony went to the library to study for his final exam. The library was quiet and he could concentrate well. However, about an hour later, two students came into the library and sat at the table next to him. They started chatting loudly. It was too noisy for him to study. He stared at them but they kept talking. In this situation, what would Tony most likely say to them?

남 일요일 오후였고 Tony는 기말고사 공부를 하러 도서관에 갔다. 도서관은 조용했고 그는 집중을 잘 할 수 있었다. 그러나 한 시간쯤 후에 두 명의 학생이 도서관으로 들어와 그의 옆 책상에 앉았다. 그들은 큰 소리로 수다를 떨기 시작했다. 그것은 너무 시끄러워서 그가 공부를 할 수 없었다. 그가 그들을 빤히 쳐다보았지만 그들은 계속해서 말을 했다. 이 상황에서, Tony는 그들에게 뭐라고 말할까?

---

01 ⑤	02 ④	03 ③	04 ⑤	05 ⑤	06 ②	07 ③	08 ②
09 ①	10 ②	11 ②	12 ④	13 ④	14 ②	15 ⑤	16 ③
17 ⑤	18 ⑤	19 ②	20 ②				

- Dictation Test -

01 with a ribbon, simple, square, whole body
02 swimming suit, sunscreen, might have missed, drawer   **03** do me a favor, give a speech, being held
04 interview, lecture, take two hours, right after
05 left my bag, a couple of, with yellow stripes
06 not supposed to, straight ahead, every weekend
07 sign up for, take part in, a piano lesson
08 arriving at, was built in, visit the museum
09 plastic frame, cooler in summer, cool wind, wave it   **10** grow up, piece of cake, supposed to bring, hurry   **11** tired of, planning to go, more exercise
12 looking at, every Monday, sign up   **13** How much, take five pairs, Anything else   **14** slight headache, desert plants survive, get some information
15 going to visit, old items, have lunch, free time
16 buy a hat, buy two, give one   **17** severe toothache, examine, treated right away   **18** read books, interested in helping, join me   **19** win the match, do your best, come and watch   **20** eat less, started to exercise, much better

01 ⑤

W   I'm looking for a mirror to put in my room.
M   How about this round one with a ribbon?
W   I don't need a ribbon. I'd like a simple one.
M   How about this simple square one?
W   I like that one, but I want to buy a big mirror. It's important that it should be big enough so I can see my whole body.
M   Then, this one is perfect for you. It's a simple full-length mirror.
W   Oh, that's prefect. I'll take it.

여   내 방에 놓을 거울을 찾고 있어요.
남   리본이 달린 이 둥근 것은 어떠세요?
여   리본은 필요 없어요. 저는 단순한 것으로 할게요.
남   이 단순한 사각 거울은 어떠신가요?

여   맘에 들지만, 큰 거울을 사고 싶어요. 제 몸 전체를 볼 수 있도록 충분히 큰 게 중요해요.
남   그렇다면, 이것이 딱 좋을 것 같네요. 이것은 단순한 전신 거울이거든요.
여   오, 완벽해요. 그걸로 할게요.

02 ④

M   Honey, how long will it take to pack your things?
W   About an hour.
M   Don't forget your swimming suit. There is a beautiful beach just in front of the hotel.
W   I already packed it with a hat and sunscreen lotion.
M   Good. Did you bring your passport and airplane tickets?
W   Oh, my! I totally forgot about them. If you hadn't reminded me, I might have missed my plane.
M   Where is your passport?
W   It is in the top drawer of my desk. My tickets are inside the passport.
M   Let me go get them.

남   여보, 짐 싸는 데 얼마나 걸릴까요?
여   한 시간 정도요.
남   수영복을 잊지 마요. 호텔 바로 앞에 아름다운 해변이 있어요.
여   이미 모자와 자외선 차단 로션과 함께 챙겼어요.
남   좋아요. 여권과 비행기표를 챙겼나요?
여   오, 이런! 난 그것들을 완전히 잊어버렸어요. 만약 당신이 나에게 알려 주지 않았다면, 나는 비행기를 놓쳤을지도 몰라요.
남   여권은 어디 있어요?
여   내 책상 맨 위에 서랍에 있어요. 비행기표는 여권 안에 있고요.
남   내가 가서 그것들을 가져올게요.

03 ③

[Telephone rings.]
M   Hello.
W   Hello, Mr. Wilson. This is Alice Brown at Green Middle School.
M   Hi, Ms. Brown. How have you been doing?
W   I've been doing well. Mr. Wilson, could you do me a favor?
M   Oh, what is it?
W   Could you give a speech at the graduation ceremony?

M Sure. When is the graduation ceremony being held?

W Next Friday. It starts at 10:30. So, please come to the teachers' office by 10 o'clock.

M Okay. I will.

[전화벨 소리가 울린다.]

남 여보세요.

여 여보세요, Wilson 씨. 저는 Green 중학교의 Alice Brown입니다.

남 안녕하세요, Brown 선생님. 어떻게 지내셨어요?

여 저는 잘 지내고 있습니다. Wilson 씨, 제가 부탁 한 가지 드려도 될까요?

남 오, 그게 뭔가요?

여 졸업식에서 연설을 해 주실 수 있으세요?

남 물론이죠. 졸업식이 언제 열리나요?

여 다음 주 금요일입니다. 10시 30분에 시작해요. 그러니까 10시까지 교무실로 와 주시면 됩니다.

남 좋아요. 그렇게 하죠.

---

04 ⑤

[Telephone rings.]

M Hi, Ms. James. This is Tom from *The Apple Times*.

W Hello, Tom. Are you calling for our interview?

M Yes. Are you free tomorrow at 11 a.m.?

W No. I'll be giving a two-hour lecture from 10 a.m. at the university.

M I see. When will you be free?

W Well, I have a book signing at a local bookstore at 1 p.m. That will take two hours, but then I'll be free.

M Good. I'll meet you at the bookstore right after the book signing.

W Okay.

[전화벨 소리가 울린다.]

남 안녕하세요, James 씨. 저는 〈애플 타임즈〉의 Tom입니다.

여 안녕하세요, Tom. 우리 인터뷰 때문에 전화하셨나요?

남 네. 내일 오전 11시에 시간이 되시나요?

여 아뇨. 대학교에서 오전 10시부터 2시간짜리 강의를 할 거예요.

남 그렇군요. 언제 시간이 나시나요?

여 글쎄요. 오후 1시에 동네 서점에서 책 사인회가 있어요. 그것은 두 시간이 걸리겠지만, 그 후에는 시간이 됩니다.

남 좋습니다. 책 사인회가 끝나면 바로 서점에서 만나요.

여 네.

---

05 ⑤

W Excuse me. I left my bag in a bus.

M What was the number of the bus?

W 70.

M All right. We have a couple of bags from no. 70 buses. What color is it?

W It's brown with yellow stripes.

M I think we have. Just a moment, please. *[Pause]* Is this yours?

W Oh, yes. I didn't expect I would find it. Thank you so much.

M You're welcome. Have a nice day!

여 실례합니다. 제가 버스에 가방을 놓고 내렸어요.

남 그 버스 번호가 어떻게 되죠?

여 70번입니다.

남 알겠습니다. 70번 버스에서 나온 가방이 두어 개 있어요. 어떤 색깔이죠?

여 노란색 줄무늬가 있는 갈색이에요.

남 저희가 가지고 있는 것 같네요. 잠시만 기다려 주세요. *[잠시 후]* 이것이 당신의 것입니까?

여 오, 맞아요. 그것을 찾을 거라고 기대하지 않았는데. 너무 감사해요.

남 별말씀을요. 즐거운 하루 보내세요!

---

06 ②

① **M** Hello. Can I buy these flowers?

　W Of course.

② **M** Excuse me. You are not supposed to pick the flowers here.

　W I'm sorry. I didn't know that. I won't do it again.

③ **M** Would you show me the way to the flower garden?

　W Sure. Walk straight ahead.

④ **M** Excuse me. Is there a trash can around here?

　W Yes, there is one near the flower garden.

⑤ **M** Do you come here often?

　W Yes, I come here every weekend.

---

① **남** 안녕하세요. 제가 이 꽃을 살 수 있을까요?

　여 물론이죠.

② **남** 실례합니다. 여기서 꽃을 꺾으시면 안 됩니다.

　여 죄송합니다. 몰랐어요. 다시는 그러지 않겠습니다.

③ **남** 화원으로 가는 길을 알려 주시겠습니까?

　여 물론이죠. 앞으로 계속 걸어가세요.

④ 남 실례합니다. 이 근처에 휴지통이 있습니까?
　여 네, 화원 근처에 하나 있습니다.
⑤ 남 여기에 자주 옵니까?
　여 네, 주말마다 와요.

07 ③

M Lisa, where are you going?

W I'm going to sign up for the summer camp.

M Summer camp? When does it start?

W It starts on July 25th. And it continues to July 28th.

M I'd love to take part in the camp, too.

W Really? Then, let's go to the camp together.

M Okay. Lisa, could you sign me up, too? I have a piano lesson now.

W No problem. I'll do it for you.

남 Lisa, 어디 가고 있니?

여 여름 캠프를 신청하러 가고 있어.

남 여름 캠프라고? 언제 시작하는데?

여 7월 25일에 시작해. 그리고 7월 28일까지 계속되고.

남 나도 그 캠프에 참가하고 싶어.

여 정말? 그럼, 캠프에 같이 가자.

남 좋아. Lisa, 나도 신청해 줄 수 있니? 난 지금 피아노 수업을 받아야 하거든.

여 문제없어. 내가 대신 해 줄게.

08 ②

M Attention, please. We're arriving at the Picasso Art Museum soon. Before you enter the museum, I'll tell you about it briefly. The museum was built in 1988. It has more than 3,000 pieces of famous art works. More than 10,000 people visit the museum every year. The museum closes at 6 p.m. So you have to come back to this bus before then. Please enjoy your visit.

남 주목해 주세요. 우리는 곧 피카소 미술관에 도착할 것입니다. 여러분이 미술관에 들어가시기 전에, 그것에 대해 간단하게 말씀드리겠습니다. 미술관은 1988년에 지어졌습니다. 거기에는 3천 점 이상의 유명한 미술 작품들이 있습니다. 만 명 이상의 사람들이 매년 미술관을 찾아옵니다. 미술관은 오후 6시에 문을 닫습니다. 그러므로 그 이전에 이 버스로 돌아오셔야 합니다. 즐거운 방문 되세요.

09 ①

M This is a flat object having a wooden or plastic frame with paper or cloth. In the old days before electric fans, people used it to make themselves cooler in summer. Sometimes, they used it as an accessory, too. In old movies, you may see some western noble ladies holding this. You can also see some noble people holding this in Korean old pictures. To make a cool wind, you hold this in your hand and wave it to make the air move.

남 이것은 나무나 플라스틱 틀에 종이나 천을 입힌 것으로 만들어진 평평한 물건입니다. 선풍기가 없었던 옛날에, 사람들은 여름에 스스로 시원하게 하기 위해 이것을 이용했습니다. 때때로, 그들은 장식품으로도 그것을 이용하기도 했습니다. 옛 영화에서, 당신은 서양 귀족 여성들이 이것을 들고 있는 것을 볼 수도 있습니다. 당신은 또한 한국의 옛 그림에서도 양반들이 이것을 들고 있는 것을 볼 수 있습니다. 시원한 바람을 만들기 위해, 당신은 이것을 손에 들고 공기를 움직이게 하기 위해 그것을 흔들어야 합니다.

10 ②

① M What do you want to be when you grow up?

　W I love animals, so I want to run an animal hospital.

② M Have you heard of the lie detector?

　W Sure, but I've never been there before.

③ M Are you saying you've already finished your homework?

　W Dad, it was a piece of cake.

④ M How much is the late fee?

　W It's two dollars in total.

⑤ M You're supposed to bring a present for him.

　W Sorry, I was in such a hurry that I left it at home.

---

① 남 너는 커서 무엇이 되고 싶니?

　여 난 동물을 좋아해서 동물병원을 운영하고 싶어.

② 남 거짓말 탐지기에 대해 들어 봤니?

　여 물론이지, 하지만 난 전에 거기에 가 본 적이 없어.

③ 남 벌써 숙제를 끝냈다는 거야?

　여 아빠, 그것은 식은 죽 먹기였어요.

④ 남 연체료가 얼마인가요?

　여 모두 합해서 2달러입니다.

⑤ 남 너는 그의 선물을 가져오기로 되어 있었잖아.

　여 미안해, 너무 바빠서 집에 두고 왔어.

11 ②

M　How was your week at school?

W　I'm so tired of studying. I think I need a break.

M　I know what you mean. I'm going to a concert this Friday night. How about coming along?

W　Sorry, but I can't. I'm planning to go to the gym to exercise with my sister. She helps me exercise.

M　I thought you don't like exercise.

W　You're right. Actually I don't. The doctor said I needed more exercise.

M　Well. Good luck. See you at school on Monday.

남　학교에서 한 주 잘 보냈니?

여　난 공부가 너무 지겨워. 휴식이 필요한 것 같아.

남　무슨 말인지 알아. 난 이번 주 금요일 밤에 콘서트에 갈 거야. 함께 갈래?

여　미안하지만, 난 못 가. 나는 언니와 함께 운동하러 체육관에 갈 계획이야. 언니가 내가 운동하는 것을 도와줘.

남　난 네가 운동을 좋아하지 않는 줄 알았어.

여　네 말이 맞아. 사실 난 좋아하지 않아. 의사 선생님이 내가 운동을 더 해야 한다고 말씀하셨어.

남　음. 행운을 빌어. 월요일에 학교에서 보자.

12 ④

M　Yuna, you're looking at the swimming classes at ABC Sports Center.

W　Yeah. I'm going to take one of the classes. Will you join me?

M　Sure.

W　Good. How about Mr. Jackson's class on Mondays and Wednesdays?

M　Sorry, I can't. I have guitar lessons every Monday and Wednesday.

W　Right. I can't take a Friday class, either.

M　Then let's take Ms. Wilson's class on Tuesdays and Thursdays.

W　Good. Let's sign up for the class.

남　유나야, 너 ABC 스포츠 센터의 수영 강좌들을 보고 있네.

여　응. 그 강좌들 중 하나를 수강할 거야. 너도 나와 같이 할래?

남　물론이지.

여　잘됐네. 월요일과 수요일마다 있는 Jackson 선생님의 강좌는 어때?

남　미안하지만, 안 돼. 난 월요일과 수요일마다 기타 레슨이 있어.

여　그렇지. 나도 금요일 강좌는 수강할 수가 없어.

남　그럼 화요일과 목요일마다 있는 Wilson 선생님의 강좌를 듣자.

여　좋아. 그 강좌를 신청하자.

13 ④

M　Hello. Can I help you?

W　Yes, please. How much is this shirt?

M　It's 20 dollars. But if you buy two, you can get them for 35 dollars.

W　Good. I'll take two of them. And I also need some socks.

M　How about these ones? We sell five pairs of socks for 20 dollars.

W　I'll take five pairs then.

M　So let me check. 35 dollars for two shirts and 20 dollars for five pairs of socks. Anything else?

W　No. That's all.

남　안녕하세요, 도와 드릴까요?

여　네, 부탁드립니다. 이 셔츠는 얼마인가요?

남　20달러입니다. 하지만 두 장을 구입하시면, 35달러에 구매하실 수 있어요.

여　좋네요. 두 장을 구입하겠습니다. 그리고 저는 양말도 몇 개 필요해요.

남　이것들은 어떠세요? 다섯 켤레를 20달러에 팔아요.

여　그럼 다섯 켤레 살게요.

남　그럼 확인할게요. 셔츠 두 장에 35달러와 양말 다섯 켤레에 20달러예요. 다른 것은요?

여　없어요. 그게 전부입니다.

14 ②

M　Cathy, you don't look good.

W　I have been in bed for three days because of a bad cold.

M　That's too bad. Are you okay now?

W　I'm okay except for a slight headache. I heard our science teacher gave us homework.

M Right. Yesterday, we learned about life in the desert. We have to write a report about how desert plants survive.

W Do you have any ideas about that?

M No, actually I'm going to the library to get some information. You can come with me.

W Okay, thank you.

남 Cathy, 너 안 좋아 보인다.

여 감기가 심하게 걸려서 3일 동안 누워 있었어.

남 안됐구나. 이제 괜찮아?

여 약간의 두통을 제외하고는 괜찮아. 과학 선생님이 우리에게 숙제를 내 주셨다고 들었어.

남 맞아. 우리는 어제 사막에 사는 생물에 대해 배웠어. 우리는 사막 식물들이 어떻게 살아남는지에 대해 보고서를 써야 해.

여 그것에 대해 무슨 생각이 있니?

남 아니, 사실 난 정보를 좀 얻기 위해 도서관에 갈 거야. 나랑 같이 가도 돼.

여 그래, 고마워.

15 ③

W Good morning everyone. Did you sleep well? We're going to visit the National Museum this morning. You can see lots of old items that local people used to use. We will then have lunch at the Chinese restaurant near the museum. After lunch, you'll have some free time. We'll meet up again during the evening to have dinner at the hotel.

여 여러분, 안녕하세요. 잘 주무셨나요? 오늘 아침에는 국립 박물관을 방문할 예정입니다. 지역 주민들이 썼던 오래된 물품들을 많이 보실 수 있을 겁니다. 그리고 나서 박물관 근처에 있는 중국 식당에서 점심을 드실 것입니다. 점심 식사 후에는 자유 시간을 갖게 되실 것입니다. 저녁 시간에 다시 모여서 호텔에서 저녁을 드실 것입니다.

16 ③

W What can I do for you?

M I'd like to buy a hat.

W How about this white one?

M Well, it's likely to get dirty too easily. How much is this blue one?

W It's 10 dollars. But if you buy two, we'll give them to you for 16 dollars.

M Good. I'll take two and give one to my brother then.

여 무엇을 도와 드릴까요?

남 모자를 하나 사고 싶어요.

여 이 흰색 모자는 어떠세요?

남 글쎄요. 그건 너무 쉽게 더러워질 것 같아요. 이 파란색 모자는 얼마죠?

여 10달러입니다. 하지만 두 개를 사시면, 16달러에 드릴게요.

남 좋네요. 그럼 두 개를 사서 하나는 동생에게 줘야겠어요.

17 ⑤

M Good morning. Please take a seat here.

W Thanks.

M What's your problem today?

W I have a severe toothache. I can't stand it any more.

M Let me examine your teeth. Please open your mouth.

W All right. Ah.

M You have some cavities. The two upper ones look serious.

W Do you think I should get them treated right away?

남 안녕하세요. 여기 앉으시죠.

여 감사합니다.

남 오늘은 무슨 문제가 있으신가요?

여 심한 치통이 있어요. 더는 참을 수가 없어요.

남 이를 검사해 보겠습니다. 입을 벌려 보세요.

여 알겠습니다. 아.

남 충치가 몇 개 있네요. 위쪽의 두 개는 심각해 보입니다.

여 그것들을 당장 치료해야 한다고 생각하세요?

18 ⑤

M Jia, I heard you do volunteer work at the children's hospital every Saturday. Is that true?

W Yes. I have been doing volunteer work there since last year.

M Wow! What kind of work do you do there?

W I usually read books to the sick children.

M How nice you are! Actually, I'm interested in helping others, too.

W Really? Then join me!

M Can I?

남 지아야, 네가 토요일마다 어린이 병원에서 자원 봉사를 한다고 들었어. 그게 사실이니?

여 그래. 작년부터 거기에서 자원 봉사를 해 왔어.

남 와! 거기서 어떤 종류의 일을 하니?

여 난 보통 아픈 아이들에게 책을 읽어 줘.

남 넌 정말 마음씨가 좋구나! 실은, 나도 다른 사람들을 돕는 데 관심이 있거든.

여 정말? 그렇다면 나와 함께 하자!

남 나도 할 수 있어?

19 ②

M Alice, I heard about your tennis match this Sunday.

W Did you? I really want to win the match, but I'm not sure I can.

M You're a very good player. I'm sure you'll win the match.

W Thank you. But the player I'm going to play is really good.

M I'm sure you'll beat her if you try to be calm and do your best.

W Okay, I'll keep that in mind. And I think I'll do better if you come and watch the match.

남 Alice, 이번 일요일에 있을 네 테니스 시합에 대해 들었어.

여 그랬니? 나는 정말 그 경기에서 이기고 싶은데, 내가 할 수 있을지 모르겠어.

남 넌 매우 훌륭한 선수야. 난 네가 경기에서 이길 거라고 확신해.

여 고마워. 하지만 나와 경기할 선수가 매우 잘해.

남 네가 침착하려고 노력하고 최선을 다하면 틀림없이 그녀를 이길 거야.

여 좋아, 그 점을 유념할게. 그리고 네가 와서 경기를 지켜봐 준다면 더 잘할 것 같은데.

20 ②

W Jack used to eat a lot of fast food. But one day he decided to eat less of it and eat more healthy foods. These days he's enjoying eating more vegetables and fruits. In addition, he has started to exercise. He jogs every day. When his old friend Emily meets him, she sees that Jack is looking much better. In this situation, what would Emily most likely say to Jack?

여 Jack은 패스트푸드를 많이 먹곤 했다. 하지만 어느 날 그는 그것을 더 적게 먹고 건강에 좋은 음식을 더 많이 먹기로 결심했다. 요즘 그는 더 많은 채소와 과일을 먹는 것을 즐기고 있다. 게다가, 그는 운동을 시작했다. 그는 매일 조깅을 한다. 그의 옛 친구 Emily가 그를 만났을 때, 그녀는 Jack이 훨씬 더 좋아 보인다는 것을 알아차린다. 이 상황에서, Emily는 Jack에게 뭐라고 말할까?

Memo

프로 혼공러의 공통점 - 빈틈없는 공부 환경

나는 오늘도 완벽한 혼공이 가능하다!

☑ 내 학교 일정에 딱 맞게 계획해
1:1 맞춤 학습관리

☑ 코딩이 재미있어서 공부 중이야
창의인재 양성 미래교육 4.0 강좌

☑ 궁금한 건 언제든 물어봐
24시간 질답 서비스 질답ON

☑ 재미있고 이해가 잘 되니 자꾸 듣게 돼
검증된 최고 실력의 강사

☑ 프로그래머라는 꿈을 정했어
진로활동 가이드 & 진로 컨설팅

☑ 우리 학교 교과서로 공부하니까 시험에 유리해
100% 전 과목 출판사 강좌

☑ 집중력이 흐트러지면 알려주셔
알파ON 라이브 코치

☑ 시간이 부족할 땐 필요한 부분만 골라 들어
스마트 콕 강의 서비스

☑ 과제나 수행평가 대비도 쉽게 할 수 있어
수행평가 만점 자료실

☑ 개인적으로 고민이 있을 땐 따로 물어봐
SKY 선배 1:1 멘토링 멘토ON

All that 올댓·중학·영어   중학영어의 모든 것이 들어 있는 올댓으로 학교 시험 완벽 대비!

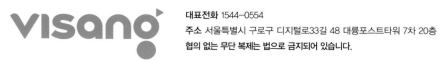

대표전화 1544-0554

주소 서울특별시 구로구 디지털로33길 48 대륭포스트타워 7차 20층

협의 없는 무단 복제는 법으로 금지되어 있습니다.